AN ARCHAEOLOGICAL HISTORY OF BRITAIN

AN ARCHAEOLOGICAL HISTORY OF BRITAIN

Continuity and Change from Prehistory to the Present

Jonathan Eaton

First published in Great Britain in 2014 by
PEN & SWORD ARCHAEOLOGY
an imprint of
Pen and Sword Books Ltd
47 Church Street
Barnsley
South Yorkshire S70 2AS

ISBN 978 1 78159 326 4

A CIP record for this book is available from the British Library

Printed and bound in India
by Replika Press Pvt. Ltd.

Typeset in Times New Roman by
CHIC GRAPHICS

Pen & Sword Books Ltd incorporates the imprints of
Pen & Sword Archaeology, Atlas, Aviation, Battleground, Discovery,
Family History, History, Maritime, Military, Naval, Politics, Railways,
Select, Social History, Transport, True Crime, and Claymore Press,
Frontline Books, Leo Cooper, Praetorian Press, Remember When,
Seaforth Publishing and Wharncliffe.

For a complete list of Pen and Sword titles please contact
Pen and Sword Books Limited
47 Church Street, Barnsley, South Yorkshire, S70 2AS, England
E-mail: enquiries@pen-and-sword.co.uk
Website: www.pen-and-sword.co.uk

Contents

Acknowledgements

This book presents an introduction to the archaeological history of Britain for the general and specialist reader alike. It does not attempt to provide a comprehensive overview of the subject, but is instead designed to inspire readers to explore their interests in greater depth. The relevant sources cited in the bibliography will serve as a useful starting point. Where possible I have cited texts which are easily accessible to the general public. The genesis of this work lies in my teaching and I am indebted to my former students for drawing my attention to the need for an introductory text covering all of British archaeological history. Their questions and discussions have shaped this book. Students, colleagues and friends at Newcastle College have stimulated my thinking and provided a congenial environment in which to work. My passion for teaching and communicating the past was inculcated by Derek Slater whose enthusiasm, encouragement and patience remain a constant inspiration to me.

I wish to thank my editors, Eloise Hansen and James Dixon, for their guidance and support in preparing this text for publication. Marcia Pointon kindly provided me with a copy of her article on the funerary topography of Princess Diana at a critical stage of my research.

The unfailing support of my family and friends has nurtured this book throughout its gestation. Jenesta, Jake and Millie have filled my life with happiness and borne my frequent absences with patience and understanding. I hope that someday Jake and Millie will share my love of our past through reading this text. This book is dedicated to my parents. It is in part payment for their love, devotion and guidance over the past thirty years. But most of all, this book is for a Christmas Eve long ago when they stayed up late into the night to make a Roman army costume for a little boy. *Optimus parentibus.*

Chapter 1

Early Prehistory

(*c.* 800,000 – 4200 BC)

Even a cursory inspection of a reasonably detailed map or satellite image of Britain will reveal two seemingly incontrovertible facts. First, Britain is an island nation separated from the European landmass by the English Channel and North Sea. Second, a considerable amount of our landscape is dedicated to agriculture of various kinds. From the viewpoint of traditional history, both of these facts are true. Yet from the longer perspective of archaeological history, Britain has been an island and its inhabitants have practised farming only for a very short space of time. This chapter covers the vast majority of British archaeological history, from the first appearance of archaic humans around 800,000 years ago through to the introduction of farming around 4200 BC. For all of this period, the inhabitants of Britain lived as hunter-gatherers, and, but for a single millennium, Britain was physically connected to the Continent. This era can be characterized as our early prehistory. It is recognized by archaeologists of consisting of two separate periods, the Palaeolithic (or 'Early Stone Age') and the Mesolithic (or 'Middle Stone Age'). Although these early inhabitants of Britain left only fleeting traces of their presence, they are crucial for understanding the struggles which our ancestors faced in colonising a landmass on the very edge of their ecological range. These were not brutish cavemen, but individuals with potentially complex social structures, hunting behaviour and even, later in this era, belief systems from which certain spiritual beliefs which persist in the modern world may be descended. Ultimately, their story is our story.

British early prehistory can be characterized as the struggle of our species to successfully expand their range in the face of considerable challenges posed by catastrophic climate change. Britain faced a period of dramatic ice ages and warmer interglacial periods which had significant ecological and geographical impacts. It has been calculated that Britain has experienced at least twenty major climatic shifts since the first appearance of archaic humans 800,000 years ago.[1] Indeed, the last ice age only ended around 12,000 years ago. The presence or absence of early humans was dictated by these drastic climactic shifts. For significant periods of time, humans retreated to the Continent to escape extreme conditions, only making fleeting visits back when climatic fluctuations led the glaciers to retreat. Archaeologists estimate that Britain has only been inhabited by humans for around a fifth of the period between 500,000 – 12,000 years ago.

BEGINNINGS

The archaeological history of Britain begins 800,000 years ago on the coast of what is now Norfolk.[2] At that time, the area around the modern village of Happisburgh was situated near to where a great estuary (the ancestor of the River Thames) flowed into the North Sea. Britain was not yet a separate island, but was instead joined to the continent by a great landmass in the south east, which archaeologists have christened 'Doggerland'. Identifying the presence of humans this far in the past is always difficult. Happisburgh provides the earliest evidence for the presence of archaic humans in Britain. But there is a problem. We do not know who exactly these early inhabitants actually were. They did not belong to the same sub-species as us, as *Homo sapiens* would not emerge from Africa until several hundred thousand years into the future. Instead, they probably belonged to a closely related group. No physical remains have been found, which means that the exact identity of these hominins is likely to remain a mystery for the foreseeable future.

Nevertheless, it is possible to reconstruct what their environment looked like. The climate was noticeably different than it is today, with warmer summers but cooler winters. The estuary flowed slowly into the North Sea. Pike, sturgeon and other fish species thrived in this environment. The river was flanked by swampy areas which gradually gave way to forest. It is not difficult to understand why archaic humans chose to visit this area. It attracted a range of fauna, whose presence is recorded by the bones they left behind. Mammoth, bison, horses and elk frequented the banks of the river. Smaller mammals such as lemmings and beavers could also be seen. Given the prevalence of prey species, it is unsurprising that predators also lurked in the area. Hyenas and sabre-toothed cats stalked the shallow pools on the fringes of the forest.

The presence of archaic humans in this landscape is revealed through the discovery of around eighty flint tools. They are relatively unsophisticated compared to the tools which would be produced later in prehistory, but nevertheless indicate that these early hominins were capable of producing tools for specific tasks. Animal bones from Happisburgh betray cut marks left by flint tools, indicating that they were being used to scrape flesh from bones and extract marrow. It is difficult to locate the role of hominins within this ecosystem. Traditionally, early humans have been viewed as apex predators, but there is little evidence to support this theory. At Happisburgh, it is likely that the hominins were scavenging from the remains of prey left behind by hyenas, sabre-toothed cats and other unidentified predators. The use of flint tools made them more effective as scavengers by allowing them to strip a carcass relatively swiftly. This would have been particularly useful if they themselves were under threat from aggressive carnivores. The hominins were probably also supplementing their diet by foraging for edible plants in the forest and along the river banks. There is no evidence at Happisburgh for the daily lives of these early hominins. We simply do not know how their society was organized, how they communicated or how they protected themselves from predators. They remain an enigmatic and ethereal presence at the very edge of our archaeological history.[3]

BOXGROVE

The first species of early human which we can clearly identify in Britain appeared around 500,000 years ago. This early form of human is named *Homo heidelbergensis* or 'Heidelberg Man', named after the site in Germany where the first clearly identified specimen was uncovered. Understanding the relationship of various archaic humans to each other and to ourselves is a complex problem, which is still taxing some of the finest minds in archaeology. However, it is reasonably certain that *H. heidelbergensis* was either our direct ancestor, or closely connected to our ancestral line.[4] The British example of this species was discovered in a gravel quarry at Boxgrove in Sussex. The landscape which *H. heidelbergensis* inhabited consisted of a coastal lagoon, surrounded by grassland and salt marshes. Inevitably, this location would have attracted a range of fauna from the surrounding habitats. A large number of animal bones have been recovered from the site, allowing us to build up a comprehensive picture of the ecosystem in which archaic humans operated. Some of the animals would be familiar to us in Britain today, namely red deer, wild horses and boar. Others were decidedly more exotic, including bison, elephants, lions, hyenas, rhinoceroses and wolves. This was a thriving ecological landscape offering a range of dietary resources for predators and prey alike.[5] The most obvious sign of the presence of *H. heidelbergensis* consists of around 300 flint handaxes which have left their mark on the bones of a range of large mammals including deer, horse, bison and rhinoceros. Geological analysis demonstrates that the handaxes were produced locally, the flint obtained from nearby cliffs. The presence of suitable flint nodes and substantial numbers of large mammals must have made this a favoured habitat for *H. heidelbergensis*.

The physical remains of a single *H. heidelbergensis* were also found at Boxgrove, in the form of a tibia from a left leg and two front teeth. At first glance, these may seem uninspiring. Yet they represent the remains of the oldest archaic human to have been found in Britain. These slight traces enable us to build a picture of the individual. He was male and stood around 1.8 m in height. He weighed approximately ninety kilograms and can be estimated to have been 40 years old when he died. Unfortunately, his cause of death cannot be clearly identified. The front teeth of this individual carry considerable tartar deposits, suggesting that he existed on a diet which contained a significant amount of meat. This is, of course, reinforced by the cut marks on the animal bones found nearby. Chemical analysis has found no evidence that seafood played a part in the diet of this individual. This is somewhat surprising given the original close proximity of this site to the coast. We must assume that *H. heidelbergensis* was attracted to Boxgrove by the presence of large terrestrial mammals rather than marine creatures. The two remaining teeth of this individual are heavily worn, suggesting that considerable damage was caused to them during his lifetime. The cause of this dental damage most likely lies in the method utilized by *H. heidelbergensis* to cut meat. It appears that he held animal flesh between clenched teeth whilst slicing through it with a flint handaxe. This rather dangerous technique inevitably took its toll on his dental health. Remarkably, we can even tell from a close examination of the surviving teeth that our *H. heidelbergensis* was right handed when using his stone tools.[6]

Attempts at understanding the behaviour and the social structures of archaic humans have often proved to be controversial. Boxgrove offers a few clues for understanding what *H. heidelbergensis* was doing at the site. There are no traces of the consumption of small mammal species here, despite their obvious presence within the landscape, nor is there any evidence for habitation at the site. This suggests that *H. heidelbergensis* was moving meat elsewhere, perhaps to a base camp further inland. The flint tools were deliberately fashioned at the site using local geological resources and appropriate implements, in the form of an antler hammer which has been recovered by archaeologists, evidence perhaps of a degree of planning in how *H. heidelbergensis* accessed food and prepared it for consumption.

Considerable debate has raged for more than a century over the extent to which archaic humans were capable of hunting prey species, rather than just scavenging kills made by predators. Some of the animal bones at Boxgrove do indicate that they were gnawed by large mammals such as lions and hyenas, as well as being marked by the handaxes of *H. heidelbergensis*. Yet close examination reveals that these mammalian teeth marks almost always overlie the marks left by flint tools. This suggests that lions and hyenas were scavenging kills left by *H. heidelbergensis,* rather than the other way round. The absence of evidence for the consumption of small mammals by archaic humans at Boxgrove indicates an element of selectivity in the meat they consumed, symptomatic of hunting rather than scavenging behaviour. Circumstantial evidence supports this view. It is unlikely that rhinoceroses had any natural predators at Boxgrove. Scavengers would therefore only have access to animals which had died of natural causes. Yet the carcasses preyed upon by *H. heidelbergensis* mainly belong to relatively healthy individuals who appear to have died in the middle of their life expectancy, rather than the weak, diseased or old. It can be assumed that *H. heidelbergensis* was consciously selecting rhinoceroses to predate on the basis of their size and weight for consumption. Hunting and killing large mammals must have required planning, teamwork and a considerable amount of risk. *H. heidelbergensis* may not necessarily have relied upon handaxes for this difficult task. A shoulder blade belonging to a wild horse killed by *H. heidelbergensis* contains a noticeable hole which may have been caused by a spear point. Such a weapon would have consisted of a flint spearhead mounted on a wooden shaft. The successful deployment of a spear designed to kill a wild horse would demand skill, strength and experience. *H. heidelbergensis* was not a primitive form of human, but rather a species capable of sophisticated hunting behaviour enabling them to thrive within the landscape they inhabited through the effective utilisation of local, natural resources. They were not just surviving, but thriving within this ecosystem.[7]

The success of *H. heidelbergensis* and other archaic forms of human did not continue for long. The period between 400,000 to around 100,000 years ago was characterized by a series of extreme climatic events which made most of Britain completely inhospitable to archaic humans. Evidence for the presence of archaic humans in Britain at this point is scant. We can expect that the descendants of *H. heidelbergensis* and related species retreated southwards to refuges on the continent. Visits to Britain are most likely to have been of a relatively fleeting nature and advancing glaciers marred any attempt at prolonged colonisation.

NEANDERTHALS

By the time that the climate of Britain became more congenial to the presence of archaic humans, we begin to find traces of perhaps the most famous of our relatives: the Neanderthals (*Homo neanderthalensis*). In the modern world, the term 'Neanderthal' has come to be seen as one of abuse, denoting someone brutish or primitive in their behaviour and social habits. Such an image has no resemblance to the Neanderthals of prehistory.[8] Indeed, it is rather a slur on their character. Neanderthals were physically distinct from how we appear today. In general, they were shorter and stockier than us, with a pronounced brow ridge and a sloping facial profile. Their physical attributes meant that they were well adapted to surviving in difficult climatic conditions. Evidence for the presence of Neanderthals has been found across Europe and parts of the Middle East.

Perhaps the most famous Neanderthal site in Britain is at Lynford in Norfolk.[9] Approximately 60,000 years ago, this was a marshy area around a river surrounded by open grassland. The British climate was considerably colder at this point than it is today. It is noteworthy that all of the sites mentioned so far are directly connected to water. Archaic humans were attracted to this type of habitat due to the presence of prey species. Conditions in marshy areas also favour preservation, meaning that archaeologists often have a stronger chance of finding prehistoric remains in such locations. The marsh and river at Lynford were visited by a range of large mammals, some of which are similar to those from Boxgrove. Rhinoceroses, bison, wild horses and wolves were all present, as were reindeer, brown bears and foxes. Yet the main attraction for Neanderthals was groups of mammoths, and it is clear that these formed their main prey species at this site. Although no Neanderthal bones have been discovered at Lynford, over fifty of their handaxes have been found. There is little evidence for flint quarrying or working locally, suggesting that the Neanderthals quarried and worked their tools at another location before transporting them to Lynford to target mammoths. This indicates a considerable degree of mental preparation for the hunt and suggests that this area was seen as a special location for the Neanderthals who visited it, perhaps as prime hunting territory.

The remains of eleven individual mammoths have been identified at Lynford, ten adults and a single juvenile animal. Injuries are most clearly visible on their ribs and vertebrae, suggesting that the Neanderthals were utilising a specific hunting strategy. The majority of the dead animals were adult males, who would have been vulnerable when they were outside of the herd. Tackling a group of mammoths would have been difficult and dangerous. Stalking lone males may have been easier and safer. It has been convincingly argued that the mammoths were attacked when they were in the swamp, and therefore vulnerable with limited avenues of escape. This would explain the large number of flint tools found at the site. Handaxes dropped into deep water were unlikely to have been recovered. Very few mammoth leg bones have survived, suggesting that parts of the carcasses were removed and transported elsewhere. The Lynford Neanderthals were well organized and capable of conceiving and implementing an effective hunting strategy which allowed them to successfully kill large and dangerous prey. Evidence from sites in Israel and Iraq hints at relatively complex Neanderthal societies which cared for the weak and old. They are thought to have been capable of sophisticated methods of communication, possibly including language itself. It has even been argued, controversially, that they possessed the capacity for language and religious belief. Neanderthals were perhaps not as dissimilar to us as we might like to think.

Neanderthals disappeared by around 35,000 years ago. The last known population of Neanderthals has been recorded in seashore caves in Gibraltar. A number of theories have been advanced to explain the extinction of Neanderthals, ranging from climate change to catastrophic disease.[10] Blame has also been apportioned to our species, *H. sapiens*, whose emergence from Africa may have been roughly contemporary with the beginning of the demise of the Neanderthals. It has been argued that our species could have caused their extinction in a number of ways, including genocide, cannibalism or by outcompeting them for resources.

Recent advances in our understanding of DNA have provided a new and startling explanation for the disappearance of the Neanderthals. Genetic analysis of modern humans from across the globe and comparison with DNA sequenced from archaeological remains has shown that all modern humans of non-African descent contain traces of the genetic sequence of Neanderthals within their DNA.[11] In other words, most of us are part Neanderthal. The most likely explanation for the presence of Neanderthal DNA within modern humans is that early *H. sapiens* interbred with Neanderthals shortly after their emergence from Africa and dispersal across the Middle East and Europe. The offspring of these unions were fertile, and thus Neanderthal DNA endured within the human line of descent down to the present day. The extent to which this interbreeding contributed to the disappearance of Neanderthals is currently unknown. It may, in fact, have been unrelated to their extinction. The demise of the Neanderthal population could have been caused by a number of different factors. It is, however, worth reflecting that a small part of the Neanderthals survives in each of us.

THE EMERGENCE OF MODERN HUMANS

The first members of our species, *H. sapiens*, appeared in Britain around 40,000 years ago. These early humans (as distinct from archaic humans who came from closely related species to our own) evolved in sub-Saharan Africa and spread through the Middle East to Asia and Europe. They are often referred to as Cro-Magnons, after a famous site of that name in France. The first early human to have been discovered in Britain was found buried in a cave at Paviland in south Wales. The burial belonged to a male who died around 30,000 years ago.[12] The care taken to bury the deceased in terms of both the arrangement of his body and the artefacts interred with him suggests that early humans possessed some form of belief system concerning the fate of the dead. The corpse had been covered in red ochre, which was still highly visible when it was first excavated. A series of artefacts were recovered in close proximity to the human remains, including a mammoth bracelet, sea shells and ivory rods. The presence of grave goods in archaeological burials tends to indicate a belief in life after death, with the objects intended to serve the deceased in the afterlife or be used to placate the gods. It is impossible to prove that this was the purpose of the artefacts at Paviland. Another feature of the burial which may be a result of some form of belief system is the absence of the skull, which may have been removed during post-mortem treatment of the body in preparation for burial.

During the period between 25,000–15,000 years ago, Britain experienced extremely harsh climatic conditions which probably pushed early humans back to the continent. When early humans began to return, the evidence shows considerable continuity with the evidence from Paviland. Excavation at Gough's Cave, part of the Cheddar Gorge cave system in Somerset, have provided further evidence for how early humans acted towards their dead. The site has revealed around 2200 flint artefacts, alongside carved reindeer antlers and mammoth ivory. Bones from a range of fauna were also present, including wild horse, red deer, wolf, brown bear and lynx. Remains of arctic foxes and hares represent the contemporary climate. It is clear that this site was used as a hunting camp during both the winter and summer months. The remains of wild horses predominate in the cave, suggesting that early humans were specifically targeting this species locally, and then using the site to butcher and prepare the carcasses. This was not a permanent camp. Indeed, scientific evidence suggests that the inhabitants ranged over a considerable territory. Mammoth ivory could not have been obtained locally in this period. Isotope analysis of remains of early humans from the cave reveals that their diet consisted mainly of the meat from red deer and wild cattle – not the horses butchered in the cave. These hunter-gatherers were adapted to utilising different aspects of the British landscape for specific aspects of the dietary and material needs.

The inhabitants of Gough's Cave left behind their dead. An assemblage of around 120 human bones was discovered during excavations at the site. Of these, one quarter display deliberate cut marks. The only logical explanation for these marks is that the bodies of these early humans were defleshed after death. There are two possible explanations for this activity. It is possible that these bones are evidence for systematic cannibalism within Gough's Cave. In this case, early humans were deliberately butchering other members of their own species, as well as wild horses and other fauna. Certainly, the technique used to deflesh the dead is similar to the technique they were using on their hunting kills. Yet there may be another explanation for this activity. There seems to be a particular emphasis on human skulls at this site, with at least five separate skulls recovered. It is noteworthy that a skull was absent from the earlier Cro-Magnon burial at Paviland. The defleshing of the corpses at Gough's Cave may have been a specific activity linked to their belief system. Recent research has suggested that the skulls found at the site may have functioned after death as skull cups, used by the relatives of the deceased.[13] The removal and post-mortem use of skulls is known from a number of sites across antiquity. This does not necessarily entail cannibalism, but rather a communal act of memory and mourning, perhaps aimed at maintaining the benefaction and wisdom of the ancestors.

Understanding the belief systems of early humans is virtually impossible. Whilst we are granted brief glimpses of possible ritual activities, these cannot be drawn together into a cohesive outline of their beliefs. A millennium after the defleshing of corpses in Gough's Cave, inhabitants of another cave, at Creswell Crags in modern Nottinghamshire, were carving images on the ceiling and walls of the cave. Ninety separate figures have so far been identified at this most important site for cave art in Britain. The vast majority depict animals with which the inhabitants would have been intimately familiar, including bison, wild horse and red deer. Hunter-gatherers were absolutely reliant upon their prey species for the survival and sustainability of their communities. It is possible that they attached spiritual significance to their relationship with such animals. Hunter-gatherer societies which have been studied by anthropologists in the modern world often practice animism, a belief system where both living and non-living things are seen to possess spirits which need to be placated and respected. In some cases, hunter-gatherers may attach particular significance to a specific species of plant or animal which forms their totem. It is possible that the cave art from Creswell Crags reflect the animistic beliefs of their early human inhabitants. Alternatively, it is possible that the images were used to teach younger members of the community about the species upon which they relied for meat and other materials. Regardless of the motives behind the creation of cave art, we can imagine that the act of creating it must have been a powerful and cohesive event for the community who used the site.[14]

THE MESOLITHIC

Around 10,000 BC by conventional dating, the Palaeolithic gave way to the Mesolithic. The latter is characterized by the sole presence of our species, *H. sapiens*, all other forms of archaic humans having gone extinct. The British climate was becoming more stable during this period. Indeed the start of the Mesolithic was probably milder than it is today. The Mesolithic people of Britain were hunter-gatherers, as early humans were during the Palaeolithic. There was a strong degree of continuity between the two eras, although there were also signs of increasing complexity in social organisation and population dynamics.

At the start of the Mesolithic, Britain looked much different than it does today. It was still physically connected to the European landmass through a forested plain stretching from the south east to the continent, which facilitated the movement of individuals and groups in and out of Britain. The landscape of Britain was characterized by birch and pinewoods, followed by the spread of ash trees in the centuries to come. Doggerland, which stretched from Britain to the continent, consisted of a forested plain with inland lakes and streams.[15] This area allowed the migration of animals, and their human hunters, over large distances. Rising sea levels ultimately led to the destruction of Doggerland and its submersion beneath the North Sea. Whether this was a result of a sudden catastrophe or a gradual process is unclear. What is certain, however, is that the submersion of Doggerland severed the physical connection between Britain and the rest of Europe, which would have a significant impact on the history of both.

STAR CARR

Perhaps the most important Mesolithic site in Britain can be found at Star Carr in Yorkshire. The importance of the site lies in the local waterlogged conditions, which support an enviable level of preservation, and the depth of research which archaeologists conducted there across the twentieth century. For this reason, we have a better understanding of Star Carr than perhaps of any other Mesolithic site in Britain. Scientific dating techniques suggest that the site was occupied from around 8770 – 8460 BC. Star Carr was positioned on the edge of a large lake within a reed fringed swamp. Beyond the swamp stood birch and poplar trees, with thick woodland beyond. An area of vegetation had been cleared within the swamp and a birch platform constructed to provide a safe foundation for a habitable area. Timber from the constructed platform provides some of the earliest evidence for woodworking in Britain.

As might be expected, this landscape supported a thriving ecosystem which was exploited by the group who used the site as a hunting camp. They were hunting red and roe deer, elk, wild cattle and pigs. Other animals were taken for furs, including bears, badgers, foxes and wolves. Prey species from Star Carr also included water birds, such as storks and cranes. The broad range of species indicates the adaptability of this Mesolithic group to their landscape setting, and the value of the site in terms of the ecological terrain in which it was situated. This probably explains why they took such pains to construct a camp site. Surprisingly, there is no evidence for the consumption or utilisation of fish at Star Carr, despite the close proximity to the prehistoric Lake Pickering. It could be that freshwater fish populations had not yet recovered since the end of the last glacial maximum. An alternative explanation is that local soil conditions could have prevented fish bones from being preserved in recognisable quantities.[16]

The people at Star Carr identified closely with red deer. Antlers were being fashioned at the site, and over 100 barbed points have been discovered. The most famous find from the site consists of twenty-one frontlets made from the top of red deer skulls with antlers still attached. These have been deliberately crafted to allow them to be worn as head dresses. Archaeologists are divided as to what the purpose of these striking artefacts actually was. It is possible that they were used for camouflage during the deer stalk, allowing hunters to approach deer closely before the kill. Presumably, in this case, they would have been worn in conjunction with deer hides. Alternatively, it has been argued that these were ritual head dresses, worn during shamanistic rituals.[17] Given the importance of the red deer to the sustainability and survival of the Star Carr group, it makes sense that they perhaps believed it was possible to commune or interact with the spirit of this animal. There is also evidence, in the form of elk mattocks, that individuals were deliberately depositing artefacts in the lake. As we will see in later chapters, watery places have long been seen as possessing religious significance through Britain. It is entirely possible that Star Carr was a site of spiritual significance to Mesolithic people as well as, or perhaps because of, its rich biodiversity.[18]

It is tempting to view Mesolithic people as being in some way fundamentally different from ourselves. It is difficult to reconcile their hunter-gatherer lifestyles and beliefs with our historic reliance on agriculture. All too often, we tend to view ourselves as the heirs of incoming populations into Britain, such as the Romans, Vikings or Normans. Yet recent genetic analysis has convincingly demonstrated that this is not the case. Almost two thirds of the British population are descendants of migrants who entered

Britain during the Mesolithic.[19] These migrants potentially travelled along two established routes. The first, across Doggerland, would have brought them westwards from eastern Europe. The second, via the Atlantic seaway, is more contentious as it entails a considerable degree of seamanship.[20] Regardless of the exact route travelled, it is clear that the modern population of Britain to a large extent owes its existence to these ambitious hunter-gatherer pioneers. The Mesolithic was the period in which the foundations of Britain, in terms of geography and society, were truly laid.

Chapter 2

The Neolithic

(*c.* 4200 – 2500 BC)

Picture your breakfast this morning. Imagine how many people played a role in bringing it to your table. Thousands of individuals probably contributed to creating your meal, from lorry drivers to graphic designers, chief executives to supermarket shelf stackers. Few of these actually grew the organic components of your breakfast. The productivity of our agricultural system ultimately means that it can support the majority of the population who play no role in farming. It is only possible for you to read this book, or me to write it, because of the agricultural surplus which means that there is little (if any) subsistence farming in modern Britain. Throughout history, complex societies with structured hierarchies have arisen only because an agricultural surplus supported specialist and elite occupations. The transition from hunting and gathering to farming is therefore one of the most important phases in the archaeological history of Britain. Arguably, it is of greater significance than the Industrial Revolution in economic and social terms. The Neolithic (meaning 'new stone age') represents the dawn of agriculture in Britain. The beginning of the Neolithic is generally dated to around 4200 BC although, as we shall see, recent scientific advances suggest that this date can be refined further.

THE IMPACT OF THE NEOLITHIC

The origins of farming in human history can be traced geographically to the Levant and southwest Asia around 12,000 years ago. It is possible that agriculture began in a number of areas independently. From a scientific perspective, the presence of farming is detected through the domestication of animal or plant species. Domesticated species are genetically or physically distinct from their wild relatives as a result of manipulation by humans. This manipulation usually takes the form of artificial selection, in choosing specimens to reproduce in order to produce offspring with particular traits. Repeated over time, this process will eventually lead to a clear distinction between domesticated and wild species. Domesticating a species may take a considerable amount of time, and need not have been a result of a deliberate strategy. It is entirely possible that the origins of farming within a particular region witnessed a considerable overlap between hunter gatherer lifestyles and agricultural practices, as the two need not be mutually exclusive.[1]

The Neolithic spread of farming across Britain prompted profound changes in landscape, society, religion and culture. In archaeological terms, these changes are reflected through a number of features, which archaeologists refer to as the Neolithic package. Most obviously, this includes evidence for crops and domesticated animals, in the form of seeds, pollen and animal bones. But it would be wrong to see the dawn of the Neolithic as representing only the arrival of new flora and fauna in Britain. On the contrary, it led to a significant shift in the mindset of the population. By their very nature, farming communities are far less mobile than hunter gatherer societies. The presence of crops indicates a personal investment by the farmer in a particular area of land. It is difficult and potentially dangerous to move domesticated animals over large distances. This reduced mobility is evident archaeologically through the presence of permanent settlements and other sites which represent particular investment in a specific landscape indicating an element of ownership or territoriality.

The Neolithic witnessed a broad diversity in material culture across Britain. Hunter gatherers tend to travel light, eschewing the burden of lots of possessions in favour of the speed and adaptability of a mobile lifestyle. With less mobility, farming communities can invest in possessions which are difficult to transport. Pottery first occurs in Britain during this period. Despite their convenience for storage, cooking and dining, pots would be prone to breaking during the travels of a hunter gatherer group. The sedentary lifestyle offered by agriculture encouraged the use of pottery and the developing economy provided an opportunity for trade. Stone tools were also further refined during the Neolithic, in terms of both form and function. They became increasingly significant not only for their utility, but also as symbols of status and objects of power.

The Neolithic presents the first evidence for the social cohesion of communities within Britain. Hunter gatherer societies inevitably leave little trace on the landscape. This changed radically with the dawn of farming. Neolithic communities marked the landscape through a range of collaborative construction projects which created a series of different types of impressive monuments, including henges, causewayed enclosures and cursus monuments. These monuments seem specifically designed to mark the presence of the community on the landscape in which they lived, to such an extent that many are clearly visible over 6,000 years later.

Less easy to trace is the change in mindset of the British population as a result of the transition to a farming lifestyle. Their entire way of life was fundamentally altered through the decline of mobile hunting and gathering. Instead of transiting across the British landscape, they now lived within a specific location which acquired critical importance for the sustainability of their community. It is almost certain that this focus on a particular area would have had a considerable impact on religious belief systems. Early farming communities from across the globe are known to have a particular focus on the worship of ancestral spirits, who were believed to have the power to provide a good harvest or prevail upon higher deities to do so. Aspects of this ancestral worship can still be found in areas of rural China today. Indeed, the custom of leaving an empty seat at a wedding in honour of a recently deceased family member is a distant echo of this belief system. Many of the monuments of the Neolithic have a connection to death and the ancestors, providing a broad range of evidence for understanding the religious beliefs of our Neolithic ancestors.

DATING THE NEOLITHIC

How did the Neolithic actually begin in Britain? Throughout the twentieth century, there were two competing theories to explain the emergence of farming. According to one theory, farmers arrived in Britain from the Continent, bringing domesticated animals and crops with them. Through population growth, these incoming farmers gradually replaced the native hunter gatherer population. As we saw in the previous chapter, there is considerable evidence for contact between Britain and the northern Europe during the late Mesolithic. An alternative viewpoint minimises the role of incomers and instead views the spread of farming as the transmission of ideas rather than individuals. In this model, hunter gatherers switched to farming as a lifestyle for the benefits it brought rather than being forcibly displaced.

Recent advances in archaeological dating techniques offer a new understanding of the origins of the British Neolithic. The most useful method for dating prehistoric remains consists of radiocarbon dating. All living things absorb Carbon 14 from the atmosphere during their lifetime. After death, these Carbon 14 reserves begin to break down at a known measurable rate (referred to as the 'half-life' of Carbon 14). By analysing the amount of Carbon 14, it is possible for scientists to provide an approximate date range for when the specimen died. Carbon 14 dating only works for organic material, such as wood, seeds and bones and it is difficult to obtain a narrow date range for material from the distant past. However, in recent years archaeologists have significantly refined dates obtained from Neolithic sites by utilising Bayesian statistics. This technique is named after the eighteenth century clergyman and mathematician who invented it. Bayesian statistics improve the accuracy of probabilities (in this case a particular date range) through applying a broader range of relevant data to inform the calculation.

Bayesian statistics have radically improved our understanding of the dawn of the British Neolithic through clarifying the chronology of early sites. Detailed analysis reveals that the so-called Neolithic package first appears around the Greater Thames Estuary between 4100 and 4000 BC. It then slowly spreads westwards, reaching Wales by around 3700 BC. The first appearance of farming within a single localised context strongly supports the possibility that it was brought to Britain by migrants from the Continent. Early animal bone and cereal assemblages show marked genetic similarities from similar material found in Brittany, Normandy, Calais and the Paris region. It is unclear how large this incoming group of farmers actually was, but the evidence seems to suggest that they assimilated into the native population relatively quickly, rather than replacing them.[2]

Some trace of the impact of the formation of agricultural communities may be found in early Neolithic tomb structures. Recent studies indicate that such sites in southern England, such as Wayland's Smithy in Oxfordshire and West Kennett in Wiltshire, were constructed and used for only a few generations between 3800 and 3700 BC. The relatively rapid utilisation of these sites during the early phases of the Neolithic suggests that they may have been purposefully used to display the status of powerful farming families. Monumentalising the residences of the ancestors would have emphasized the ownership of particular dynasties over specific territories.[3]

Causewayed enclosures are some of the most important monuments from this period.[4] These sites are found mostly in southern England and vary considerably in size and layout. In general, causewayed enclosures are formed through the digging of between one to four enclosing ditches. Their name comes from the fact that not all of the ditches were continuous, leaving untouched ground (or causeways) in some sections of the perimeter. Earth dug from the ditches formed internal banks. The diameter of causewayed enclosures ranges between 200 – 400 m. The function of these sites is disputed. Similar structures are known from central and northern Europe. There is no evidence of permanent structures within the enclosures, indicating that they were not established as settlement sites. The permeability of the surrounding ditch systems means that they could not have had a defensive function. Some causewayed enclosures contain burials, indicating a potential link with religious belief and the realm of the ancestors. The interior of the enclosures may have been used for ceremonies, perhaps involving religious specialists with the rest of the community spectating from beyond the ditches.

Causewayed enclosures flourished between 3700 and 3600 BC. They were usually built on virgin sites, away from any previous Palaeolithic or Mesolithic activity. It therefore seems likely that the construction of causewayed enclosures played a crucial role in establishing and sustaining early farming communities. The discontinuous nature of the surrounding ditches could have been a result of particular lengths of ditch being dug by individual families. This would make the construction of causewayed enclosures particularly important for cementing family unity within the context of larger communities. The construction of large scale sites usually indicates some form of command authority overseeing the project, in the form of chieftains or elders. The significant investment of labour in constructing causewayed enclosures demonstrates a desire to inscribe the landscape, which would fit with the mindset of a community permanently based within a specific area.

It may be noteworthy that, around 3500 BC, a new form of landscape monument became prominent. Named cursus monuments, these enigmatic sites defy easy explanation.[5] Cursus monuments consist of two parallel ditches running for up to 10 km. In some cases, the ditches are connected at either end, although there is no evidence for any monumental entrance. In contrast to causewayed enclosures, cursus monuments were often constructed close to earlier sites. The layout of these sites suggests that they may have been used for religious processions. The emergence of the cursus monument, perhaps in opposition to the earlier form of the causewayed enclosure, may indicate a deliberate attempt to present a new communal identity within the landscape. It is possible that they were created by emerging groups eager to distinguish themselves from established farming communities.

The term 'prehistoric' is traditionally applied to societies which are incapable of recording their own history. In Britain, this is generally taken to be the case for all periods prior to the Roman conquest. Yet the use of Bayesian statistics allows a tantalising glimpse of a possible historical framework for the early Neolithic. Incoming farmers established themselves around the Thames Estuary and grew crops and domesticated animals imported from the near Continent by 4000 BC. These farmers soon assimilated into the native population and their lifestyle replaced hunting and gathering over the next few centuries. Neolithic communities sought to display their new relationship with the landscape and other groups through constructing monuments to display their status. Although we cannot identify specific individuals or families, we can begin to understand how the arrival of farming and the social structures it encouraged impacted on the archaeological record.

SKARA BRAE

Our discussion of the Neolithic has focussed initially on broad trends. Much can be learnt by examining how these trends are reflected on a local level. The most spectacular Neolithic settlement in Britain can be found at Skara Brae in the Orkneys. It was established in approximately 3000 BC and occupied for around 600 years. The impressive level of preservation is a result of the settlement being covered by sand dunes until its discovery in the nineteenth century and the fact that many of the structures, and indeed furniture, were made of stone. Skara Brae provides a fascinating insight into the daily lives and social structure of early farming communities.[6]

The settlement at Skara Brae was dug into pre-existing midden mounds, formed by the accumulation of rubbish over time. This meant that most of the structures were actually beneath the level of the ground. This construction method is also present at other Neolithic sites in Orkney. Sinking the settlement into the midden mounds would have provided some protection against the elements. Skara Brae contains a total of eight separate buildings, all but one connected to each other by a single central passage. There are great similarities in the size and layout of the individual houses. The close proximity of the houses and their uniform design promote a clear sense of community within Skara Brae.

Most of the houses follow a standard pattern in their layout. Each house has only one entrance, leading off the main passage through the settlement. One central room dominates the interior of the house and was clearly a focal point for the lives of the inhabitants. Facing the entrance stands a stone dresser providing space for storage and display. The centre of the room holds the hearth. Stone box beds can be found next to the walls on either side of the hearth. The bed on the right is always slightly larger than its counterpart on the left, perhaps suggesting that it was occupied by the male inhabitant. Stone cupboards are set into the walls, particularly next to the beds. In several places, stone tanks were set into the floor. These were probably lined with clay. It is possible that these held water to be used for drinking and in food preparation. There is evidence that some of the tanks may have contained limpets, perhaps kept to be used as fishing bait. Leading off the central room are a series of small cells. These were used as storage spaces. In some instances, cells have drains connected to the main settlement drain. This suggests that they could have functioned as lavatories. The roof structure has left little trace. Most probably it consisted of turf or thatch supported on a framework made from driftwood or even whalebone.

Two of the structures at Skara Brae differ markedly from the usual design. House 8 stands separately from the rest of the settlement, and is the only structure to stand completely above ground level. The walls are unusually thick, up to two metres in width. The building contained no stone dresser or box beds, although there was a hearth and cupboard spaces. It has been suggested that this may have functioned as a workshop for the community. Alternatively, it is possible that this building was a later addition to the site. House 7 is probably the oldest structure within the settlement. It is reached its own side passage, making it more remote than the rest of the houses. The bodies of two women were found buried beneath the floor during excavation of the structure. This indicates that ritual and religion may have played a role in the function of the building. The door to this house was strangely locked from the outside. It is evident that House 7 was unique within Skara Brae and had a specialist function for the community. Its purpose was clearly to isolate individuals from their peers. It has been suggested that this structure was used as a retreat for women during their menstrual cycle, a practice which has been noted in other early societies.

Daily life at Skara Brae was dominated by membership of the community as a whole, which would have felt much stronger than it does for most people today. All of the houses are directly linked to each other promoting an intimate communal spirit. There is no evidence within the architecture of the settlement to identify a specific chief or leader of the community. None of the houses is much larger or more elaborate than the others. Indeed, there is very little evidence for social hierarchy. The inhabitants of Skara Brae seem to have possessed remarkable equality. It is possible that status was displayed through possessions rather than the size of a house. The stone dresser was the first aspect of each house visible upon entry. This was possibly used to display items of value to visitors, including pottery, beads or other artefacts which have left no trace. Gender roles seem important at Skara Brae. The distinction in the size of stone beds may reflect a divide within the house between female and male spheres. It is noteworthy that visitors were often channelled towards the male area of the house on entry from the main passage. The unusual nature of House 7, which was possibly used to isolate individual females, may also indicate a defined gender divide within the community.

PERSONAL VIOLENCE IN THE NEOLITHIC

The egalitarian community of Skara Brae can mislead the unwary into assuming that the Neolithic was a peaceful agricultural Eden. In fact, the evidence suggests that the Neolithic may have witnessed the emergence of organized warfare in Britain. From an archaeological perspective, it is difficult to clearly distinguish warfare from other forms of violence, including murder, execution and human sacrifice. In the absence of historical records, evidence for violence in the Neolithic can be deduced from human remains and through the excavation of defensive sites.[7]

One research study has examined the evidence for cranial trauma inflicted on Neolithic individuals. Three-hundred and fifty individual crania were examined, mostly dating from the early Neolithic period. From this sample, a total of thirty-one showed healed or unhealed injuries. There is an equal occurrence of cranial trauma in both male and female individuals, indicating that violence was not gender specific. The nature of the injuries indicates that most were probably caused through blunt force trauma, probably inflicted through the use of clubs made from stone, antler or wood. Not all of these individuals died as a result of their injuries as, in a number of instances, the wound clearly healed. From this sample, it has been estimated that around 2% died as a result of blunt force trauma, with another 4 – 5% surviving such an assault. Not all of these may have resulted from organized warfare, but it is nevertheless clear evidence that life in Neolithic Britain could be violent.[8]

The most devastating weapon utilized in the Neolithic was probably not the club, but rather the bow. This weapon would have been used primarily for hunting but its devastating effectiveness would have made it useful during periods of conflict. Neolithic bows were made from yew and stood between 1.5 – 2 m tall. Experiments have demonstrated that a Neolithic bow was capable of penetrating a target at a distance of 60 m. One scholar has argued that archery played a significant role in Neolithic warfare.[9] Leaf arrowheads have been found in association with a number of individual burials. An adult male skeleton recovered at West Kennet Long Barrow, for instance, was found with such an arrowhead lying in his throat area.[10]

Arrowheads have also been found in large numbers at a number of Neolithic enclosures.[11] Crickley Hill causewayed enclosure, for example, seems to have come under sustained arrow attack on at least two occasions during its history. The earliest attack seems to have resulted in part of the enclosure being burnt. After rebuilding, a section of the enclosure was attacked again. This assault resulted in over 400 arrowheads being discovered grouped around two entrances to the enclosure. Clearly, this was a coordinated attack involving multiple individuals. Similarly, at Carn Brea enclosure in Cornwall, over 800 arrowheads were found during excavation along with evidence of burning. Excavations at Hambledon Hill causewayed enclosure revealed two male individuals who had been buried beneath a collapsed rampart. Both men had arrowheads lodged in their throats.

The emergence of organized warfare during the Neolithic is not surprising. Farming requires investment in a specific area through the cultivation of crops and the raising of herds. Inevitably some areas would have been more productive than others through soil type, climate and the prevalence of natural resources. Whilst some hunter gatherer societies also protect territories or hunting ranges, Neolithic farmers had far more at stake in defending a specific area from incomers. The growth of larger societies, indicated by the monuments erected during the period, may also have encouraged tensions between rival groups which could erupt into open warfare.

STONEHENGE

Perhaps the most famous monument associated with the Neolithic stands as a prime example of the collaborative efforts of social groups during the period. The story of Stonehenge in fact encompasses the centuries both before and after the Neolithic. All too often, the monument is seen in isolation when it was actually part of a much larger ritual landscape (Fig 1). Our understanding of the site has been revolutionised in recent years by fieldwork conducted by the Stonehenge Riverside Project, made up of academics and students from a number of universities led by Professor Mike Parker Pearson.[12] A key aim of the project was to test a theory developed by Parker Pearson and his collaborator Ramilisonina, an archaeologist from Madagascar. This theory connected the meaning of Stonehenge with timber circles at the nearby site of Durrington Walls. In many societies, including those of Madagascar, wood is associated with life and stone with death. By this reckoning, the timber circles at Durrington Walls represented the domain of the living with Stonehenge forming the domain of the dead. Linking the two domains is the River Avon, which perhaps functioned as a route for transiting between the realms of the living and the dead.[13]

The site of Stonehenge as we currently see it is the result of a series of modifications made to the site throughout Prehistory. The first evidence for ritual activity at Stonehenge consists of four holes, discovered beneath the modern visitor car park, which held timber posts aligned on a single axis. The discovery of monuments erected by hunter gatherers is extremely unusual, indicating that this landscape held religious significance prior to the

Neolithic. Construction at the site began during the middle Neolithic (3000 – 2920 BC) and continued through to the middle Bronze Age (*c.* 1520 BC). Throughout this period the site changed rapidly with standing stones being removed and rearranged into new groups. The phases of construction at the site entailed a significant level of investment in terms of manpower and management structure.

The largest stones within the monument are the sarsens, which weigh up to thirty-five tons. Although sourced from the local area, the transport and erection of these stones was a considerable feat of engineering. The smaller stones set within Stonehenge are named 'bluestones'. These were the earliest stones to be erected at the site. Geological analysis has indicated that these stones were quarried in the Preseli Hills of south west Wales. This would have involved a journey of around 250 km to transport the stones, the largest of which weighs up to ten tons. For centuries, debate has raged about the method by which these stones were transported. Some scholars have argued that they were moved naturally to the area through glacial action. Recent analysis of the movement of glaciers across Britain indicates that this is unlikely. Movement by sea and rivers would have required less manpower but raises considerable practical problems. Transporting the stones over land would have required significant manpower and organisation, but would have emphasized the special nature of the task being undertaken. In some ways, the journey of the bluestones may have been similar to the journey of the Olympic Torch through Britain in 2012, in terms of promoting a sense of communal celebration and pride. A number of archaeologists have suggested that the bluestones were believed to have special healing powers, based on a number of folklore sources, which would have also explain the great effort invested in transporting them.[14]

The monument at Stonehenge is aligned on the solstice axis, meaning that sunrise and sunset at the midsummer and midwinter solstices was reflected in the architecture and arrangement of the stones. This deliberate marking of the seasons is as important to some people today as it evidently was to the Neolithic population near Stonehenge. During fieldwork conducted by the Stonehenge Riverside Project, a surprising feature was discovered which may explain the alignment of the stones. Archaeologists discovered parallel gullies running through the chalk bedrock. These features are entirely natural, having been created by the movement of water and the freeze-thaw mechanism. Yet despite their natural creation, they are also aligned with the solstice axis. It therefore seems extremely likely that Stonehenge was constructed as a means of monumentalising an existing natural phenomenon. This may also explain the erection of the line of posts by Mesolithic hunter gatherers in the same area. Even when buried beneath the soil, the gullies would still have been visible on the grass above during dry summers through inhibiting the growth of vegetation above.

Yet Stonehenge is about far more than the midsummer and midwinter solstices. It is the largest known cemetery from the period between 3000 – 2000 BC, with over sixty known cremation burials. There is the potential for many more cremation burials to reside within the area which has not been excavated due to legal protection. This significantly reinforces Parker Pearson's argument that Stonehenge represented the domain of the dead. Reverence for the ancestors is particularly important in early agricultural societies and it is possible that the cremation burials interred at Stonehenge represent the ancestors of the community which laid claim to the site.

If Stonehenge was dedicated to the ancestors, then the nearby site of Durrington Walls may represent the domain of the living. At least three timber circles are known to have stood within the vicinity of the site. Durrington Walls consists of a henge, which is defined as a large enclosure ditch with a bank raised outside. Strictly speaking, Stonehenge cannot be defined as a henge as its bank lies inside the surrounding ditch. The Stonehenge Riverside Project focussed on understanding what had happened at the site prior to the construction of the henge. Excavations revealed one of the largest settlements ever discovered from Neolithic Europe. It is estimated that there may have been up to 250 houses on the site, housing a potential population of 4000 individuals. Despite its size, this was not a permanent settlement. Analysis of the copious amount of pig bones found during the excavation demonstrates that the settlement was probably occupied at midwinter and midsummer, the same period of the year when Stonehenge would have been particularly important. The animals were not reared locally, but seem to have brought to the site specifically for consumption. Very few human bones were recovered at Durrington Walls, suggesting a clear emphasis on the living rather than the treatment of the dead. It seems likely that Durrington Walls functioned as a seasonal settlement, where communities gathered to celebrate key events in their annual calendar. This perhaps would have been when animals could be traded, deals done and marriages arranged. It would have provided a welcome respite from the harsh lives of the early farming communities.

Parker Pearson believes that the Stonehenge sacred landscape was deliberately shaped to represent unity. The natural bedrock gullies in alignment with the solstice axis perhaps indicated that the area represented the unity of the earth, sun and heavens. The transport, shaping and erection of the stones would have required communal unity on a massive scale, as witnessed by the size of the Durrington Walls settlement. Parker Pearson has theorised that there may have been a migration of early farming communities from the Preseli region of Wales to Salisbury Plain during the Neolithic period. If this is the case, than the inclusion of Preseli bluestones at Stonehenge would have clearly identified the site as belonging to the ancestors and would have demonstrated the unity of the living with the dead and the wider cosmos. It is possible that we will never fully understand the meaning and significance of the monuments of the Stonehenge landscape. What is clear, however, is that the monuments represent a complex belief system supported by an advanced understanding of engineering and the movement of celestial bodies.[15]

The Neolithic represents possibly the most important period of change in Britain. The transition from hunting and gathering to farming facilitated a number of changes in social organisation, from the small community of Skara Brae to the great mass of people who gathered twice a year at Durrington Walls. The surplus provided by effective farming practices supported the creation of a range of distinct monuments including henges, causewayed enclosures and cursus monuments. Yet this change came at a cost, in the form of significant intercommunal violence.

Chapter 3

The Bronze Age

(*c*. 2500 – 800 BC)

One of the closing acts of the story of King Arthur and his knights consists of the disposal of the sword Excalibur. As the king lies mortally wounded, his trusted companion Sir Bedevere takes the sword and tosses it into a lake where it is grasped by a mysterious hand rising from the water. Arthur will soon make a similar journey, as he is conveyed to the mysterious Isle of Avalon to await his return at our greatest hour of need. The sword Excalibur, beyond its obvious role as a weapon, can be viewed as an artefact which represents Arthur's status, strength and kingship. It therefore seems appropriate that it will have no other owner and will instead disappear in magical circumstances. The story of Arthur, as we shall see in a later chapter, is a myth without factual basis. Yet the scene of the disposal of Excalibur in a lake reaches back into prehistory and owes much to religious belief and ritual practice in the Bronze Age.

The system of dividing prehistory into three separate periods, namely the Stone Age (Palaeolithic, Mesolithic and Neolithic), Bronze Age and Iron Age has been in use since the nineteenth century. Whilst this system is a convenient method of delineating the vast span of prehistory, it has increasingly been viewed as overly simplistic. The boundary between the Neolithic and Bronze Age is particularly problematic in this regard. The developments at Stonehenge, for example, continue through the late Neolithic and into the early Bronze Age, with little to suggest any radical differences between the two eras. It should also be noted that there are significant variations in the archaeological record on a regional basis meaning that some areas could be classed as Neolithic whilst others should, more properly, be considered to show the characteristics of the Bronze Age. Indeed, many archaeologists view the late Neolithic and early Bronze Age as one distinct period. There does seem to be a clear transition around 1500 BC between this early period and the middle and late Bronze Age. The reasons for this will be examined later, but it is clear that there were three elements to this transition.[1] The cultivation of land became increasingly concentrated on areas with productive soils, with less useful areas abandoned from an agricultural perspective. The internment of the dead became less visible in the landscape as Bronze Age people ceased to use round barrows as funerary monuments and instead used cremation cemeteries or urnfields. It is also possible that they disposed of their dead using methods which leave no archaeological trace, such as scattering their ashes in lakes, rivers and other watery places. The amount of metal artefacts deposited with the deceased also radically decreased after 1500 BC. Instead, metal artefacts tended to be deliberately deposited in hoards not directly associated with funerary monuments. Whilst acknowledging that the Bronze Age consists of at least two phases, studying the period as a self-contained unit of time allows us to understand the origins of metalworking in Britain and the impact which this had on society, culture and the landscape.

THE SIGNIFICANCE OF BRONZE

The key difference between the Bronze Age and the preceding periods consists of the use of metals, as opposed to stone, for the creation of tools and weapons. In fact, the earliest use of metals in Britain probably belongs to the late Neolithic. Artefacts made of gold and copper have been dated to between 2700 and 2000 BC. Even this early date is considerably later than the appearance of metalwork in the Near East and Europe, which can be traced back to almost 2000 years before their use in Britain. In some areas of Europe, archaeologists have been able to identify a separate Copper Age, prior to the advent of bronze. From a British perspective, the sole use of copper was probably too short to classify as a specific period in its own right. Copper is a relatively soft metal and does not possess many utilitarian advantages over the earlier stone tools. For this reason, bronze became increasingly important as a resource. Bronze is produced by mixing copper with tin through a ratio of around 8:1. In Britain, lead was often added to the mix as well.

The creation of bronze required a renewed emphasis on mining. Tin was available in sufficient quantities in Cornwall, where it continued to be mined into the modern period. Copper appears to have been mined at a number of sites, the most interesting of which can be found at the Great Orme near Llandudno. The Great Orme mine was one of the largest Bronze Age mines in Europe. Mining at the site continued from around 1800 – 900 BC: an extremely long lifespan for an individual mine, perhaps indicating how important it was in Bronze Age Britain. Copper ore was extracted by heating the rock through the use of fire. It was then rapidly cooled by throwing water upon it leading to cracks being formed. Tools made of bronze, bone and antler were then used to break it down further. The mine consisted of two separate categories of activity. Opencast working on the surface required the removal of around 40,000 cubic metres of material. Below ground, a series of horizontal and vertical shafts run to a depth of 70 m below ground level. The narrow width of some of the tunnels makes it almost certain that children were used as miners. It has been estimated that the Great Orme mine would have produced up to 235 tonnes of copper during its working life. The extent of the workings and the long span of the mine's existence demonstrate the value which was placed on bronze during this period.[2]

It should be appreciated that the process of creating metals, from material taken from the ground, and converting it into a useful object can be seen as magical. The skill necessary to perform this task would have given the metalworker considerable status. A good example of this can be found in a barrow (or burial mound) at Upton Lovell in Wiltshire. This barrow dates to between 1900 and 1700 BC. The male individual buried within the mound was surrounded by an array of unusual objects including a cloak decorated with thirty-six boar tusks, axe heads and stone cups. He also possessed a set of hammers for working metals and a collection of polishing stones. It is almost certain that the Upton Lovell burial represents an early metalworker. It has also been suggested that he may have been a shaman, based on some of the other items within his burial assemblage. The magical power which a shaman was believed to possess could easily be ascribed also to his metalworking abilities, which could be seen as a form of alchemy in producing new useful materials from what appeared to be stones. Throughout prehistory and in later periods, the modern distinction between the sacred and secular did not exist. Daily activities were infused with ritual actions and religious belief to maintain a sense of harmony with the deities.[3] The extraction and use of metals would also have had deep ritual significance, particularly due to the level of danger and risk associated with these activities.

BEAKER CULTURE

The appearance of metalworking in Britain raises the issue of how such knowledge and skill was transmitted. A number of archaeologists have assumed that the advent of the Bronze Age indicates the arrival in Britain of a migrant population who brought an understanding of metalworking with them. It is noteworthy that across most of Europe the appearance of metalworking is roughly contemporary with a new style of pottery in the forms of finely decorated beakers. Material evidence for metalworking alongside beaker pottery has been identified as signifying a Beaker Culture. Evidence for this Beaker Culture has been found from across Europe from as far east as Hungary to Ireland in the west. Beaker pottery tends to be found in graves from around 2500 – 2200 BC, in other words around the start of the Bronze Age. Beaker Culture is not simply a case of finding beaker pottery. Instead, it seems to be represented by a complex package of artefacts which are repeated across multiple sites. Typical Beaker assemblages contain beaker pottery, copper knives, flint arrowheads and stone wrist-guards, to protect the individual's wrist and arm during archery. The frequency with which these artefacts are found together indicates that they were of more than practical value. On first glance they perhaps suggest a hunter or warrior identity, but they may also have been symbolic of the values prized by the Beaker Culture rather than demonstrating the attributes of the deceased individual.

Over 2000 sites in Britain and Ireland have produced Beaker pottery. In Britain, evidence for the Beaker Culture is particularly concentrated around Wessex and the Upper Thames Valley, as well as along the eastern coast. A recent scientific project has studied the remains of Beaker people from British graves in order to understand their diet and lifestyle.[4] These individuals seem to have had a specific diet, not necessarily linked to their particular environment. Very little evidence for a seafood or marine diet was found, even from individuals found close to the coast. Analysis of dental wear suggests that they did not consume bread made from stone ground flour, although it seems like their diet was high in green vegetables. Pottery analysis has revealed high levels of consumption of a range of dairy products. Overall, these individuals seem to have been of relatively good health. There is far less evidence for personal violence than during the Neolithic period. Analysis of oxygen and strontium isotopes in dental enamel allows scientists to trace the likely region in which an individual was raised as a child, based on the drinking water which they consumed. When this technique is applied to Beaker people in Britain, it suggests a reasonably mobile population. A high proportion of them were not raised in the area in which they were buried. Some certainly had links with the Continent.

Three of the most important burials for understanding Beaker Culture have been found close to Stonehenge at Amesbury and Boscombe Down.[5] The grave of the so-called Amesbury Archer contains the largest assemblage of grave-goods ever discovered within a Beaker burial. He was buried with Beaker pots, a wrist-guard, arrowheads, flints, a copper knife and a stone for working metal. Two gold earrings were also placed in the grave. The Archer was between 35 and 45 years old at the time of his death. Radiocarbon dating indicates that he was buried between 2380 – 2290 BC. Analysis of his dental enamel indicates that the Amesbury Archer probably grew up on the

Continent, most likely somewhere close to the Alps. Another grave was found close to that of the Archer. This individual, nicknamed the Companion by archaeologists, died between 2350 – 2260 BC. Both the Archer and his Companion possessed the same congenital foot condition indicating a genetic relationship. It seems highly likely that these individuals were father and son. Interestingly, the Companion was raised locally in Wessex but seems to have spent some of his teenage years on the Continent. The third grave, from Boscombe Down, consists of a communal burial of a group named the 'Boscombe Bowmen'. A group of several adults, teenagers and children were buried together, possibly over a long period of time. The grave has been tentatively dated to 2510 – 2300 BC. It seems highly likely that these individuals were all part of a family group. All of the individuals in the grave were male. Eight Beaker pots were discovered alongside the burials, the largest number known from a single burial. A boar's tusk and arrowheads were also recovered from the site. Like the Archer, scientific analysis indicates that these individuals were not raised locally. We cannot be sure where they come from exactly, although the Lake District or Wales are possibilities. Some archaeologists have argued that they could have originated in mainland Europe.

The burials at Amesbury and Boscombe Down indicate a surprising degree of mobility during the early Bronze Age. Only the Companion was raised locally and he had spent a considerable amount of time in mainland Europe during his youth. There is clear evidence in these burials of prolonged and sustained contact with the mainland. It is noteworthy that the analysis of strontium and oxygen isotopes in dental enamel can only trace movements during the youth of an individual. Journeys made during adulthood cannot be traced. It is evident that the Beaker people were at least a semi-mobile population with considerable social links across Britain and Europe. The journey which the teenage Companion made to Europe would have entailed crossing the English Channel and a number of different territories. The fact that such an itinerary was possible demonstrates the existence of complex social networks connecting Beaker individuals across Britain and mainland Europe. Not all of the Beaker people were of Continental origin. It seems likely that there was an initial arrival of a small number of individuals who carried knowledge of metal working with them. The Amesbury Archer was potentially one of these first arrivals. They assimilated into the local population but their descendants maintained their traditions and status markers through the artefacts with which they were buried. The Beaker people also maintained their semi-mobile lifestyles which included, in some instances at least, travel across and beyond Britain.

Contact with mainland Europe flourished throughout the Bronze Age. In part, this was due to the demand for bronze and other metal objects. Trading networks between Britain and the Continent became increasingly sophisticated to serve this demand. Although it is difficult to trace the mechanics of this early trading system, it should not be viewed as one-way traffic. Cornish tin would have been of particular demand on the Continent as a necessary part of the bronze production process. Similarities are apparent in the archaeological record on both sides of the Channel in terms of material culture and settlement types, indicating widespread and prolonged interaction between communities. Artefacts recovered through underwater archaeology provide an insight into the scale of trade taking place across the Channel. Such finds often come from presumed shipwrecks, although others could be a product of deliberate deposition at sea as a ritual act. One find at Langdon Bay off Dover consisted of around 360 bronze tools and weapons dating to around 1300 – 1150 BC. It is likely that these objects were being transported to Britain for resmelting. Recycling is not a new concept, particularly where metals are concerned. A number of shipwrecks have been discovered in Salcombe estuary in Devon. One boat carried 259 copper ingots and twenty-seven tin ingots, along with a sword and gold bracelets. This particular find has been dated to 900 BC, close to the end of the Bronze Age. The presence of copper and tin ingots strongly suggests that this was a shipment of raw materials quarried in Britain being transported to the Continent to be converted into bronze.[6]

BRONZE AGE LANDSCAPES

The Bronze Age had a profound impact on the British landscape, particularly through agriculture. Whilst the Neolithic witnessed deliberate attempts to impose monuments upon the landscape, the Bronze Age saw the first successful attempts to control the landscape through dividing it for agricultural use in a managed process. Bronze Age settlements consisted of roundhouses, usually in groups of between two and ten. Roundhouses, despite their appearance, had a sophisticated design.[7] They could possess up to 100 m^2 of floor space. Doorways tended to face south, to maximise the amount of daylight entering the dwelling. The roofs were thatched with rushes or turf. Contrary to popular depictions, chimney holes were not provided in the thatch. Experimental archaeology has demonstrated that chimney holes are a safety hazard as they encourage sparks to fly up to the thatch. Instead, the smoke would have gently dissipated through the thatch. Meat and fish may have been hung in the rafters to be smoked. Some roundhouses also had purpose built gullies outside to catch and channel rainwater pouring from the thatch. Roundhouses tended to be accompanied by outhouses and sheds for holding livestock.

Buildings of increasing complexity begin to appear in the late Bronze Age in the form of the so-called ring forts, which were built *c.* 1000 – 800 BC.[8] These were large circular structures containing one or more timber buildings, surrounded by concentric ditches. Some appear to have possessed timber palisades. Impressive examples have been excavated at Thwing in Yorkshire and Mucking in Essex. The purpose and function of the ring forts is a matter of continuing debate. Some archaeologists dislike the term ring forts, for its martial undertones, and prefer to describe them as ring works. Regardless of the term used, they were clearly imposing structures which involved a form of display. It is possible that they were elite residences with a defensive function. On the other hand, they do bear a marked resemblance to Neolithic henges. Indeed, some ring forts have been previously misidentified as henges. They could have had similar functions, as communal places for public ceremonies.

Bronze Age farmers began a deliberate process of creating field systems to divide the land between them. To a certain extent, this laid the foundations for the field systems still in use in the British countryside today. Deliberate woodland clearance had been undertaken during the Neolithic. Indeed, there is evidence of burning being used to clear areas at Star Carr during the Mesolithic. However, the early Bronze Age saw acceleration in the pace of woodland clearance across Britain, particularly in upland areas. For example, the lowlands of Cumbria were cleared of forest by 1700 BC and much of the Pennine uplands by 1200 BC.[9] This deliberate programme of woodland clearance from 2500 BC represents a clear attempt to increase the amount of land available for agricultural use through the cultivation of crops or raising of livestock.

One of the best examples for understanding Bronze Age field systems can be found on Dartmoor in Devon. Woodland clearance on Dartmoor began around 4000 BC and was completed by 1500 BC. The landscape of Dartmoor visible today owes much to the actions of Bronze Age farmers. The clearances consisted not just of removing trees and bushes, but also stones and rock which were strewn across the landscape, requiring a considerable amount of labour and organisation. Removing these rocks not only eased ploughing, but also increased the area available to vegetation and provided building materials. Bronze Age Dartmoor was characterized by the regular layout of fields over large areas. Farmers grew cereal crops and raised livestock, mainly sheep and cattle. The process of dividing Dartmoor into individual fields shows clear evidence of careful management, whether through the control of a single leader or the collaborative activities of a group of farmers.[10] In total, around 10,000 hectares of land were enclosed. Dartmoor was divided into five major territories, subdivided into large strips of land. In some cases, these were then divided into even smaller fields. The earliest field boundaries were probably built of timber. However, this would become increasingly scarce as the clearances progressed. Later boundaries consisted of 'reaves' or low straight stone barriers holding an earth bank. A hedge probably ran along the bank which, through careful management and regular pruning would prove a formidable obstacle for wandering livestock. Settlements were usually located within or close to the fields, indicating a sense of ownership over individual parcels of farmland. There is some evidence to suggest that monuments to the dead, in the form of burial cairns, were usually found close to the boundaries between different farming territories. This suggests that the role of the ancestors in watching over and protecting agricultural land, which seems to have been a prevalent belief during the Neolithic, was of continuing importance during the Bronze Age as well. Most of the settlements on Dartmoor seem to have been abandoned by around 1200 BC. This was not an isolated event, as most of the British uplands seem to have been abandoned by Bronze Age farming communities by 1000 BC at the latest. Farmers seem to have returned to the lowlands and not repeated their attempt to exploit upland areas for agricultural purposes. The abandonment of the uplands may have had an ecological cause. These areas were unsuitable for long term grazing or crop cultivation due to poor soil conditions. It is therefore possible that they were abandoned as they were no longer productive or efficient to farm. On the other hand, climate change may also have played a role in encouraging farmers to abandon their land. It has been calculated that there was a significant drop in temperature in Britain sometime around 1000 BC.[11] This climatic change would have made upland farming increasingly difficult, particularly during the winter months. It seems likely that poor soil conditions combined with an increasingly harsh climate forced Bronze Age farmers to return to the lowlands.[12]

Lowland farms were not without their own problems. The Fenlands of East Anglia, for example, were prone to flooding during the winter months. A long standing research project has studied the Bronze Age landscape around Fengate near Peterborough. Farms tended to be located on the higher land to prevent them from being flooded. The field system was defined by boundary ditches. Droveways, for facilitating the movement of livestock to summer pastures, were located every 200m or so across the landscape. These droveways were clearly marked through ditches and banks.[13]

FLAG FEN

An insight into the religious beliefs of these early Fenland farming communities is provided by the site of Flag Fen. This site would have been a shallow lake during winter months, although it probably dried out somewhat during the summer.[14] Excavations have revealed a timber trackway which connected dry ground at Fengate to an island at Whittlesey, a distance of just over 1 km. This trackway was not a light undertaking. Over 60,000 timber posts were used in its construction, requiring the felling of over 20,000 trees. Given the local environment, this timber must have been transported a considerable distance to the site. The trackway was probably at least partly submerged during the winter, meaning that it would have been in use during the summer, when sand and gravel were spread along it to prevent slippages. Dendrochronological dating of the timbers indicates that it was in use from 1300 – 924 BC.

Excavations at Flag Fen revealed far more than the timber causeway. Over 300 separate finds of Bronze Age metalwork were recovered from the site, including swords, daggers, spearheads and metal working implements. Shale bracelets and a surprising quantity of dog bones were also discovered. These objects had been deliberately thrown into the water from the timber trackway. The dog bones indicate that these animals were sacrificed at the site. Many of the objects had been deliberately broken or put beyond use prior to being deposited in the water. Some of the spearheads, for example, had been partially melted down. The range of finds recovered from the site indicates that deliberate depositions were taking place at Flag Fen for almost 1300 years. This was clearly a site of great ritual significance.

What was going on at Flag Fen? We started this chapter by considering the disposal of the sword Excalibur in a lake, in circumstances which are remarkably similar to Bronze Age rituals at Flag Fen. It is possible that a similar mindset was held by the local Bronze Age population. Weapons and tools are markers of status and social identity, as is evidenced by the arrowheads interred with the Amesbury Archer and Boscombe Bowmen. They can represent the strength, martial prowess and authority of the individual, or the values of a particular society. The deliberate vandalism of these objects was perhaps designed to prevent them being used by humans again. It could be that a warrior would dedicate his weapons to a deity on the completion of his fighting career (in a way similar to the story of King Arthur) or in fulfilment of a vow after a victory. It could be that these objects were dedicated because of their intrinsic value as objects fit for the gods, rather than for the personal history of the individual concerned.

The deliberate deposition of artefacts in the ground as hoards is particularly common in the Bronze Age and beyond. Although it was once believed that these objects had been hidden for later retrieval, it is now almost certain that these hoards represent deliberate ritual activity. It is possible that the demand for trade with the Continent was encouraged through the removal of metal from circulation to be interred in hoards. Although hoards were also buried on dry land, watery sites were a particular focus for ritual depositions.[15] Bronze Age artefacts have been recovered from a number of rivers in Britain, including the Thames and Trent, indicating that this was not a localised phenomenon. The concept of liminality is important for understanding the ritual significance of watery places in the Bronze Age. The term 'liminal' refers to a place, person, event or object which sits at the boundary between two worlds or domains. Halloween is a liminal event, as it is the time when the boundary between the living and the dead is believed to be permeable. Likewise, a shaman is a liminal individual as he or she is believed to possess the ability to travel to the divine realm. Watery places can be identified as liminal locations, in that they appear to represent the boundary between this world and that of the supernatural. It is impossible to understand exactly what a Bronze Age community may have believed about a specific location, but it is likely that the concept of liminality explains why they deposited objects in the water at Flag Fen. They were literally sending it to the gods. It is interesting to note that we are essentially echoing this behaviour whenever we throw coins into a wishing well.

SEAHENGE

The most enigmatic Bronze Age site in Britain has been erroneously nicknamed Seahenge, although it is certainly not a henge. Seahenge consists of a series of oak posts which were discovered on a beach near Holme-next-the-Sea (Fig 2). In the Bronze Age, this site was situated close to the sea, on an area of mudflats protected from the fury of the waves by sand and gravel banks. The posts were arranged in a rough circle or ellipse with a diameter of around 6.5 m. A total of fifty-five different timbers formed the perimeter. These posts would probably have risen 3 – 4 m into the air. In contrast to the timber circles of the Neolithic, these were not designed to surround a public area. The surrounding timbers form a solid wall with a narrow entrance formed only by a forked timber post. This entrance faces the south west which, perhaps deliberately, is the direction of the midwinter sunset. The activity conducted within was clearly not meant for public consumption. Each of the timber posts had been carefully debarked. Around fifty separate axes were used in felling and shaping the timbers. In the centre of the ellipse was an oak trunk which was deliberately placed upside down, with its root system in the air. This tree was 167 years old when it was felled. Clearly the decision to invert this trunk was of central significance for the meaning of the site. Dendrochronological dating indicates that the trees were felled between April and June of 2049 BC.

Understanding the meaning of Seahenge is difficult.[16] The location of the site by the sea strongly suggests that it was understood as a liminal location, in other words a boundary between two worlds. It has been suggested that the site could have functioned as an excarnation enclosure. Some communities in Bronze Age Britain did practice excarnation, which consists of leaving bodies to be defleshed by scavengers so that the bones can be removed later for burial. In this theory, the body could have been placed in the roots of the inverted trunk at the centre of the site. The concept of inverting a tree trunk is known from European folklore, where it was believed to grow in the other world. Another way to understand the site may be to consider the theory that wood was used in prehistoric religion to symbolise life, as opposed to stone which represented death.[17] In this case, Seahenge would be the focus for ceremonies and rituals concerning the living rather than the deceased.

The people of Bronze Age Britain seem tantalisingly close to us and yet, at the same time, remarkably alien. Looking at their farms and field systems, it is easy to recognise that they would have shared many of the problems experienced by modern farmers: the climate, flooding and soil conditions. Their connections with European communities and, in some instances, their mobility may also seem familiar. However, many of their beliefs defy our attempts to understand them through their complexity and sophistication. Our interpretations often rely heavily on comparative material from other periods and locations, which are not necessarily sound indicators of religious practice in prehistory. What is clear is that the population of Bronze Age Britain had a profound impact upon our landscape. Their activities do not reflect a break with those of their Neolithic ancestors, but instead represent a continuing development of the agricultural practices and belief systems of earlier prehistory. The attempted shift to upland farming, even though ultimately unsuccessful in the long term, indicates a desire to maximise the amount of land under agricultural exploitation. This, in turn, would lead to a greater agricultural surplus which could provide for a more diversified society. There are glimpses of status and rank in the Bronze Age, through the ring forts and the weapons deposited in hoards or burials. The more stratified and hierarchical societies of the Iron Age and beyond would be fed by an agricultural surplus created by the innovative developments in farming begun during the Bronze Age.

Chapter 4

The Iron Age

(*c.* 800 BC – 43 AD)

Around the year 320 BC, an explorer named Pytheas left his home in Massalia (modern day Marseilles) to travel to the northern extremities of the known world. Massalia, a Greek colony in southern Gaul, was an appropriate starting place for such a venture. The city, with a population of between 30,000 – 40,000 individuals, was a leading centre of the wine trade and probably controlled much of the maritime commerce along the northern shores of the western Mediterranean. The personal history of Pytheas remains obscure. Although a later source described him as poor, he was certainly well educated with an enquiring scientific mind. Pytheas published an account of his journey in a text entitled *On the Ocean*, scraps of which are preserved in the works of later Classical authors.

On leaving Massalia, Pytheas probably crossed southern Gaul to reach the northern coast of Brittany. A day's sailing took him northwards to Britain, where he possibly landed in Devon or Cornwall. Pytheas was attracted to Britain by the tin reserves of the south-west, which lured merchants and traders from mainland Europe. According to Pytheas, the main island of Britain was known as Albion and was inhabited by the *Pretani* (or painted ones). Pytheas' account of the tin trade, preserved in the later work of Diodorus Siculus, refers to a small island called *Ictis* which acted as a trading zone for the exchange of tin with European merchants. Such an island would have served as a safe location for both local traders and Gallic merchants. Tin purchased on *Ictis* was transported across the Channel and through Gaul to the mouth of the Rhône, where some of it would eventually have been conveyed to Massalia. It is likely that Pytheas may have first heard of the existence of Britain from conversations with tin traders in his home city.

Pytheas' journey continued along the western coast of Britain, probably through a series of short voyages. Fortunately for us, Pytheas attempted to calculate the distance he had travelled from Massalia through a series of measurements of the sun's height undertaken at separate points on his journey north. These measurements allow us to track his progress. The first measurement in Britain was probably conducted on the Isle of Man, the second on Lewis in the Outer Hebrides and the third near the northern tip of the Orkney Islands. Whilst we cannot be sure how much time Pytheas spent at these locations, his descriptions of the *Pretani* were incorporated into later accounts of Britain by Classical authors. He describes Britain as thickly populated with a people who generally lived a modest lifestyle. They stored grain in purpose built granaries and deployed chariots in combat. British society was controlled by an elite composed of kings and aristocrats who were mostly at peace with each other. It is difficult to know how accurate Pytheas' account was, or whether it was conceived from his personal observations or discussions with people he met during his journey. The northern extremity of his journey was a location he calls *Ultima Thule*, which has been identified as Iceland, although it is unclear whether he personally visited it or merely noted its existence. Pytheas' return journey took him along the eastern coast of Britain, with a possible excursion to Jutland, before passing through the English Channel and returning to Massalia via Brittany.[1]

BRITAIN & THE CLASSICAL WORLD

The significance of the Pytheas' journey lies in the fact that it marks the entry of Britain into history through the writers of the Classical period. Before Pytheas, the very existence of Britain was subject to rumour and supposition. The publication of his *On the Ocean* brought Britain and its inhabitants firmly into the known world. To a certain extent, this mirrors the shift of the wider importance of Britain during the Iron Age. For the first time, British archaeology can be supported with references to historical and literary sources. By 43 AD, many of the *Pretani*, particularly those from the southern tribes, were firmly connected to the rising superpower of imperial Rome.

It is important to note that Iron Age Britain was not a homogeneous entity, but rather was subject to significant regional variations. A leading scholar of Iron Age archaeology has identified five key regional zones across Britain during this period, namely the north-western (Scottish highlands), north-eastern (Scottish lowlands and northern England), eastern, central southern and south-western zones.[2] These regional zones are reflected in distinct changes in economic productivity and settlement patterns. Across Britain, therefore, the nature of Iron Age society and culture varied considerably. The historical sources which shed light on the period were written by Classical authors who were most interested in the tribal territories of south eastern Britain, which had the most contact with Rome. Their accounts provide a glimpse of life in the Iron Age from a narrow geographic perspective and do not necessarily reflect reality across the rest of Britain.

Across Europe, there is considerable evidence for economic decline at the end of the Bronze Age. Bronze seems to have played a decreasing role in contemporary societies as an object of value for exchange mechanisms. The dwindling supply of bronze may be linked to the end of major copper mining projects across Europe. Iron had numerous advantages over bronze as a material. The process of smelting iron ore was discovered in the Middle East by about 1500 BC. Its spread across the western world was slow, with iron smelting technology in use in Britain around 800 BC. Iron ores are commonly found across Britain, in contrast to the more restricted distribution of tin and copper. The accessibility of iron ores would have promoted the use of the material. Whilst iron can be smelted at a much lower temperature than copper, it tends to be worked at an equivalent temperature. It seems likely that smiths who formerly produced bronze switched to working with iron, utilising their existing knowledge of metalworking. In practical terms, iron formed weapons and tools which were considerably stronger, harder and sharper than their bronze counterparts.[3]

Classical sources provide us with insight into life in Britain at the end of the Iron Age. However, caution is essential when dealing with such accounts. The Roman and Greek authors who mention Britain were writing from a Mediterranean perspective. They were part of the rapidly expanding Roman Empire and therefore many of their texts are infused with an imperialist theme. Britain stood at the edge of the known world and was seen as a mysterious and strange place. Like many societies, Rome used negative stereotypes of those living beyond her borders to assert her own cultural superiority. The evidence provided by Classical authors needs to be treated carefully, particularly in terms of their source of information. In some cases, information on British geography and society was taken from earlier authors, such as Pytheas, or from discussions with traders or soldiers who may have visited Britain. Only rarely does such information come directly from personal experience.

Strabo was a Roman geographer who published a sweeping study of his subject at the end of the first century BC and beginning of the first century AD. Strabo was born in Asia Minor and certainly never visited Britain. Instead, he relied on the works of earlier authors. He claims that the lifestyles of the British were similar to those of the Gauls, if only more barbarous. However, Iron Age Britons were significantly taller than their counterparts across the Channel. Strabo supports this assertion by citing the cases of British slaves that he saw in slave markets in Rome, who stood over half a foot above the rest of the population, despite being otherwise physically unimpressive. The presence of British captives in Rome is explained through the inclusion of slaves on Strabo's list of prized British exports, alongside hunting dogs, hides, corn, cattle, gold, silver and iron. This evidence for the British slave trade is a poignant reminder of the realities of life in Iron Age Britain. Strabo states four major crossing points are used to connect the European mainland to Britain. All were centred on the mouths of major river systems, namely the Rhine, Seine, Loire and Garonne. The geography of Britain, according to Strabo, was mainly low lying and heavily wooded. He claimed the British population resided within the forests, where they built large circular stockades to serve as settlements.[4]

Some of Strabo's account is clearly fictitious. He claimed, for example, that the British 'know nothing of planting crops or of farming in general'. This is clearly nonsense, as the archaeological record demonstrates the longevity of agriculture in Britain. Yet, even despite this, Britain does emerge in better shape in Strabo's account than the inhabitants of Ireland. The Irish, he claimed, were cannibals who consumed their own fathers after death. Moreover, they frequently indulged in incestuous relationships. Needless to say, Strabo's scandalous claims concerning Ireland demonstrate the difficulties in dealing with Classical accounts of lands at the edge of their comprehension.

A more useful account of Iron Age Britain can be found in Julius Caesar's account of his Gallic Wars. Caesar was eager to present the Roman people with his version of his campaigns in order to cement his popularity and further his political career. In the course of his campaigns in Gaul, Caesar twice raided Britain in 55 and 54 BC. It is critical to note that Caesar was not a dispassionate observer of events but an author eager to emphasize his leading role and, in this case, the innovative nature of his attack on Britain, which was the first to have been carried out by Roman troops. He was keen to portray himself as a general who had expanded the boundaries of Roman power. Nevertheless, Caesar does include a brief overview of the customs of the British, which may at least have been informed by his time amongst them.

Caesar claimed that Britain possessed a large population, most of whom were native to the island. Their settlements were similar to those he had visited in Gaul. Caesar claimed that the inhabitants of Kent were the most civilized of the British. Cattle were reared in large numbers. The British were forbidden from eating hares or waterfowl, though they still reared them as pets. Tin and iron were naturally occurring, although most copper was imported. Bronze and gold coins, along with iron ingots, served as currency. Caesar claimed that the Britons daubed themselves in blue dye named woad and shaved their bodies. He showed particular interest in British sexual habits, claiming that wives were shared amongst groups of males, particularly those related by blood. Like Strabo, Caesar's interest in sexual habits of societies beyond the empire indicates a desire to depict such groups as wholly alien and uncivilized compared to the inhabitants of Rome.

POPULATION MOVEMENTS DURING THE IRON AGE

Caesar, intriguingly, stated that immigrants from Belgic Gaul had settled near the coast. Originally visiting Britain to wage war, they decided instead to remain as farmers. Caesar gave no indication of when this population movement took place and archaeologists are divided as to whether these Belgic settlers even existed. The movement of individuals and groups between Britain and the Continent during the Iron Age was not unknown. Indeed, Caesar's self-proclaimed motive for invading was that British tribes had provided reinforcements for the Gauls during his campaigns. High profile Gallic nobles frequently sought refuge in Britain during times of political and military strife. During the Roman period, the British tribe of the *Belgae* were located in Hampshire with a tribal capital at Winchester. The location of this tribe does correspond with Caesar's description. It is therefore possible that the British *Belgae* were descendants of settlers from Belgic Gaul who arrived at some point during the Iron Age.[6]

Evidence for the arrival of Continental migrants during this period can also be found on the Yorkshire Wolds. Inhumation burials are relatively rare during the Iron Age. Most of the dead seem to have been disposed of in ways which leave little trace in the archaeological record, such as through excarnation. From around 400 BC, cemeteries begin to appear in the south-west and Yorkshire. Those in Yorkshire are particularly interesting for the links they potentially demonstrate between the local population and contemporary societies in the Ardennes, Moselle region and Seine Valley. These burials on the Yorkshire Wolds have been identified as belonging to an Arras Culture (named after one of the original sites near the town of Market Weighton), common to inhabitants of both geographic areas. The most significant feature of the Arras Culture burials in Yorkshire consists of the deposition of two-wheeled vehicles (described either as chariots or carts) within graves of elite individuals. So-called chariot burials have been found elsewhere in Britain, even as far north as Edinburgh, but never in as great a frequency as they are on the Yorkshire Wolds. Another potentially anomalous feature to be found in the same region consists of square barrow mounds which often contained grave goods of European origin. These square barrows are delineated by shallow ditches which preserve their outline shape.

The most important site for understanding Arras Culture is the Iron Age cemetery at Wetwang Slack in Yorkshire. One of the burials, for example, belongs to a mature female. She was buried with an iron mirror, pork joint, dress pin and bronze box. These grave goods are indicative of her status. A dismantled cart complete with harness fittings was added to the grave. The cemetery was in use between the fourth and first centuries BC, and was carefully laid out next to a linear earthwork, close to an existing settlement. The structure of the site was carefully managed so that the distribution of barrows reflects social stratification and possibly wider cosmological beliefs. Some of the graves contain weapons deposited with the deceased. The local tribe was named the *Parisi*. Interestingly a similarly named tribe, the *Parisii*, are known to have lived in the Seine Valley. Does this suggest the Continental origins of the inhabitants of Wetwang Slack and the Yorkshire Wolds?

There are some anomalies which must be considered in understanding the meaning of Arras Culture. The fact that the vehicles which were interred in the Yorkshire burials were dismantled contrasts with similar burials on the Continent where they are usually buried in full working order. The settlement at Wetwang Slack is indistinguishable from contemporary sites across northern England. Neither the material culture nor the architecture of the site indicates that the community was in any sense distinct from any other. The roundhouses are in keeping with those from across British during the same period. There is little evidence for individuals of high status within the settlement, in contrast to some of the burials. The presence of weapons as grave goods is not reflected in the structure of the settlement, which is not overtly militarised. In other words, though the burials at Wetwang Slack are distinctive, the settlement is not. Perhaps the best explanation is that the Yorkshire Wolds was settled at some point in the Iron Age by migrants from the Seine Valley region. These individuals, probably from a very small group, assimilated into the local population. Their Continental origins were reflected not in their daily lifestyle, but through the identities they displayed in death.[7]

HILLFORTS

The landscape of the Iron Age was dictated by agricultural intensification. The roundhouse was the predominant form of housing structure. By the beginning of the Iron Age, roundhouses were increasing in size to between 10 and 15 m in diameter. This increasing size indicates that larger social groups were co-habiting. Up to twenty individuals, potentially, could live within roundhouses of this size. In some cases, roundhouses may even have possessed two storeys. There is increasing evidence that livestock were stabled within the roundhouses, requiring distinct zones of activity to be observed within the structures. Roundhouses were constructed with increasing frequency from the fourth century BC with increasing concentrations in river valleys. This suggests a burgeoning population across Britain.[8]

A symptom of the intensification of agriculture may be found in the appearance of hilltop enclosures across central Britain. These sites are identified through their large size and relative absence of interior features, in contrast to most hillforts. Whilst hilltop enclosures may be surrounded by perimeter ditches, they often utilize features of the surrounding landscape to act as a boundary. The hilltop enclosure at Walbury in Wessex consists of a trapezoidal parcel of land enclosing eighty-two acres. Archaeological investigation of the interior has revealed a scarcity of interior structures.[9] It seems likely that hilltop enclosures were used primarily for gathering livestock, essentially acting as cattle ranches. This may have taken place at certain times of year, for example to count the herd or select individual animals for slaughter. Alternatively, it could be have been used as a secure location for corralling livestock during times of war. The existence of such large enclosures, and the number of livestock which they housed, demonstrate the effectiveness of contemporary livestock rearing techniques and reveal something of the complexity of Iron Age societies.

The most famous type of sites from this period are undoubtedly hillforts. These sites are generally characterized by their physical location, which tends to dominate the surrounding landscape, and the ditch and rampart which defines the area under enclosure. Hillforts were constructed from the sixth century BC across a broad swathe of England (from the south-east through to north Wales) and Scotland (generally around the east coast). Hillforts can be found in a variety of shapes and sizes. Some, like Danebury, demonstrate a considerable amount of internal planning including roads, storage pits and dwellings. Others were far smaller and less impressive.

The purpose of hillforts has been the topic of great debate among archaeologists. It cannot be denied that many hillforts do have a violent history. Fin Cop, an imposing hillfort in Derbyshire, was constructed between 440 and 390 BC. Recent excavations uncovered an 11 m section of the surrounding ditch.[10] Nine human bodies were discovered in the ditch, buried among the remains of the surrounding wall which appears to have been deliberately collapsed into the ditch around the same time as their burial. All of the Fin Cop bodies were female. Two of the skeletons represent adults, alongside four babies and a single teenager, toddler and individual of indeterminate age. There is no evidence for trauma on their bones, indicating that they were killed through a method which would leave no skeletal trace. Strangulation or throat cutting remain distinct possibilities as potential causes of their deaths. Skeletal analysis indicates that this group had experienced considerable dietary stress and anaemia, perhaps as a result of starvation. The rampart wall had not been standing for long prior to its destruction, suggesting that it was constructed as a response to a specific threat and was destroyed during a single violent episode. The hillfort may have been established as a secure place of refuge for the local community. Unfortunately, it failed to provide them with adequate security. Given the relatively small section of ditch excavated, Fin Cop may potentially hold hundreds of bodies. The lack of male burials may be significant. It is possible that the male population was executed elsewhere on the site or disposed of in another manner. In many ancient societies, women would be enslaved by the victors.[11] The fate of the female inhabitants of Fin Cop suggests that the attack which destroyed their hillfort was motivated by a desire to commit genocide against the inhabitants. It is a salutary reminder of how dangerous life in Iron Age Britain could be.

It may be too simplistic to view all hillforts as solely defensive structures. It used to be widely assumed that hillforts represented the residence of an elite, who perhaps ruled over the farmers of the surrounding territory. Yet not all hillforts contained internal structures suggesting that they were dwellings of any great significance. Some may have been inhabited seasonally or infrequently on particularly important occasions. The dramatic location of many hillforts emphasizes their visibility. This could be because the inhabitants wished to maintain surveillance over the landscape. Yet it can also be argued that they were meant to be seen as status symbols for the groups who built them. The act of digging the perimeter ditches and constructing the surrounding rampart would have required the involvement of the wider community. These were large scale construction projects. Similar to the great monuments of the Neolithic, the act of bringing the community together with a common purpose and objective may have been as significant as what they constructed. The hillfort may have continued to play a key role in the life of the community, not only as a refuge in times of trouble but as a venue for festivals and ceremonies. Perhaps the value of hillforts lay in their function as a geographical centre for a tribal group dispersed over a large area.[12]

DANEBURY

From around 300 BC, there is considerable evidence for a shift in the usage and meaning of hillforts. A large number of smaller hillforts seem to have been gradually abandoned. In most areas, only a single hillfort remained.

This may indicate the increasing dominance of elite groups over their local areas. Danebury in Hampshire is one of the best understood hillforts due to a longstanding research project which analysed the site within its landscape setting.[13] Almost 20% of the site has been fully explored by archaeologists, giving an unparalleled insight into the growth, development and decline of an important hillfort. The site was established around the middle of the sixth century BC, remodelled significantly during the fourth century BC and thrived until the end of the main phase of its existence around 100 BC. The hillfort lies 143 m above sea level, making it visible from a considerable distance over the surrounding landscape. Thirteen acres of land are enclosed within three major earthworks. Danebury's ramparts were clearly designed for a defensive purpose. The rampart was originally topped with a timber fence up to 4 m in height. Later, the timber wall was replaced and the rampart rebuilt to form a descending slope up to 16 m in height crested by a flint wall. Pits within the hillfort, clustered close to the rampart, held stores of slingshots to be used when the site was under attack. One such pit held 11,000 separate stones.[14]

Danebury was clearly an important location during the Iron Age. Investigations have demonstrated that a large number of contemporary hillforts from the local region were abandoned by 300 BC, leaving Danebury as one of the few remaining. Excavations have revealed that Danebury's interior contained a large number of storage pits and structures. Over 18,000 separate post holes have been identified across the site. Post holes mark the original locations of timber posts which have long since rotted away. Roundhouses were the most prominent structures, usually around 6 – 9 m wide. Granaries were also present. These were raised up to 1 m above ground level to prevent the grain within from being spoiled by pests or damp. Most of the granaries appear to be a relatively late addition to the site. Given that Danebury was occupied for over 500 years, it is unsurprisingly difficult to estimate the population at any one time. In all likelihood, the population was between 200 – 300 individuals for most of its existence.

Danebury was peppered with around 5000 storage pits which were dug into the earth to store grain over the winter months. Storage pits provided an efficient method of storing grain in the absence of granaries, provided that they were adequately sealed. The act of digging into the earth and trusting that the sealed grain would not be ruined was surrounded in ritual. Around a third of excavated storage pits contained some form of offering, including human and animal remains. Sheep, cattle, horses, pigs, dogs and a single cat and goat were discovered, either as whole skeletons or individual body parts. Pots, iron tools and burnt grain were also deposited.

It is possible that the inhabitants of Danebury viewed the storage pits as liminal locations, perhaps between the human world and the realm of the gods below. These offerings would therefore be perceived as a method for ensuring divine protection for the interred grain. Similar offerings may have been involved during the construction of the ramparts. A quarry pit close by contained the bodies of three male individuals. Not all of the human remains buried in storage pits consisted of whole skeletons. Individual body parts were also commonly found. This suggests that excarnation was practised by the local population. The emphasis on the storage of grain at the site is intriguing. It has been calculated that Danebury held at least twenty times the amount of grain stored by local farming communities. Perhaps Danebury functioned as the residence of a local elite who monopolised local grain production and whose stores would provide them with considerable influence and power.

The main phase of the occupation of Danebury came to a sudden and dramatic end around 100 BC. The main gate of the hillfort was destroyed by fire. Most of the interior was abandoned at around the same time, although limited occupation seems to have continued into the Roman period on a very basic scale. Did Danebury fall as a result of a hostile assault by enemy forces? The inhabitants of the site were not immune from violence. A number of bodies recovered from the site show evidence of combat. One male was killed through a spear smashed through his forehead and another had a cranial wound caused by a sword. One male skull displays a prominent smashed eye socket caused by a blow from a blunt object. Around 100 BC, the remains of twenty-one individuals were hurriedly buried in two pits close to the main gate. The group included men, women and children. Most of the remains show signs of mutilation. Is this evidence for a massacre at the site, with the dead hurriedly disposed of into mass graves? It is possible these burials could also represent the disposal of the dead from a local excarnation site as Danebury was being abandoned. Although the firing of the main gate can be viewed as a hostile act of aggression, it can also be seen as a symbolic act to mark the end of occupation at the site, possibly carried out by the inhabitants themselves. It is, however, worth noting that another hillfort at Bury Hill, only 6 km away, seems to have been reoccupied and its defences reinforced around the same time that Danebury was in decline.[15] Archaeological excavation at Bury Hill indicates that the occupants had a distinct profile from those at Danebury. In particular, large numbers of horses seem to have been kept at the site. Chariot fittings have also been recovered. Could the inhabitants of Bury Hill have been an emerging horse riding elite who inflicted a devastating defeat on Danebury's defenders?[16]

In Scotland, the Iron Age witnessed the creation of two new forms of settlement structures, namely brochs and crannogs. The earliest broch seems to have been constructed around 600 BC, although most date from between 200 BC – 200 AD. Brochs consist of a tall tower-like structure up to above 9 m in height, often with surrounding buildings.[17] The wall of the broch contains the staircase leading to the upper floors. In many instances, broch entrances are flanked by a guardroom. Whilst some brochs were clearly the residence of a single family unit, others show evidence for larger social groupings. The Broch of Gurness on Orkney, for example, is surrounded by a double walled enclosure which contains fourteen separate buildings. Analysis of space and movement within the site indicates that it was constructed to reflect and reinforce an existing social hierarchy.[18] Movement through the broch and surrounding buildings seems to have been tightly controlled. The broch tower offered the possibility for surveillance over the enclosure. It seems likely that the broch housed an elite family, surrounded by the homes of their retainers who were offered the protection of the enclosure from external attack. Brochs offered an opportunity for their owners to demonstrate their status over the surrounding landscape.

Crannogs are waterside settlements, often in the form of artificially constructed islands, found across Scotland. Timber posts would be driven into the bed of the lake or loch, enclosing a foundation of rubble and brushwood. Oak logs would then form a platform on which a large hut could be safely constructed. Crannogs were usually joined to the shore by a timber walkway. Crannogs continued in use into the Roman period. Their isolated location meant that they could be easily defended. Moreover, the effort which went into their construction probably reflects the status and power of their inhabitants. The connection between crannogs and water may also indicate a religious significance in their location.[19]

By the late first century AD, hillforts were gradually superseded by a new type of settlement named an *oppidum* (plural *oppida*). *Oppida* are rather mysterious archaeological sites. In contrast to hillforts, they were established on low lying ground. The reason for the establishment of *oppida* is unclear. It has been suggested that their construction may have been prompted by increasing trade links with mainland Europe, which prompted local elites to attempt to control trade routes through their territory. Lofty hillforts would have been completely unsuitable for such a purpose. *Oppida* are difficult to trace archaeologically, although a number have been identified including Colchester, Silchester and St Albans. It is no coincidence that each of these sites became important Roman settlements. Most *oppida* appear to have been clearly defined by earthworks. Those at Colchester enclosed an area of around 32 km^2. Earthworks of the *oppidum* at Chichester run for over 10 km. It has been estimated that constructing the ramparts would have required the movement of over 340,000 tonnes of soil.[20]

RELIGION

Religion and ritual permeated all areas of life in Iron Age Britain to the extent that it cannot be separated easily from other aspects of the archaeological record.[21] Iron Age religion is famously linked to the Druids. Our best surviving source for their organisation, power and belief system is Julius Caesar who described Gallic Druids in his account of the conquest of Gaul. Whilst Caesar was not describing Druids in a British context, he emphasizes that they originated in Britain and young Gauls still travelled to Britain to become learned in their lore. Caesar believed that Gauls held incredible influence within Gallic society. He claims that the Druids oversaw acts of worship, sacrifices and ruled on religious matters. Outside of the religious sphere, Druids acted as judges pronouncing sentences on individuals and tribal groups. Anyone who failed to follow the rulings of the Druids was prohibited from attending sacrifices, leading to them being shunned from wider society.

Caesar states that the Druids were led by a single leader. Becoming leader usually involved an election, although sometimes single combat was preferred. The Druids assembled each year near modern Chartres. Many young men were eager to join the Druids. Training involved memorising a large number of verses and lasted for up to twenty years. To protect their rites, the Druids refrained from committing any of their beliefs to writing. This poses considerable problems for modern scholars. Caesar suggests that their main belief was in the immortality of the soul through reincarnation. Perhaps as a result of his military interests, Caesar argued that this made the Gauls better fighters as they were less terrified at the prospect of death. The Gauls also maintained an interest in the cosmos and the gods.[22]

Another Roman writer, Pliny the Elder, portrays a particular aspect of the Druidic belief system. Pliny was an experienced Roman statesman with a passion for science. Unfortunately, this was to be his downfall as he died whilst venturing to investigate the eruption of Mount Vesuvius in AD 79. Pliny describes Druidic rituals associated with mistletoe, which he probably came into contact with during military service on the Rhine. The Druids believed that there was a direct connection between mistletoe and the type of tree on which it grew. They particularly venerated the growth of mistletoe on hard-oaks, which they believed had been sent directly by the gods. When such a plant was found, the Druids would gather around the tree. Often this event was arranged to coincide with a date of particular religious significance. A ritual banquet would be prepared beneath the tree and two white bulls would be brought for sacrifice. The chief Druid, clad in white robes, would ascend the tree and cut the mistletoe with a gold sickle. The mistletoe was caught on a white cloak and used to make a drink which acted as a fertility aid and antidote to poisons.[23]

Druids have frequently been associated with the practice of human sacrifice. In the absence of Druidic texts, it is extremely difficult to prove whether this connection is justified. Caesar claims that the Druids officiated at human sacrifices, which were used to appease the gods or save the life of another. He describes how some Gallic tribes constructed huge wicker frames which they filled with unfortunate victims and then burnt. This description clearly influenced British horror film 'The Wicker Man'. It must be remembered, however, that Caesar was writing from a specific sociocultural perspective. Emphasising the Gallic propensity for human sacrifice depicted them as less human and therefore inferior to Romans. Finding archaeological evidence for human sacrifice is problematic. Yet one British site may provide an insight into this murky aspect of Iron Age religion. (Druids have attracted a number of scholarly treatments, of varying quality. Two recent studies are Hutton, 2009 and Aldhouse-Green, 2010)

LINDOW MAN

In 1984, the well preserved body of an Iron Age man were recovered from a peat bog on Lindow Moss in Cheshire. Nicknamed Lindow Man, this was the most complete of at least four bodies to have been interred at the site during this period. Radiocarbon dating demonstrates that he died at the very end of the Iron Age or beginning of the Roman period, between 2 BC and 119 AD. The body displays a remarkable level of preservation due to the chemical environment of the bog. Lindow Man was around 25 years old when he died and stood approximately 1.7 m tall. There is no evidence that he was malnourished and his beard and nails were well trimmed. His lifestyle was not one of arduous daily labour. On the contrary, his physique and personal grooming may indicate that he was a man of status.[24]

Lindow Man died a violent death with a number of serious wounds displayed on his body. He was struck on the head at least twice by a blunt object. One of his ribs was broken and he was probably strangled. Lindow Man's throat was also slit at the time of his death. The excessive level of violence poses interesting questions about his final moments. There are a number of competing theories to explain why Lindow Man was killed in this way. Given Lindow Man's status, it is possible that he was the victim of a robbery. His body entered the bog naked save for a fox fur armband. Yet this doesn't explain the various acts of violence perpetrated on his body. Lindow Man was dumped face down in the bog. This suggests contempt for his corpse and possibly even an attempt at post-mortem punishment. Execution could explain this punitive aspect of his death. The choice of a watery location for his grave may indicate a religious context for his violent end. As noted in an earlier chapter, water was associated with the realm of the gods in ancient Britain. Was Lindow Man ritually sacrificed? It is interesting his stomach contained a small amount of mistletoe pollen. Mistletoe was regarded as possessing ritual significance and acts as a muscle relaxant, which would potentially have been useful in preparing someone for sacrifice. The period of his death, marked by the wider involvement of Rome in British affairs, would have been a time of considerable stress in contemporary societies. Human sacrifices usually occur at times of societal stress, as the ultimate act of seeking the support of the gods. Bodies have been found in bogs across northern Europe dating from around this period, many of which show evidence of violence. Whilst we may never know the circumstances of Lindow Man's murder, it seems highly likely that it had a ritual significance.

BRITAIN AND ROME

The wider involvement of Rome in British affairs was facilitated by the raids of Julius Caesar in 55 and 54 BC. Whilst Caesar's landings are often referred to as 'invasions', as we shall see, they were really no such thing. Julius Caesar was an ambitious Roman general and statesman. In 58 BC, he initiated the conquest of Gaul which was a natural step in the strategic expansion of Rome, although it also suited Caesar's political ambitions to establish a reputation as a proven commander. By 55 BC, he had accomplished enough in Gaul for him to begin to look for new avenues to glory and renown. On the edge of the known world, Britain offered a particularly attractive opportunity. Caesar claimed that the support offered by Britons to the Gauls was sufficient to warrant a Roman attack. Caesar began his campaign by sending Commius, the king of the Atrebates of Gaul, to seek the submission of the British tribes prior to his arrival. Caesar crossed the Channel in late summer with two of his legions. His campaign appears to have resulted in an embarrassing lack of success. The British tribes had seized and detained his envoy Commius. The crossing proved particularly difficult. His geographical sphere of activity seems to have been limited to Kent. Although the unfortunate Commius was released, the British tribes proved difficult to deal with. Caesar hastily negotiated treaties with the some of the tribes and returned to the Continent. Only two of the tribes provided hostages to demonstrate their loyalty to Rome.[25]

The following year, Caesar launched a larger attack on Britain with an assault force consisting of five legions and over 2000 cavalry, giving him an army of 30,000 troops hardened by campaigns in Gaul. The British had not been idle in the intervening period. A new military leader had emerged named Cassivellaunus and had organized a coalition of resistance against the Roman attack. It is not clear to which tribe Cassivellaunus belonged, although later Roman forces refer to him as a king. His tribal heartland appears to have been located north of the Thames. Caesar's landing was unopposed by native resistance, although a storm ruined part of his fleet. Caesar forced his way northwards towards Cassivellaunus' stronghold. Caesar's campaign was assisted by a political asset under his protection, in the form of Mandubracius, a young tribal prince. Mandubracius belonged to the Trinovantes, one of the larger tribes of the south-east region. The Trinovantes had been increasingly pressurised by Cassivellaunus' expansionist policies, ultimately resulting in the assassination of the king. Fearing for his life, Mandubracius had fled to Gaul where he sought refuge with Caesar. Now, Caesar used him to win the support of the Trinovantes who offered their surrender and cooperation in return for the installation of Mandubracius as their king. The defection of the Trinovantes was a significant coup for Caesar. Five other tribes came to terms with him as a result, namely the Cenimagni, Segontiaci, Ancalites, Bibroci and Cassi. In desperation, Cassivellaunus convinced four kings from Kent to attack Caesar's landing zone. This final attempt at resistance failed, forcing Cassivellaunos to negotiate surrender through Caesar's envoy Commius. In return for the promise of annual tribute, a guarantee of safety for the Trinovantes and the provision of hostages, Caesar embarked his forces for the return to Gaul to deal with a growing rebellion.[26]

Caesar had successfully taken Roman soldiers across the ocean to the edge of the known world. He had received the surrender of a number of British kings, obtained hostages and the promise of annual tribute. The installation of a friendly king in the form of Mandubracius was also potentially valuable in political terms. Yet his campaign was geographically limited and any influenced he had won was localized to the south-east. A Roman perspective on the British campaigns can be found in the letters of Cicero, a famous orator whose brother Quintus accompanied Caesar on the campaign of 54 BC. Cicero wrote as both an anxious relative and a politician with an eye on Caesar's political ambitions. Alongside expressing concern for Quintus' safety, Cicero noted that no silver could be found in Britain and any slaves captured would inevitably be depressingly uncultured. On completion of the campaign, Cicero recorded that, whilst hostages had been taken from the British tribes, the tribute was levied as no booty was available for the troops.[27] After Caesar's raids, Roman troops would not return to Britain for almost a century. The main reason for this lack of further military activity is that Britain was too peripheral to the empire to require invasion. The emperor Augustus did indicate a willingness to conquer Britain, but focussed instead on consolidating the German frontier. The emperor Caligula gathered an army on the Channel coast in preparation for an invasion attempt, but changed his mind and returned to Rome. Yet despite the absence of a military presence, Rome continued to play a role in British affairs.

Caesar's envoy Commius, king of the Atrebates, returned to Gaul with the Roman expeditionary force. Yet he appears to have switched sides during the Gallic revolt led by Vercingetorix and became one of the leading Gallic rebels. After the collapse of the revolt, Commius narrowly surivived an assassination attempt by a Roman officer and eventually came to terms with Rome. Commius' history as both a Roman ally and a Gallic rebel made him both useful and dangerous. Numismatic evidence suggests that Commius was settled in Britain as a king who would owe his loyalty to Rome.[28] This practice was widely used by Roman generals to assert their influence over territories beyond the frontier of the empire. Commius took up residence south of the Thames, exerting his power over Hampshire and Sussex. Coins reveal that Commius was succeeded by a number of other rulers who claimed to be his heirs, namely Tincomarus, Eppilus and Verica. It is impossible to prove whether these later rulers were related to Commius or merely sought the political advantage of claiming membership of his dynasty. To the north of the Thames, a second dynasty became established under a ruler named Tasciovanus. He was succeeded by his sons Cunobelin and Epaticcus. Roman sources indicate that Cunobelin produced two sons, Amminus and Caratacus, who later ruled in his stead.

Dissecting the murky politics and dynastic histories of the late Iron Age is a murky task. Some insight is provided by coins minted by emerging rulers. The first coins arrived in Britain from Gaul during the second century BC. The arrival of coinage was accompanied by the appearance of spectacular gold torcs, probably also a result of Gallic influences. Coins and torcs share a common purpose in displaying status, particularly through their display and distribution by rulers. Early coins minted in Britain tended to display abstract designs which were possibly influenced by shamanic rituals. After Caesar's raids, the imagery on coins becomes increasingly sophisticated and closely mirrors that displayed on Roman coins.

Roman imagery first appears on British coins during the reign of Tincomarus (c. 20 BC – AD 10), one of the self-styled 'sons' of Commius. One of the first Roman images used consisted of a mounted horseman thrusting his spear downwards. This image may have had particular resonance with British rulers due to their increasing reliance on horses, as evidenced by the horse bones and fittings from Bury Hill. The emperor Augustus left an account of his reign, the *Res Gestae*, which records the presence of two British nobles, Dumnobellaunus and Tincomarus, at his court.[29] The latter is almost certainly the son of Commius and this may explain his eagerness to use the imagery of imperial propaganda for his own purposes. The practice of taking hostages or *obsides* from tribes on the edges of the empire was frequently used by Roman authorities. These hostages were meant to ensure the compliance of their tribes. However, their exposure to Roman culture and society made them particularly valuable as future client kings. The Boscoreale Treasure, a pair of cups recovered close to Pompeii, depicts a group of barbarians presenting their children to the emperor Augustus. In all likelihood, this scene represents submission to the emperor and the presentation of hostages. Tincomarus' presence in Rome as a hostage would explain his understanding of imperial imagery which, in some instances, materialised as playful manipulation. One particular image, a boy riding a dolphin, is probably a witty play on his name which meant 'big fish'. As the use of coins became more common across the south-east, the range of Augustan propaganda utilised also increased. Visual representations of imperial concepts such as the Sphinx, Victory, the return of a Golden Age through fertility symbols and the healing of the state through sacrifices were mimicked on British coins.[30] The depictions of kings such as Cunobelin, Tasciovanus and Verica also mirror those of emperors. British kings were consciously emulating the symbols and imagery of imperial power to reflect their own status.

The display of status by the late Iron Age was not limited to coins. A timber structure established at Hayling Island in Hampshire may have been dedicated to a ruler cult linked to Commius.[31] This would have significantly strengthened the influence of his successors by reinforcing their dynastic links to a deity. It may be significant that Julius Caesar and Augustus claimed descent from a deity in the form of the goddess Venus, and both would be deified themselves after death. Around 10 BC, the cremated remains of an adult male were interred in a barrow mound close to the entrance of the *oppidum* at Colchester. The Lexden tumulus would have been a conspicuous local monument over 20 m in diameter. The deceased was buried with a significant assemblage of grave-goods. The burial included locally produced pottery alongside imported amphorae from the Continent. A Roman medallion depicting the emperor Augustus, produced within the last decade, accompanied the corpse. Chainmail armour, which had been ritually destroyed prior to deposition, was scattered across the 8 m burial pit. A folding stool, bronze cupid and silver studs also filled the grave. The individual buried within the Lexden tumulus was clearly of considerable status. The influence of Rome is clear from their burial assemblage, not only from the Augustan medallion but also the luxury goods imported from the empire.[32]

The Iron Age was a period of substantial transition. British societies changed considerably to more hierarchic structures, where individual rulers become recognisable in the archaeological record and historical sources.[33] It would be wrong to claim that Britain has ever been isolated from the Continent for any significant period of time since the last Ice Age. Movement of individuals and groups to and from the European mainland is a frequent feature of the British archaeological record. But from the late Iron Age, European involvement in British politics became more pronounced through the expanding superpower of Rome and the campaigns of Julius Caesar. This facilitated high level contacts between the elites of south-eastern Britain and the imperial court in Rome. Yet the geographic impact of these links should not be over exaggerated. Caesar's raids did not take him beyond the south-east of Britain. It is debatable to what extent Rome's influence was able to penetrate the northern and western regions beyond the territories of its client kings. The heterogeneous nature of Iron Age Britain belies easy generalisations. Only actual invasion would bring Britain firmly within the orbit of Rome.

Chapter 5

The Roman Period

(43 – 410 AD)

In the museum at the Roman fort of *Arbeia* (South Shields) can be found a large tombstone belonging to a lady named Regina, which colloquially translates as 'Queenie'. Regina is depicted on the tombstone as an elegant and respectable Roman matron. She sits on a throne like chair, clothed in a tunic and robe. Distinctive jewellery can be seen displayed on her neck and wrist. A distaff and spindle are placed on her lap and a box of wool is placed to her left. Regina's right hand rests on an ostentatious jewellery box. The inscription beneath the carving of Regina provides us with an insight into her life:

> D(IS) M(ANIBUS) REGINA LIBERTA ET CONIUGE BARATES PALMYRENUS NATIONE CATUALLAUNA AN(NORUM) XXX

> *'To the spirits of the dead, and to Regina, his freedwoman and wife, of the Catuvellauni, aged 30 years, Barates of Palmyra erected this'*[1]

Regina began her life as a member of the Catuvellauni, formerly one of the most important tribes of southern Britain during the Iron Age. She had been a slave, perhaps as a result of poverty or warfare. Her husband, Barates, had bought Regina and then freed her in order to marry her. She evidently ended her days as a relatively wealthy lady. Barates came from Palmyra, a rich trading city in Syria. Beneath the Latin inscription can be seen a heartbreakingly short Palmyrene inscription reading '*Regina, the freedwoman of Barates, alas*'. The presence of this Palmyrene inscription demonstrates the multicultural society of Roman Britain. Barates came from the other side of the empire, yet had made a comfortable life for himself on the edge of the northern frontier. Barates died further up the Tyne at Corbridge aged 68 years.[2] His profession as inscribed on his tombstone is recorded as *vexillarius*. This would normally indicate that he was a standard bearer in the imperial army. However, the absence of any other mention of military service may suggest that he received the honorific title of standard bearer for a trade organisation and that his actual profession was as a merchant. This would explain the internment of Regina at South Shields, which was a busy port throughout the Roman period. The biographies of Barates and Regina emphasize the geographic and social mobility available in the Roman world. Barates had travelled across the Empire. Regina rose from being an anonymous slave to become a wealthy lady. In some sense, they represent the social vitality and cultural diversity of Britain during the Roman occupation.

THE ROMAN INVASION

The incorporation of Britain under Roman imperial control was primarily motivated by political factors.[3] Britain posed no strategic threat to the Empire and Caesar's raids had demonstrated that its economic significance was minimal. In 41 AD, Claudius became emperor after the assassination of his nephew Caligula. Claudius had been originally been ignored in the conventional line of succession due to his physical infirmity, which may have been a result of cerebral palsy. Lacking the usual military and political experience expected in an emperor, Britain offered a perfect opportunity for Claudius to demonstrate his competence as a commander in chief and strengthen his relationship with the imperial army.

Events in Britain provided appropriate grounds for launching an attack. Cunobelinus was one of the preeminent ruler of south west Britain during the late Iron Age. The Roman biographer Suetonius identifies him as 'king of the Britons'.[4] Although it is not clear to which tribe Cunobelinus belonged, the Cassivellauni seem the most likely group. He minted coins at Colchester which suggests that his tribe had considerably expanded their territory into that of neighbouring groups. This expansion appears to have caused significant political repercussions. Around 40 AD, Cunobelinus exiled one of his sons, the unfortunate Adminius, who fled to the court of the emperor Caligula. Cunobelinus died at some point during the next three years and was succeeded by his remaining sons Caratacus and Togodumnus. By 43 AD Verica, a ruler who formerly exerted control over Hampshire, also fled Britain and sought the protection of Claudius. Whilst the exact circumstances of Verica's flight are unclear, it could be linked to further aggression by the Cassivellauni. The requests of exiled British kings for support provided Claudius with a pretext for launching an invasion.

The invasion of Britain was led by the general Aulus Plautius who commanded an army of around 40,000 troops. The army probably landed at Richborough in Kent, although some scholars have argued that Chichester may be a more likely location for the beachhead. Plautius' immediate target was the *oppidum* at Colchester, the heartland of Cunobelinus' sons. The beachhead was secured with little resistance from British forces. Instead, the Britons appear to have faded into the landscape in preparation for a guerrilla war, anticipating a similar cycle of events to Caesar's raids almost a century before. Plautius made a concerted attempt to locate Caratacus and Togodumnus. Two hard fought river crossings, of the Medway and Thames respectively, opened the way to Colchester.[5]

Plautius halted his army to await the arrival of the emperor, who would preside over the capture of Colchester. Claudius thus became the first emperor to visit Britain.[6] He arrived accompanied by a number of elephants, which he thought may be of use during the conquest. Claudius' visit was brief, only around sixteen days in total. The storming of Colchester essentially demonstrated the symbolic achievement of the professed aim of the conflict, to relinquish the power of Cunobelinus' tribe. Eleven British kings surrendered to the emperor, thus granting him a significant propaganda victory which he was not slow to utilise. Back in Rome after his visit to the front, Claudius celebrated a ceremonial triumph. His young son was granted the name Britannicus in honour of his father's victory. Arches were erected in Rome and Gaul to celebrate the conquest and the submission of the British kings. The victory significantly boosted the popularity of the emperor. Inscriptions in honour of his successful campaign have been found at a number of locations across the empire. Perhaps the most striking illustration of Claudius' victory can be seen in a stone relief from Aphrodisias in modern Turkey.[7] The relief depicts an idealised form of Claudius, young and muscular, physically restraining a young maiden. The exposed breast on the unfortunate female communicates a brutal symbolism. Claudius is raping Britannia in a ruthless analogy of the conquest of Britain.

COLLABORATION & RESISTANCE

Yet for all the imperial propaganda, the invasion was far from over. In fact, to a certain extent it would never be finished. Northern Scotland would always be outside of imperial control and Roman troops never landed in Ireland. Subduing the rest of Britain required a series of hard fought campaigns across the rest of the first century AD. The future emperor Vespasian, serving as a legionary commander, is alleged to have fought thirty separate battles and captured twenty hillforts.[8] Maiden Castle is believed to have fallen to Vespasian's legion. Early excavators discovered a series of burials which they dubbed a war cemetery on account of the presence of male individuals with violent wounds. Caratacus, son of Cunobelinus, slipped away and became a guerrilla leader of the British resistance. Captured eventually by imperial forces, he was paraded in Rome before being pardoned in a magnanimous act by Claudius. The Silures of Wales proved particularly difficult to subdue. Wales was only secured by 76 AD, around the same time that northern England was also pacified. The difficulties which the imperial army faced in Britain over decades of campaigns are crucial for our understanding of Roman Britain. Regional differences were more profound under the occupation than they had been during any earlier period.

Kings did not disappear from Britain immediately after the invasion. Indeed, one king in particular thrived under the occupation. Togidubnus is named by the Roman historian Tacitus as a king famed for his loyalty to Rome.[9] Togidubnus' base of power was Chichester, as is evidenced by an inscription from the town:

> NEPTUNO ET MINERVAE TEMPLUM PRO SALUTE DOMUS DIVINAE EX AUCTORITATE TI(BERI) CLAUD(I) TOGIDUBNI REG(I) MAGNI BRIT(ANNIAE) COLLEGI FABRORUM ET QUI IN EO SUNT D(E) S(UO) D(EDERUNT) DONANTE AREAM … ENTE PUDENTINI FIL(IO)
>
> *'To Neptune and Minerva for the welfare of the Divine House, under the authority of Tiberius Claudius Togidubnus, great king of Britain. The guild of smiths and those who belong to it gave this temple from their own resources. The site was given by (missing)...ens, son of Pudentinus.'*[10]

The context of the erection of this inscription seems clear. A guild of smiths funded and built a temple to Neptune and Minerva. This project was undertaken with the approval of their king, Tiberius Claudius Togidubnus. His name is particularly interesting. Roman citizens required three names, as opposed to the single name used by Iron Age Britons. The prefix 'Tiberius Claudius' indicates that Togidubnus was awarded citizenship by the emperor. The Divine House indicates the imperial family. This inscription is therefore infused with loyalty to the emperor. The deities are Roman and the inscription itself is Latin. This is a profoundly Roman monument. There is little here of the Iron Age. The title 'great king of Britain' may even indicate that Togidubnus was granted special status as a reward for his fidelity to the occupying forces. He is depicted here as more of a Roman official than a British king.

No coins are known to have been issued by Togidubnus. Perhaps the Roman authorities wished to limit the dissemination of his personal imagery and preferred to circulate imperial coinage. Togidubnus may be linked to the proto-palace at Fishbourne, close to Chichester. This remarkable site offers a fascinating insight into the acculturation of Roman art and architecture within the newly conquered province. Fishbourne, originally, seems to have been used by the Roman military. Whilst some archaeologists have argued that the site was a Roman military base protecting a client king before the invasion, this seems highly unlikely. The presence of Roman troops in Britain would be a propaganda coup for any earlier emperor. It seems more logical that Fishbourne was briefly home to a Roman unit during the initial invasion phase. When it was no longer of military use to the occupying forces, the site was converted into a substantial Roman style palace. By the 60s AD, a residence had been constructed which would not have looked out of place in Italy. Consisting of a large courtyard house with Corinthian columns, the site also held a bathhouse. The house was decorated with black and white mosaics, according to the contemporary style favoured in Rome. The bathhouse, which would have consisted of a series of baths of varying temperatures, is particularly fascinating. Bathing was an essential component of Roman life. The inhabitants of Fishbourne clearly wished to express their identity as Romans rather than Britons. By the end of the first century AD, the residence had been replaced by a palatial structure which closely resembled the Flavian Palace constructed in Rome. It seems likely that Togidubnus died before 70 AD, suggesting that the later palace was constructed by his successors.

Togidubnus was clearly of importance to the imperial authorities. Client kings were useful in assisting in the pacification of newly conquered territories. Granting them control of specific areas freed up Roman troops to operate elsewhere. Cooperation with native rulers also furnished the occupying forces with an air of legitimacy. Their use was usually of a temporary nature. No client kings ruled in Britain after the first century AD. The identity of Togidubnus remains obscure. It is interesting that neither Adminius nor Verica appear to have been installed as client kings by the invaders. His name is strikingly similar to Togodumnus, one of the sons of Cunobelinus. The historian Cassius Dio, writing over a century later, claimed that Togodumnus was killed during Plautius' initial campaigns.[11] Given the time that had elapsed, it is possible that Dio was mistaken. The Romans had forgiven Commius after his disloyalty, so perhaps Togodumnus was similarly rehabilitated. Alternatively, it is possible that Togidubnus was a previously unknown scion of a British noble family. The rewards showered on Togidubnus, including citizenship, royal title and a palatial residence, demonstrated the benefits of loyalty to the new regime.

There appears to have been considerable division, even within tribes, concerning loyalty to Rome. In the early stages of the occupation

Cartimandua ruled as queen of the Brigantes. This tribe was the largest in northern England with a territory which perhaps even contained part of southern Scotland. Cartimandua is unusual in that she seems to have ruled in her own right, rather than as the consort of a king. She was a loyalist of the new regime, and may even have possessed Roman citizenship. Cartimandua had been responsible for handing the fugitive Caratacus over to the imperial authorities. At some point around 51 AD, Cartimandua replaced her husband Venutius with his armour bearer Vellocatus. The original marriage may have been designed to unite pro- and anti-Roman factions within the tribe. The incensed husband mounted a coup, supported by followers who were hostile to Cartimandua's involvement with the imperial administration. After serious fighting, Cartimandua was reinstated by Roman forces in 54 AD. Fifteen years later, Venutius again seized power and displaced the queen. In contrast to his earlier coup, Venutius appears to have rapidly consolidated his grip on the Brigantes. An ill-fated intervention by Roman forces failed to reinstall Cartimandua as tribal ruler. She was instead evacuated by the imperial administration and Brigantes were ceded to Venutius. The tribe would not be brought under full imperial control until the late 70s AD.[12] Cartimandua's eventual fate is unknown. Some scholars have argued that she retired to Chester on the basis of a fragmentary inscription. Alternatively, she may have lived out her days in Italian exile, ironically a fate shared by Caratacus.

The most famous act of resistance to Roman rule after the initial phase of the conquest is the Boudiccan Revolt which broke out in 60 AD.[13] The Iceni tribe were based in East Anglia. Their king Prasutagus appears to have been loyal to the imperial authorities. On his death, he left half of his kingdom to the emperor Nero and the remainder to his wife Boudicca and two daughters. The custom of leaving half of a kingdom to the emperor was a relatively widespread practice. Such a bequest was intended to induce the emperor to protect the estate and other heirs. In the case of the Iceni, Prasutagus' gamble did not pay off. The procurator, senior financial officer in the province, and his staff appear to have been intent on annexing the kingdom and proceeded to plunder Icenian resources. Boudicca was flogged by Roman officials and her daughters raped. Icenian nobles were treated like slaves. Other factors beyond the immediate Icenian context appear to have aggravated the nature and scale of the rebellion. Another local tribe, the Trinovantes, were filled with hatred for the imperialist attitudes and abuses of the Roman veterans who had been settled in Colchester. Furthermore, the procurator had begun to demand repayment for sums which had been granted to influential figures among the tribes as gifts from the emperor during the invasion. Whilst the immediate cause of the rebellion was the appalling treatment of the Iceni, an undercurrent of tension between the tribes and the provincial administration contributed to its severity.

The rebels first attacked the Roman colony at Colchester, butchering the inhabitants and burning the settlement. Most of the legions were involved in campaigns in Wales, limiting the potential for a rapid military response beyond localized attempts at crushing the insurgency. London and St Albans were abandoned to the rebels, and suffered the same fate as Colchester. The layer of burning is still evident in the archaeological record of London. Suetonius Paullinus, the provincial governor, eventually met the insurgents with his army at an unknown location in the Midlands. The outcome was a crushing defeat for the rebels. Boudicca committed suicide rather than be captured. It is estimated that around 40,000 individuals, both Roman and British, were killed in the course of the rebellion.[14] The Roman response to the insurgency was brutal. Paullinus put the territories of the rebels to fire and sword. According to the historian Tacitus, famine spread across the countryside.[15] Whilst Tacitus claims that this was due to the British failure to sow sufficient crops, it seems more likely that it was a result of punitive action by the Roman legions. The famine became so severe that the procurator, Julius Classicianus, convinced the Emperor Nero to recall Paullinus on account of the harsh nature of his reprisals.

ROMANIZATION

For all the horror of the Boudiccan revolt, it is significant that no serious revolts broke out in within the province of Britain after the first century AD. To this extent, the Roman occupation was remarkably successful. To understand the lack of serious revolts, it is necessary to examine the benefits to the native population in cooperating with the new regime. The Romans coined the term '*romanitas*' to indicate the essential qualities of being Roman. Being a Roman was not necessarily an indication of geographic origin or ancestry. On the contrary, it was linked to the acceptance and display of a package of customs and lifestyle choices, including architecture, art, culture, literature and language. Romanization indicates the process by which conquered societies absorbed this new identity. Romanization has been conventionally viewed as something forced on subject populations by the imperial administration. Tacitus, for example, describes the governor Agricola conducting a range of activities which encouraged the Romanization of the Britons. He is described as assisting in the construction of temples and public squares. Agricola is also reputed to have encouraged the education of noble youths, in order to inculcate them with the Roman worldview.[16] Yet it is interesting that Tacitus claims the accoutrements which the native elite amassed were a symptom of their slavery, rather than evidence for their civilised outlook.

Undoubtedly, individual officials would have encouraged Romanization through their own initiatives. Yet the process of conversion was more complex than this one sided approach. In the modern world, it is commonplace for people to adopt particular lifestyles based on other cultures reflected in clothing, possessions and personal habits. Romanization potentially worked in the same way. The British elite may have wanted to display Roman habits, customs and lifestyle in order to demonstrate that they were fashionable and 'civilized'. Togidubnus is an excellent example of a Briton who was thoroughly Romanized at an early stage in the conquest. In part, this was probably due to political realities. However, when looking at the ostentatious display of wealth, status and culture evident in his possible residence at Fishbourne, it seems almost certain that he was deliberately seeking to communicate his Roman, as opposed to British, identity. In simple terms, it was fashionable to be Roman. Inevitably, the pace and depth of Romanization was not uniform. Native elites, for example, possessed the resources and political motivation to display a Roman identity to an extent which is preserved in the archaeological record. It should not be assumed, of course, that the possession of Roman artefacts indicates political alignment with the imperial administration. Likewise it is difficult to trace the scale of Romanization among poorer sections of society who often leave little trace from an archaeological perspective. As we shall see, the prevalence of Romanization varied considerably on a regional level across the province. Yet the scarcity of serious insurgencies within the province after the Boudiccan Revolt strongly suggests that the native population was willing to acquiesce with the provincial administration.

THE IMPERIAL ADMINISTRATION

When organising newly conquered provinces, Rome perfected a system of provincial political organisation which it was able to use across the empire. The senior official in the province was the governor, who acted as the representative of the emperor. The Roman political career path insisted that senators gain military experience in the provinces alongside their progression within the Senate. The governor was therefore an individual with command experience, knowledge of life in the provinces and an understanding of the political realities of the empire. Governors were expected to serve as commander in chief within the bounds of their province and the senior administrative official. Governors usually served for less than five years. This limited tenure was specifically designed to prevent them becoming a political threat to the emperor by winning over the loyalty of the provincial army. Governors were based in the provincial capital at London although, as commanders-in-chief, during the first century AD they were often on campaign in the north and west of Britain.

Julius Agricola is the most well-known governor of Britain due to the account of his command in Britain written by his son-in-law Tacitus. Agricola held the governorship *c.* 78 – 84 AD. The career of Agricola is unusual for a number of reasons. First, for the wealth of information we have on his activities in Britain as recorded by Tacitus. Second, his gubernatorial tenure was longer than any other British governor on record and indeed many others from the rest of the empire. Third and last, he is the only individual known to have held a series of military commands with in the same province, as legionary officer (tribune), commander (legate) and finally commander-in-chief. According to Tacitus, Agricola's tenure in Britain included a series of spectacular military campaigns and a series of initiatives to support the civil administration of the province.

Agricola pursued an aggressive policy of conquest during his governorship, with a particular focus on extending Roman power northwards into Scotland. But there is reason to doubt Tacitus' emphasis on his father-in-law's military abilities. Recent archaeological research demonstrates that the major northern advances in the first century AD were probably made during the earlier governorship of Petillius Cerialis. Dendrochronological dates for timbers from the fort at Carlisle prove that it was built under Cerialis, and excavations in Scotland hint at an earlier occupation before Agricola's governorship.[17] Petillius Cerialis, the son-in-law of the emperor Vespasian, is a more suitable candidate for advancing into Scotland, particularly in light of his previous unimpressive performance during the Boudiccan revolt. The climax of Agricola's Scottish campaigns was the battle of Mons Graupius in 83 AD, where he vanquished a vast army of Caledonian warriors.[18] Yet Agricola's great battle can be significantly downgraded from the importance attached to it in much modern scholarship. It is suspicious that the existence of the battle is based only on Tacitus' account. Contemporary writers such as Pliny and Suetonius, both of whom can be assumed to have read the *Agricola*, are silent on the matter. The historian Cassius Dio emphasizes Agricola's circumnavigation of Britain (which was embarrassingly first accomplished by a group of deserters) rather than his martial achievements. The ominous silence concerning the battle in other ancient sources suggests that it was little more than a skirmish. No convincing archaeological evidence has been found to prove that Mons Graupius even took place.

Financial affairs of the province were controlled by the procurator who acted as senior financial officer. Procurators were recruited from the equestrians, the wealthiest group in Roman society after the senatorial order. The equestrian class was generally composed of wealthy businessmen and traders who were perfectly suited to the role of procurator, which included overseeing the collection of taxes and balancing the provincial budget. The selection of governors and procurators from different social classes was deliberate as a means of achieving a balance of power between the two arms of the provincial government. Both procurator and governor were independent of each other and reported directly to the emperor. The benefit of this system is evident in the career of Julius Classicianus, who persuaded the emperor Nero to remove Suetonius Paullinus as governor after the Boudiccan Revolt.[19] Classicianus' funerary monument was discovered in London with the following inscription:

> DIS MANIBUS C(AI) IUL(II) C(AI) F(ILII) FAB(IA) ALPINI CLASSICIANI ... PROC(URATORIS) PROVINC(IAE) BRITA[NNIAE] IULIA INDI FILIA PACATA INDIANA(?) UXOR F(ECIT)
>
> *'To the spirits of the dead and to Gaius Julius Alpinus Classicianus, son of Gaius, of the Fabian voting tribe, (some text missing) procurator of the province of Britain. Julia Pacata Indiana(?), daughter of Insus, his wife, had this constructed.'*[20]

Classicianus' name indicates that he was of Gallic origin and probably came from a noble family. His wife also came from a prominent Gallic family. Given his family background, it is tempting to speculate that Classicianus' opposition to Paullinus was motivated by his affinity with the Britons. Sadly, it is more likely that he was driven by the negative economic implications of Paullinus' repressive policies. Classicianus probably died within a few years of the Boudiccan Revolt. The presence of his funerary monument in London indicates that the city was already the financial centre of the province, and perhaps the provincial capital at this early date.

MILITARY LIFE

The provincial administration was staffed by imperial slaves and freedmen who supported the governor and procurator in the execution of their duties. Manpower was also provided by the army, which contributed soldiers on secondment as clerks, couriers and bodyguards. The Roman army was therefore critically important in supporting the administration of the province, as well as securing it. The army was of fundamental importance in the Romanization of Britain. In the second century AD, the army in Britain consisted of around 55,000 men, roughly 10% of the total strength of the imperial army.[21] For most of the Roman occupation, three legions of around 5500 men each were based in the province. VI Victrix was stationed at York, XX Valeria Victrix at Chester and II Augusta at Caerleon in Wales. The legions formed the heavy infantry of the Roman battle line. Legionaries were Roman citizens who served for twenty-five years before retirement. Recruits were drawn from across the empire; in particular Germany, Gaul, Spain and the Balkans, meaning that the legions brought a multicultural feel to the areas in which they were based. Over time, British recruits also fed into legions based within the province. Each legion was commanded by a legate drawn from the senatorial order. The legates assisted the governor and appear to have had some authority over the area in which their unit was based. The legions were supported by the *auxilia*. These units tended to be recruited from societies living on the periphery of the empire. Recruits were normally non-citizens, who would be rewarded with citizenship on completion of their term of service. Auxiliary units could be composed of cavalry or infantry, with a nominal strength of between 500 – 1000 men. Ethnic units often took advantage of native fighting styles or techniques, for example the Syrian archers who were deployed on Hadrian's Wall. The auxilia tended to be provided with officers from the equestrian class. Britain also possessed a small fleet, the *Classis Britannica*, which facilitated movement between the province and mainland Europe. The role of the fleet seems to have been to act as a coastguard and logistical asset, rather than an offensive naval force.

The army had a significant impact on provincial society. In the early history of the province, the soldiers were probably perceived as occupiers. A startling tombstone from Lancaster belongs to a cavalryman named Insus, originally from the Treveri tribe in Germany.[22] The relief on the stone depicts Insus as a victorious warrior riding down an enemy, who is depicted beneath the hooves of Insus' steed. It is unique for a tombstone of this kind, that the fallen barbarian has been decapitated and Insus brandishes his severed head as a trophy. Given that this tombstone was erected during the first century AD, probably shortly after the conquest of northern England, it must have had a significant impact on the native population. Despite the fearsome nature of images like this, the army soon became integrated into provincial life, eventually welcoming local recruits. Military life offered social mobility, status, relatively secure income and – for most of the period in question – little fighting.

The Roman army offered a strong sense of a military community.[23] Whilst recruits were drawn from across the empire, the ethos of military units was infused with *Romanitas*. Latin was the language of the camps. A military calendar was adhered to, which emphasized dates associated with the ruling dynasty. Each unit swore an oath for the safety of the emperor on an annual basis. At Maryport in Cumbria, a large number of stone altars were discovered. These altars had been erected to give thanks for the safety of the emperor each year, and therefore demonstrated the loyalty of the troops to their commander-in-chief.[24] Wear patterns on the altars indicates that they had stood outside in rows for a considerable amount of time. This suggests that the altars were conspicuously displayed. The wages, decorations and discharge benefits which were provided to soldiers were believed to come directly from the emperor, further binding the soldiery to the imperial house.

The emerging military community had a wider impact on provincial society. As the recipients of a stable income, soldiers had considerable economic power. Traders and merchants were attracted to forts which became more permanent in nature as the conquest drew to a halt. Settlements grew up outside the walls to offer inns, shops and brothels to the troops. Since the reign of the emperor Augustus, soldiers had been prohibited from marrying. This prohibition would not be legally repealed until the third century AD. Yet the rule was widely flouted and it is clear that soldiers did marry local women, many of whom would have lived in the *vici* outside auxiliary camps or *canabae* outside legionary forts. There is even some evidence from Vindolanda, in the form of preserved shoes, which suggests that women and children may even on occasion have lived within the forts. Male offspring from these marriages may have been recruited into the army. Official documents record some recruits whose place of origin is listed simply as 'camp', indicating that they were the children of serving soldiers. The benefits in terms of recruitment may explain why married soldiers appear to have gone unpunished. After twenty-five years of service, soldiers were discharged as veterans. They were usually rewarded with sums of money or parcels of land. Whilst some veterans did return to their place of origin, the majority seem to have remained close their place of service, perhaps because they did not wish to be separated from the military community. The immersion of veterans within provincial society would have aided Romanization, as they were inevitably individuals comfortable with Roman customs and lifestyle choice. Of course, they were not always seen in a positive light. The Trinovantes were motivated to join the Boudiccan Revolt by the abuses of veterans living in Colchester. Within a newly conquered province, it suited the imperial administration to have retired soldiers living locally who could be recalled to service in extreme conditions.

The disposition of the army in Britain was regional in nature. Inhabitants of Devon and Cornwall, for example, would have encountered very few soldiers after the initial pacification of the region. Those in northern England, on the other hand, lived in a highly militarised frontier zone. Since the reign of the emperor Augustus, Roman ideology had the trumpeted the concept of *'imperium sine fine'* meaning empire without limit in either time or space.[25] Yet by the end of the first century AD it was clear that this concept was not applicable to the realities of Roman Britain. The conquest of Scotland was never completed. Agricola's victory at Mons Graupius did not invoke a new era of pacification. Rome had neither the will nor the resources to continue northern expansion. Conflict appears to have broken out at the start of the reign of Hadrian *c.* 117 AD. A tombstone from Vindolanda records a centurion who died during the war. Historical sources refer to considerable losses inflicted on the army during this period. As a result, it seems that the emperor decided to formalise the frontier system in Britain and visited the province in 122 AD to oversee the project in person. As such, Hadrian's Wall represents a failure of Roman policy in failing to complete the conquest of Britain.

Roman frontiers tended to coalesce around natural features. Elsewhere in the empire, great river systems like the Rhine, Danube and Euphrates proved suitable barriers to further expansion.[26] Britain lacked a convenient watercourse for this purpose, but two isthmuses at the Tyne – Solway and Forth-Clyde offered attractive alternatives. The initial frontier appears to have been based around the Stanegate, a Roman road which ran between Corbridge and Carlisle. Although much remains unclear about the operation of this frontier, the Stanegate was populated with an embryonic system of forts, fortlets (formerly known as milecastles) and watchtowers. The importance of the Stanegate lays in its value as a communication route. When Hadrian decided to formalise the frontier system, his wall was placed within a viable distance of the existing Stanegate. It seems likely that Hadrian's Wall was originally intended to be manned by troops from the existing forts, although these were later moved onto the frontier itself.

The construction of Hadrian's Wall was led by the governor Platorius Nepos. The Wall, running for a total of 117 km, connects Wallsend in the east to Bowness-on-Solway in the west, with a series of forts and signal stations running along the Cumbrian coast to Maryport. The fort at South Shields acted as a supply port for the frontier army (Fig 3). The structure of the Wall varies considerably along its course. Originally, the section of Wall from the Irthing to the Solway Firth was constructed in turf, whilst the remainder was made of stone. By the end of the second century AD, work began to replace the turf section with stone. Watchtowers were placed every 500 m along the Wall, with fortlets placed at 1.6 km intervals. The purpose of the fortlets was to garrison gateways through the Wall. At a later stage in construction, the forts of the Stanegate were moved on to the Wall itself. Around the same time, a large earthwork named the Vallum was constructed to the south of the Wall. The Vallum essentially created a militarised zone, by limiting the approach to the Wall to a number of designated crossing points. The remains of a Vallum crossing can be seen close to the Temple of Antenociticus at Benwell. Around 6 m to the north of the Wall lay a ditch and bank, which controlled access from the north. It is a matter of considerable debate whether the Wall was equipped with a walkway. The area between the Wall and the ditch, named the berm, was originally believed to have been empty. However, excavations in Byker have revealed that, in some sections at least, the berm was filled with *cippei*, or large pits holding sharp stakes and other obstacles. Presumably these were intended to prevent anyone approaching the Wall from the north and impede an organized assault.[27]

The forts on the Wall were significant communities in their own right.[28] Housesteads covers an area of around two hectares. It was designed to house up to 1000 soldiers and possesses a considerable civilian settlement. The fort was occupied for at least two centuries after the reign of Hadrian. A number of units were based in the fort during its history, originating from Germany and Belgium in particular. The fort follows the traditional 'playing card' design used by the Roman army. Internal buildings within forts included the headquarters building, commanding officer's house, granaries and barracks (Fig 4). The civilian settlement contained inns, shops and houses. One of the latter was found to contain human remains buried beneath the floor, indicating the violent realities of life on the frontier.

In the 140s AD, a series of successful campaigns led to an advancement to a new frontier system on the Forth-Clyde isthmus. Running for a length of 60 km between Carriden in the east and Old Kirkpatrick in the west, the Antonine Wall was closely modelled on its Hadrianic precursor. A stone foundation over 4 m high was topped by a turf bank. A ditch and bank were constructed to the north. Nineteen forts were constructed along the length of the Wall connected by a single road. The chronology of the Antonine Wall is complex, but it seems likely that the troops were withdrawn to Hadrian's Wall around 158 AD. A second occupation is possible but it is certain that the Antonine frontier was not reoccupied after 214 AD.

Hadrian's Wall is often perceived to be a physical barrier delineating Roman territory from the unconquered north. In fact, the role of the frontier is difficult to interpret. The Wall was permeable, with numerous gateways and crossings. The presence of the Vallum indicates the army were as interested in the south as they were in the north. Roman soldiers were traditionally adept in formation fighting, not the defence of a liner barrier. It is unclear how much of a barrier the Wall would pose to a concerted assault. Rather than a physical barrier, the Wall may have had an economic role. Controlling the movement of individuals across the frontier would have facilitated the collection of customs duties and taxes. It would also have prevented cattle rustling and raiding, which would become endemic in the same region in later centuries. The construction and maintenance of the Wall would also have occupied troops stationed in northern Britain who, in the absence of campaigns, may otherwise have become restless. This may explain localised variations in the fabric of the Wall as tinkering by individual units.

We are fortunate to possess a unique insight into life on the frontier through the Vindolanda tablets. The fort of Vindolanda is situated 3 km to the south of Housesteads on the Stanegate.[29] It continued to be occupied after the construction of Hadrian's Wall. As may be expected, the headquarters building processed a large amount of correspondence and records relating to the operation of the fort. These texts were written on thin slices of wood. During a period between 90 and 120 AD, unwanted documents were disposed of in a ditch which fortunately happened to be waterlogged. These watery conditions preserved the documents for centuries, allowing them to be read by archaeologists. More than 1000 fragments have been recovered at Vindolanda.[30] Over eighty can be dated to the command of Flavius Cerialis, who commanded the Ninth Cohort of Batavians between 97 AD and 104 AD. Cerialis was a member of the equestrian order, whose command at Vindolanda was a necessary step in his career within the imperial administration. As an officer, Cerialis was permitted to be accompanied by his wife, Sulpicia Lepidina, and children. Small shoes found in the headquarters building may belong to the latter, as may tablets which appear to be writing exercises based on Virgil's epic poem the Aeneid. In one tablet, Cerialis is referred to by one of his soldiers as *rex* or king.[31] Whilst it is unlikely that he was of royal descent, it is certainly possible that he may have been sprung from a noble Batavian family. Cerialis would therefore be a thoroughly Romanized member of a native elite.

The tablets provide valuable information on the daily operation of the unit based at Vindolanda. One of the tablets consists of a strength report, outlining the dispositions of the troops on a single day. A total of 752 men were currently serving in the unit. However, only 296 were actually present within the fort. The remaining 456 were on duties elsewhere[32] in locations including Corbridge, London, York and Gaul. Forty-six are specifically mentioned as being seconded to the governor as bodyguards. Of the soldiers remaining at

Vindolanda, almost 10% were unfit for duty including ten individuals suffering from an inflammation of the eyes. The dispersed nature of the unit is a salutary warning to archaeologists that the size of a fort does not necessarily indicate how many soldiers were actually serving there on a daily basis.

An enigmatic document appears to refer to the native population. The tablet describes their fighting technique, which relies on unarmoured cavalry who use spears rather than swords. The emphasis on British horsemanship is interesting given the connection between horses and status in the late Iron Age. The context of this document is unclear. It could represent an intelligence report on the techniques adopted by insurgents. Yet it could also have been a report on the progress of British recruits to the army. The natives are referred to as *Brittunculi*, an otherwise unattested term meaning 'little Britons'.[33] Whilst this could be a term of almost affectionate endearment, it also reflects the perceived superiority of soldiers over the local population. This sense of superiority sometimes led to unpleasant consequences. A highly emotive text contains an appeal by a foreign merchant for justice after an assault by soldiers which also led to his goods being damaged.[34] The assault seems to have involved a beating with sticks, which hints at the involvement of at least one centurion. The merchant has sought redress in vain from the other officers within the unit. Claiming his innocence, the merchant now appears to have appealed to the governor. It is unfortunate that we do not know the outcome of his case.

The tablets refer not only to the daily activities of the army, but also to the world which they inhabited. Vindolanda was connected to a wider social network of soldiers, officers and veterans serving elsewhere. A recently discovered tablet referring to financial transactions was written by an individual named Ascanius with the title '*Comes Augusti*' meaning companion of the emperor.[35] This title was frequently assigned to mounted guards protecting the emperor, many of whom would have had the same ethnic origin as the soldiers stationed at Vindolanda. It is therefore possible that soldiers at Vindolanda even corresponded with comrades serving the imperial court. Social connections were not limited to serving soldiers and officers. Perhaps the most famous tablet is an invitation to a birthday party, sent to Sulpicia Lepidina, wife of Flavius Cerialis.[36] The sender, Claudia Severa, was the wife of a fellow equestrian commanding officer named Aelius Brocchus. Brocchus and Cerialis appear to have been close friends. Whilst we do not know where the former was stationed, it is likely to have been reasonably close to Vindolanda as the two families are known to have visited each other. The text conveys a measure of excitement at the forthcoming party and the hope that Lepidina could attend. As wives of commanding officers, they were not permitted to mix with serving soldiers or lesser officers. It would be unthinkable for them to associate with the women from the civilian settlement. Life for Severa and Lepidina must therefore have been rather lonely and their affection for each other is perhaps a product of their need for female companionship and support.

ECONOMY

Many of the tablets from Vindolanda refer to the economic and logistical requirements of operating a garrison on the frontier. Securing and transporting provisions and clothing appear to have been a constant problem for the military. Soldiers were provided with 880 g of unground wheat and 620 g of additional rations including vegetables, nuts, cheese, meat or fish per day. In addition, the army required horses and mules, as well as leather for tents and uniforms. Overall, the presence of a large provincial army in Britain demanded an intensification of agriculture to meet the material and dietary requirements of the military. There appears to be a shift in preference from raising sheep to cattle, perhaps as a result of military demand. Spelt, barley and oats continued to be grown, although the sowing of bread wheat increased considerably. Modifications were made to the Iron Age plough to increase its efficiency. In the long term, the imperial administration required the province to become economically viable to avoid becoming a drain on the rest of the empire. The emperor Nero is reputed to have considered withdrawing from Britain due to his concern over the economic viability of the province, but was prevented by his desire not to be seen as decreasing imperial territory. This was particularly important given the large military presence in the province. Recent estimates suggest that, with regard to Britain, around 10% of the entire imperial army was based within only 4% of the empire as a whole.[37] The presence of the army would have been a boon for local farmers.

Romanization encouraged a demand among the civilian population for luxury items and exotic goods from the empire. The conquest would therefore have boosted trade with the Continent by creating a new market for exports from mainland Europe. Olive oil, wine, fine clothes and artworks would have been particularly prized by newly Romanised sections of provincial society. Samian ware pottery was imported in large quantities from Gaul and the German provinces. Garum, a fine sauce made from rotting fish guts, was particularly popular as a condiment. Continental merchants evidently grew rich from trading with the province. The following inscription comes from third century York:

NEPTUNO ET GENIO LOCI ET NUMINIB(US) AUG(USTORUM) L(UCIUS) VIDUCIUS VIDUCI F(ILIUS) PLACIDUS DOMO CIVITATE VELIOCASSIUM PROV(INCIAE) LUGD(UNENSIS) NEGOTIATOR BRITANN(ICIANUS) ARCUM ET IANUAM PRO SE ET SUIS DEDIT GRATO ET SELEUCO CO(N)S(ULIBUS)

'To Neptune and the Spirit of the place and the Divine Powers of the Emperors. Lucius Viducius Placidus, the son of Viducius, from the Veliocasses in the province of Lugdunensis, trader with Britain, presented the arch and gate in the consulship of Gratus and Seleucus'[38]

Placidus was evidently a merchant who transported his wares from the Continent to Britain. He originated from the area around modern Rouen, suggesting that he shipped goods from Gaul. Placidus' wealth allowed him to construct an arch and gateway in York, the most important city in northern Britain. Evidence for Continental trade with Britain can also be found on the Continent. The area around Domburg in Holland has produced a remarkable number of altars dedicated to the goddess Nehalennia by merchants giving thanks for shipments which survived the Channel crossing.

'To the goddess Nehalennia, on account of goods duly kept safe, Marcus Secundinius Silvanus, trader in pottery with Britain, fulfilled his vow willingly and deservedly.'[39]

It is interesting that Placidus also dedicated at altar to Nehalennia on the coast of modern Holland.[40] Unlike Placidus, Silvanus clearly identifies his profession as pottery trader. He probably sold Samian pottery, high quality tableware which was an essential component of a provincial dining set. Native pottery styles developed during the occupation, although it never reached the quality of imported tableware. Pottery industries grew in particular areas, including the Nene Valley, producing coarse and fine ware for the local population. Continental trade was not all one way. The Rhineland was home to a major army group protecting the north western frontier from tribal incursions. By the late third century AD, British merchants were supplying the Rhine legions with produce, including leather and corn. The most famous export produced by Britain was a particular garment named the *birrus Britanicus*. This was a long hooded cloak, which bore a passing resemblance to modern 'hoodies'. A mosaic from the villa at Chedworth displays a figure wearing the *birrus Britannicus*.

The mineral resources of Britain, known throughout mainland Europe since the Bronze Age, were ripe for exploitation. Initial mineral extraction operations were overseen by the military and later conducted by private contractors. Gold mines were opened in Carmarthenshire and lead deposits extracted in Shropshire and the Peak District. Iron, copper, tin and lead were also exploited. Certain metals were exported elsewhere in the empire. A Roman shipwreck which sunk off Ploumanac'h in France contained over twenty-two tonnes of lead ingots. Many of these were stamped with British tribal names, including the Brigantes and Iceni.[41] These tribal stamps indicate that the lead was mined or trafficked through their respective territories.

ART

During the Roman occupation, Classical art engaged with native artistic style derived from Iron Age and earlier. In doing so, a vibrant new art form was created which represented a fusion of Roman and British styles. Iron Age artists were capable of producing astonishing works in the 'Celtic' style, employing intricate loops and knots, as demonstrated by the Battersea shield which was deposited in the Thames. Iron Age stone carvings can often appear rather crude and unsophisticated. This is particularly the case with stone heads, which are particularly common during this period and probably are connected to specific religious beliefs.[42] Whilst the meaning of these heads is uncertain, their unsophisticated design may reflect an abstract approach. Roman craftsmen appear to have followed the legions to Britain. An early Roman tombstone, dated to within five years of the initial invasion, belongs to Marcus Favonius Facilis, a centurion of XX Valeria Victrix based at Colchester.[43] The tombstone was dedicated by two of his freedmen. Facilis is depicted on the tombstone is almost lifelike detail in the parade uniform of a legionary centurion. His body is well proportioned and his facial features clearly defined. Even his hairstyle is portrayed in the contemporary fashion, as evidenced by portraits of the emperor Claudius. The depiction of Facilis emphasizes his status as an army officer. His left arm rests on his sword, a visible reminder to the provincial population of the military power of life and death. Facilis' right hand grasps his vine stick, wielded by centurions as a symbol of their authority and used to beat recalcitrant soldiers. The detail on Facilis' tombstone means that it is almost certain to have been carved by a stonemason familiar with Classical art who had travelled to the province soon after the conquest. Another tombstone from Colchester was contemporary to that of Facilis. It was carved for Longinus Sdapeze, a cavalryman from Thrace.[44] Sdapeze is depicted in the typical pose of a Roman cavalryman, riding down a fallen barbarian. This so-called '*reiter*' design (from the German for rider) was commonly used by cavalry units across the empire. The top of the stone depicts themes from Classical mythology including a sphinx and lions catching snakes. Yet there are signs that the stonemason responsible for Sdapeze's memorial may have been of British origin. In particular, the horse bridles and pommels feature Celtic elements including rosettes.

The tombstone of Aurelia Aureliana from Carlisle provides an insight into the stonemason's trade.[45] Depicted in a long robe, which may even have been a *birrus Britannicus*, Aureliana's features are indistinct. She carries poppies which symbolise sleep and pine cones were carved on the side of the memorial, which were believed to represent life. The emphasis on sleep and life rather than death and sorrow may indicate that Aureliana was Christian and therefore believed to enjoy eternal life. Aureliana's robe is rather long for a Roman female and her undetailed features are also suspicious. It seems likely that the generic nature of the tombstone is a result of it being a general design which was purchased by her husband from the stonemason's yard already carved. Such a memorial would have been cheaper than a bespoke creation. Aureliana's memorial represents an economic approach to death.

The temple of Sulis Minerva was elaborately decorated with images taken from Classical mythology, if the pediment is anything to go by. The pediment or front face of the temple supported by columns, contained reliefs of tritons (mermen), Victories standing on globes and a gorgon. The gorgon head, which was the centre piece of the pediment, is particularly interesting with regard to Romano-British art. The gorgon was a figure from Classical mythology, a monster with hair made of snakes capable of turning the unwary into stone. According to myth, Perseus defeated the gorgon Medusa with the assistance of the goddess Athena. The Romans equated Athena with Minerva and, in Britain, Sulis. The inclusion of the gorgon on the temple therefore makes logical sense. However, the gorgon was female, whilst the figure depicted at Bath is clearly male with piercing eyes and flowing beard. The relief must represent a British interpretation of Classical myth. The male may represent a native river god or Oceanus, deity of the seas. A remarkably similar individual can be seen on a silver plate which formed part of a fourth century hoard from Mildenhall in Suffolk. The wild eyes and unkempt appearance also evoke the wild man of the woods, a familiar figure from British folklore. Whilst the execution of the pediment is in a profoundly Classical style, there are elements of a native belief clearly embedded within it.

Roman culture is firmly associated with mosaics as a decorative approach to flooring, which was used to emphasize the social identity, beliefs and cultural tastes of the owner. A number of impressive mosaic floors have been uncovered in British villas including the Christ mosaic from Hinton St Mary and the winter mosaic from Chedworth. Rudston villa in Yorkshire possessed a mosaic depicting the goddess Venus. The deity is shown holding the apple she won in the beauty contest judged by the Trojan prince Paris and accompanied by a triton. Around the central scene are four animals; a lion, stag, leopard and bull. The animals are pursued by four naked hunters. There are a number of elements which are unusual. Two of the animals receive titles on the mosaic. This was a common practice in North Africa, but in the case of Rudston the Latin contains glaring spelling mistakes. Venus is normally shown holding her mirror, emphasising her divine attributes as the goddess of love and desire. Yet the Rudston mosaic depicts the mirror as being dropped by Venus. Her portrayal is unusual. Unlike Classical images of the goddess, her figure is not in proportion. Venus' curvaceous hips are emphasized and her legs taper away to tiny feet. Given the geographic location of the villa near the edge of the empire, it is to be expected that the mosaic would emphasise native style in contrast to mosaics from more Romanised areas. A similar portrayal of Venus, this time accompanied by nymphs, can be seen on a relief from High Rochester.

RELIGION

Contrary to popular opinion, Romans were not religious imperialists. On the contrary, they believed in a world full of gods.[46] They had no desire to compel others to follow their own theological beliefs. The only exception to this religious tolerance lay in fidelity to the imperial cult. Ruler worship was alien to Rome. Originating in the East it had been exploited by Alexander the Great as a means of winning political support of subject peoples. After the fall of the Republic, emperors had seen the potential of the imperial cult as a means of legitimising their rule and securing their dynastic line. Provincial societies were therefore expected to engage with the imperial cult. It is therefore no surprise that a temple dedicated to Claudius was one of the most imposing buildings in Colchester prior to its destruction during the Boudiccan Revolt. The Roman army had taken steps to initially suppress and later eradicate druids, culminating in their final destruction on Anglesey described by Tacitus. Yet the downfall of the druids was not motivated by religious differences. Instead, their political power and influence over the tribes meant that they posed a threat to Roman rule and a potential focus for resistance.

Roman religion emphasized a contractual relationship with the gods. A Roman would seek assistance from a deity with the offer of something which would be given in return, if the prayer was answered. A large number of inscriptions from across the province were created in response to the beneficence of a divine being. A large number of lead curse tablets have been recovered from the sacred springs at Bath.[47] These consist of messages to a god begging for assistance which were inscribed on lead tablets, rolled up and deposited in the springs. The watery location of deposition demonstrates continuity with the religious significance of water going back at least to the Bronze Age. Most curse tablets in Britain refer to instances of petty theft and offer an insight into the beliefs and literacy of the provincial population. Native gods tended to be highly localised in nature, often linked to natural features such as a spring or sacred grove of trees. On encountering new deities, Romans utilized *interpretatio Romana*. In essence, this meant an acceptance the Roman and British gods may in fact be the same deities under different names. This was usually indicated by merging the Roman and native names. Cocidius was a deity popularly worshipped in northern England. Depictions of the deity show a male figure armed with a shield and sword. Romans therefore equated him with Mars, the god of war, in the form of Mars Cocidius. In some instances, soldiers entering new areas were unable to ascertain the identity of the local deity. Instead, dedications would be made to '*genius loci*' or the spirit of the place, a useful method of supplicating the local unknown god.

Roman tolerance and even adoption of native deities provides us with an insight into previously unknown Iron Age gods. The god Antenociticus was worshipped at Benwell, near Newcastle. A fort was established at Benwell to support the monitoring of Hadrian's Wall. Antenociticus appears to have been a local deity, although some scholars have suggested that he was imported by recruits from Germany. Most likely, Antenociticus was associated with a local spring. The head of his cult status shows strange swirls in his hair, which may indicate that he was a horned deity. A small temple was constructed by Roman officers and soldiers based at Benwell to venerate the local deity.[48] Although small in size, the temple was of classic Roman design emphasising the cult statue of Antenociticus. Stone altars were erected by officers and soldiers serving locally (Fig 5). Although Antenociticus almost certainly pre-dated the invasion, he was worshipped in an ostensibly Roman manner. Similarly, the native goddess Sulis was associated with the thermal spring at Bath. The spring would have been a prominent natural phenomenon for centuries and was undoubtedly the focus of prolonged ritual activity. Roman equated Sulis, as a divine mother figure, with the Classical goddess Minerva. Sulis Minerva was honoured with an impressive temple and ostentatious cult status. Over 12,000 separate objects, including curse tablets, were deposited as offerings to the goddess at Bath. To a certain extent,

Roman incomers monumentalised existing religious beliefs through the construction of temples, erection of altars and ostentatious approach to ritual behaviour. For the archaeologist, this means that religion and ritual becomes more visible in Britain than it had been before. Unlike most modern religions, those present in Roman Britain often did not revolve around a central sacred text. This makes understanding the belief systems of individual cults particularly difficult.

New cults were also imported into Britain. During the first and second centuries AD, eastern cults became particular popular across the empire, such as the cult of Serapis in evidence at York. These cults usually contained a central mystery, or body of sacred knowledge which was only available to believers. This emphasis of the benefits of membership and religious community proved particularly attractive. In contrast to traditional belief systems, eastern cults tended to offer salvation after death through access to a pleasant afterlife. One of the most prominent eastern cults recorded in Britain worshipped Mithras.[49] The cult of Mithras originated in the region of modern Iran. It spread rapidly across the empire during the second and third centuries AD. The central act of the story of Mithras was his killing of a sacred bull in a cave. In slitting the bull's throat, Mithras released something of great sacred power into the world. In some accounts, the blood of the bull represents the secret of eternal life. In others, the blood created the universe as we know it. Without any Mithraic sacred texts, it is impossible to prove either way. The scene of Mithras killing the bull was repeated wherever he was worshipped. Mithras is depicted wearing a Phyrgian cap (reflecting his geographic origins) sitting astride the bull, usually gripping a knife to its throat. This scene was clearly of great religious significance to the cult, similar to the Christian cross.

The cult of Mithras was particularly popular among soldiers. Women were excluded from worshipping him. The cult was hierarchical in nature with a series of ranks through which an initiate progressed. Promotion to a more senior rank appears to have been based on trials of endurance and strength. This would particularly appeal to a military audience. Mithras was worshipped within specialist temples called *mithraea* (the singular is a *mithraeum*). *Mithraea* have been found in a variety of sizes, yet the layout is always identical. *Mithraea* attempted to recreate the setting of the killing of the sacred bull through creating a cave-like environment through excluding as much natural light as possible. A central aisle runs down the *mithraeum* which benches or seats on either side for initiates to sit, probably for the consumption of a communal meal. It seems likely that cult members sat according to their rank. The aisle led to the main altar, on which sacrifices were conducted, and the central relief of Mithras killing the bull. The mithraeum at Carrawburgh on Hadrian's Wall was founded in the third century AD. The temple is around 70 m^2 in size. Designed in the usual Mithraic fashion, it would have attracted soldiers from the nearby fort. Interestingly, a sacred well belonging to the native goddess Coventina is nearby, demonstrating the eastern cults could co-exist with native forms of religion. Priests of Mithras were not vocational, meaning that it is likely that soldiers took this role in a voluntary capacity. The mithraeum was destroyed in the fourth century AD, probably as a result of the persecution of the cult by Christians.

The rise of Christianity can be viewed as part of the spread of eastern cults across the empire. Whilst the origins of Christianity lie in Judaism, it has much in common with mystery cults including the promise of salvation and an emphasis on social aspects of worship. Vocational priests and its inclusive approach attracted converts from across Roman society. Christianity appears to have spread reasonably rapidly, with Christians living in Rome in the 60s AD. From an archaeological perspective, it is often difficult to identify conclusive evidence of a Christian presence during the first and second centuries AD due to their persecution. An enigmatic wordsquare, discovered on wallplaster in Cirencester, is identical to similar puzzles found across the empire.[50] Although its meaning appears to be nonsensical, when rearranged the letters form a text of Christian significance (PATER NOSTER with the letters for alpha and omega). Dating to the second century AD, this wordsquare may have been a furtive method of communication between Christians whose worship had been forced underground through the threat of persecution.

In late Roman Britain, the evidence for Christianity becomes more explicit after the conversion of the empire under the emperor Constantine.[51] It is interesting to note that Constantine was elevated to imperial power in York, giving a British origin to an event of global historical significance. Christian churches have been discovered at Lincoln and Silchester. A Roman cemetery at Poundbury in Dorset has been tentatively identified as a Christian site on the basis of the east-west orientation of the deceased. However, this alignment may have been common across Britain during this period, irrespective of individual beliefs. Evidence for private Christian worship can be found at Lullingstone Villa in Kent. During the fourth century AD, part of the residence was converted into a Christian chapel containing the earliest Christian wall paintings discovered in Britain. These paintings depict worshippers and a large Chi-Rho symbol evoking Christ, unequivocal evidence of Christian beliefs. Mosaics showing scenes from Classical myth may have been designed to highlight the battle between good and evil. It is intriguing a cult room has been discovered beneath the chapel which appears to have been in contemporary use for pagan (i.e. non-Christian) worship. The significance of this is unclear. Was there a division within the villa between two competing belief systems? An alternative explanation could be that the owner saw no conflict between worshipping a new deity whilst retaining his fidelity to the old gods. The distinction between monotheism and polytheism was not necessarily clearly defined in Roman Britain.

The most impressive Christian mosaic was discovered at a villa in Hinton St Mary in Dorset. The mosaic was originally laid in two sections of a large room. The design fuses Classical mythology was Christian imagery. One scene, from the smaller section of the room, depicts the Classical hero Bellerophon spearing a monster whilst mounted on his magical horse Pegasus. Similar to the mosaics at Lullingstone Villa, the artist may have intended to communicate the inevitable victory of good over evil. The larger section of the mosaic is flanked by the images of four male individuals, who could represent the four winds or evangelists. The central image shows a clean shaven male figure with the Greek letters Chi-Rho. The identity of this figure is unclear. It could represent a late emperor. However, the presence of the imperial face on the floor, exposed to the dirty boots of visitors, residents and pets alike, could be considered an act of treason. The Chi-Rho letters point to the figure being Jesus Christ, which would make it one of the earliest of his depictions. This identification is also not without problems, not least in the perceived sacrilege in displaying him on the floor. However, it should be remembered that Britain lay at the edge of the empire and it should therefore not be surprising that early British Christians interpreted their beliefs and rituals in unorthodox ways.

URBANIZATION

Perhaps the most significant innovation introduced by Rome to Britain was urbanization.[52] Prior to the conquest, there were no settlements which could be definitely classified as towns, even when large *oppida* are considered. Rome required the presence of towns to support administrative processes, in particular the collection of taxes. The imperial administration designated three classifications of towns in Britain. Colonies were settlements initially populated by veterans from the legions and *auxilia*. Colonies therefore possessed a significant proportion of Roman citizens. The political constitution of individual colonies was closely linked to that of Rome itself. Three colonies have been identified in Britain at Colchester, Gloucester and Lincoln, although York and London were also awarded the same status later as an honorific title. *Municipia* were towns which were governed by Roman law. Political office holders (known as magistrates) were eligible for citizenship on completion of their duties. St Albans is the only firm *municipium* identified in the province. For administrative purposes, the province was divided up into regional territories, named *civitates*, of which sixteen have been clearly identified. *Civitates* were closely modelled on existing tribal territories. Each *civitas* had a principal town, known as the *civitas* capital, which was the administrative centre for the territory. Examples of *civitas* capitals include Wroxeter, Caerwent and Silchester. In contrast to other forms of town, *civitas* capitals were permitted to enforce native law. As towns grew, it was theoretically possible for them to be awarded higher status with the agreement of the imperial administration. A number of towns were constructed on the sites of Iron Age *oppida* (including Canterbury and Silchester) or Roman forts (including Carlisle and Gloucester).

Roman towns varied in size, layout and sophistication. The classic Roman town contained a number of essential features, examples of which can be found in Britain. The forum acted as the political and business heart of the town, where important citizens would gather. The basilica acted as a civic centre, with council chambers and administrative offices. A market was usually situated close to the forum, offering both imported goods and produce from the surrounding farmland. Towns were often provided with a sustainable water supply through the construction of aqueducts. Bathing was an essential component of Roman daily life. Public baths were established across the empire, as places for socialising, recreation, exercise and washing. Many bath complexes contained sophisticated engineering to facilitate the maintenance of hot and warm baths. In larger towns, amphitheatres offered entertainment to the masses in the form of gladiatorial shows. In Britain, most amphitheatres consisted of a sunken fighting floor surrounded by a turf seating area. Towns were connected through the road network with promoted trade, communication and travel. Roads were constructed initially by the army during the conquest and pacification of the province. The military invested time and manpower in constructing roads in order for them to be used for the movement of reinforcements in case of trouble. Roads also facilitated the movement of messengers connecting all areas of the province to the governor and Rome itself. The road network also had economic benefits in allowing the movement of goods across the province. Few towns possessed defences in the first century AD, except for those which had previously been military sites. By the third century AD, a large number of towns had begun to construct defences, perhaps symptomatic of military problems within the province.

COLCHESTER

Colchester was one of the earliest towns in the province. As the target of the initial phase of the conquest and the site of a considerable *oppidum,* the imperial administration perhaps wished to make a clear statement about the benefits of Roman rule and urbanisation. After the *oppidum* was seized under the gaze of the emperor Claudius, a fort was established on the site. Within six years, the military garrison was transferred to support ongoing campaigns in Wales. Colchester was therefore designated as a colony for discharged veterans. This conveniently maintained a military presence in the area. Considerable investment seems to have been made in the town, perhaps at the expense of the local Trinovantes who expressed their ire during the Boudiccan revolt. The centrepiece of the town was the temple dedicated to Divine Claudius, one of a very small number of Classical temples established in the province. Most temples built during the Roman period possessed a Romano-British style represented in a circular form within a compound. The temple in Colchester however would not have looked out of place in Rome itself. The developing town of Colchester was clearly used to demonstrate the benefits and amenities of Romanization. A recent discovery at the site has been a chariot race track or circus, the only known example from Roman Britain.

Colchester was probably intended to be the provincial capital at the time of the invasion. However, the residence of the governor was soon transferred to London. This may have happened as a result of the Boudiccan revolt, and is further evidenced by the discovery of the procurator Classicianus' funerary monument. London is unusual for a provincial capital in that its origins lie not in a major Iron Age settlement or deliberative imperial policy, but rather the decision of the business community. The crossing point of the Thames was important for trade, and the area may also have acted as a neutral meeting point for different tribal groups. A large community of merchants had established themselves near the river crossing by 60 AD, when they were attacked by Boudiccan rebels. The thriving business community ensured that it would attract the attention of the provincial administration as an economic hub. The status of London grew rapidly and the town would eventually cover over 120 hectares. As may be expected, investment in public buildings (much of it by wealthy private individuals) included a grand forum deliberately raised to increase its visual appeal. A fort was constructed at Cripplegate to house the soldiers visiting the town as bodyguards for the governor and messengers from other military bases.

SILCHESTER

Silchester was the *civitas* capital of the Atrebates and possibly came under the jurisdiction of Togidubnus. On the site of an impressive Iron Age *oppidum*, the Roman town grew to over 40 hectares in size. A regular grid plan was laid out demonstrating a structured approach to urban planning even at an early stage in the development of the province. Several buildings were constructed outside of the generic alignment of the town, which may indicate a passive attempt at resistance or simply individuals emphasising an identity distinct from their fellow townspeople. The main street of the settlement was aligned with the major road running from the south west to London, providing a valuable opportunity for passing trade. Public baths were constructed within the town. An amphitheatre on the edge of the town held between 3,000 and 7,000 spectators. Whilst the amphitheatre provided entertainment to the population of Silchester, it would also have attracted visitors from the surrounding region thus boosting the urban economy. A religious sanctuary, possibly of Iron Age origin but monumentalised by Romano-British temples was also an important feature of the settlement.

CORBRIDGE

Not all towns in Roman Britain were as large or as impressive as the examples outlined above. Corbridge, close to the northern frontier, began as a military fort sitting on the Stanegate road. After the withdrawal from the Antonine Wall *c.* 163 AD and the reemphasis on the Hadrianic frontier, the fort was abandoned. A military presence was still maintained on the site through two legionary compounds, which probably functioned as storage depots for units based on Hadrian's Wall. These depots appear to have been garrisoned by soldiers from different units. The inevitable problems caused by troops from different units living in close proximity is evidenced by an unusual inscription dedicated to *Concordia*, the personification of concord or agreement, by soldiers from VI Victrix and XX Valeria Victrix legions. Gradually a small town grew around the military compounds, perhaps encouraged by business opportunities provided by soldiers with little to do and money to spare. Aside from the military buildings, the town was dominated by a large courtyard building of unknown purpose. The structure may have been intended to serve as a forum, but was never fully completed. Two large granaries were also constructed next to the Stanegate. Other buildings included a prominent fountain house which provided a public water supply facilitated by a small aqueduct. Three well-used buildings facing on to the main street may have been temples, inns or even brothels. The rest of the settlement was comprised of houses, shops and workshops. A large building close to the Tyne river crossing may have been the residence of a provincial official. The growth of Corbridge was driven by the economic benefits of the military presence in the immediate vicinity and around Hadrian's Wall. Whilst a range of factors contributed to the origins and spread of towns in Roman Britain, urbanization promoted the benefits of *romanitas* to the provincial population as a whole.

RURAL LIFE

When analysing Roman Britain, there is a tendency to view it as a world of mosaics, fine dining, lavish architecture and exotic goods. Yet it must be remember that for most of the population, particularly those living in the countryside, life would have gone on much as it did before 43 AD. This is particularly the case in more remote, and therefore less, Romanized regions of the province. Devon and Cornwall were relatively untouched by the imperial administration after the initial pacification phase. There were few large towns and little military presence. Chysauster, a village in west Cornwall, is an excellent example of a settlement which was relatively untouched by the Roman occupation (Fig 6). Chysauster was established in the second century AD, though the architecture of the site is similar to other local villages such as Carn Euny which were constructed during the Iron Age. There is some evidence to suggest that there may have been an earlier Iron Age settlement on the site, possibly associated with a local hillfort. Chysauster consists of at least nine houses arranged in a regular layout. The buildings are conventionally described as courtyard houses, a style particularly common in this area of Cornwall and the Isles of Scilly. The houses were built of stone, with thatched roofs. A single main entrance to the house led to an inner courtyard, which was probably open to the sky, with at least three rooms opening off the courtyard. This style of house originated in the Iron Age and continued in use throughout the Roman period. The community at Chysauster was agricultural in nature and the village was surrounded by an extensive field system. Some of the inhabitants may have been involved in panning for tin, though not on a large scale. No luxury or exotic goods have been discovered at Chysauster. Indeed, there is little to distinguish this Roman period settlement from local Iron Age sites. For the inhabitants of Chysauster, Rome and the provincial administration would not have had a significant impact on their worldview or daily lives beyond the collection of taxes. The site is a salutary reminder that the inhabitants of Britain engaged with the Roman occupation in a variety of different ways. There was no single Roman Britain or indeed Roman Briton, but rather a kaleidoscope of distinct identities and experiences.[53]

VILLAS

Romano-British society was predominantly rural in nature.[54] Approximately 80% of the population resided in the countryside, pursuing an agricultural lifestyle. The countryside of Roman Britain would not have differed massively from that of the Iron Age, at least to the casual observer. More land would be under the plough as a result of economic demand and innovative changes made to ploughing technology, but the majority of dwellings would resemble roundhouses. Villas, the structure most often associated with Roman rural living, made up only around 2% of rural residences. Their presence is strong evidence of Romanization as their construction was often the result of a desire to show *romanitas*. Roman culture has always advertised the benefits of country living, in contrast to the strain of city life. Villas mostly functioned as holiday homes for the wealthy elite, acting as places where they could relax and entertain guests. As such, they tended to be located close to the road network to allow easy commuting. Whilst they did possess an agricultural function and, in some cases, could be highly productive, their social aspect was also important. Extravagant dining rooms, ostentatious mosaics and luxurious bathhouses demonstrate that many villas were designed to impress guests and advertise the status and cultural tastes of the owner. In this respect, the villa at Fishbourne with its palatial appearance is particularly relevant for its links with Togidubnus and his family.

In Britain, the largest proportion of villas occurs in the south and east, with fewer found in the north and west. The overwhelming majority occur to the east of the Fosse Way, the road which connected Exeter and Lincoln. Why the distribution of villas appears linked to a particular road is something of a mystery, although one suggestion is that the Fosse Way was an early frontier during the conquest of the Britain and areas behind it therefore tend to be more Romanized. Villas are found beyond the Fosse Way, including one at Rudston near Hull featuring the Venus mosaic. Some unexpected areas are noticeably devoid of villas, including the Fenlands of East Anglia. It is possible that such areas may have been imperial estates owned by the emperor. Another problem with identifying the distribution of villas is defining them as a class of structures. Villas in Britain display a significant range of styles, sizes and design. They range from a simple corridor building (i.e. a rectangular building with a corridor running in front) to structures with several ranges and courtyards. Elaborate villas belonging to the latter group are relatively few.

CHEDWORTH

The villa at Chedworth grew over two centuries from the second century AD to become a particularly impressive country residence for a member of the elite. The site is close to the Fosse Way and the large settlement at Cirencester. The area around the Cotswolds hosted a large number of villas, probably because of the favourable agricultural conditions and the proximity of large Roman towns, including the colony at Gloucester. The villa began as a group of separate buildings in the early second century AD with a bathhouse located close by. Water was provided by a local spring, which may have been a sacred site during the Iron Age. There is evidence for at least one Romano-British temple close to the villa. A serious fire in the third century AD prompted rebuilding of the existing structures and the renovation of the bathhouse. By the following century, Chedworth had evolved into a sophisticated villa with five ranges connected to each other A second bath complex was added and the site boasted an inner garden and outer courtyard. Excavations revealed a particular emphasis on dining within the complex. The *triclinium* was the dining room of a Roman house, named after the three couches which were normally situated within it. At Chedworth, the *triclinium* was particularly ornate with an elaborate mosaic depicting the four seasons. Most of the mosaics in the villa contained geometric designs, leaving the decoration of the *triclinium* to stand in stark contrast to the rest of the building. The mosaic survives in fragmentary condition, with the figure of winter being the best preserved. Winter is shown wearing the *birrus Britannicus*, indicating his British identity (perhaps an ironic statement on climatic conditions in the province compared to elsewhere in the empire). Winter brandishes a bare branch and a dead hare, indicating that he brings death and barrenness to the landscape. Spring, on the other hand, was shown holding a plump bird. A renowned mosaic workshop operated at nearby Cirencester and it is likely that it provided the four seasons mosaic. The witty decoration of the dining room indicates that it was a prime location for the owner to entertain guests. Villas like Chedworth convey the status and tastes of the British elite, as they sought to emulate the lifestyles of the imperial regime.

Beyond the northern frontier, the Roman occupation had a significant impact even on areas which had not been pacified. Occasional military campaigns, such as those led by Agricola in the late first century AD and the emperor Septimius Severus in the early third century AD, would inevitably have caused disruption and casualties to the native population of Scotland. Recent research on the Northumberland plain to the north of Hadrian's Wall indicates that the creation of the frontier had a long term impact on the local population.[55] Originally an area with relatively prosperous inhabitants during the late Iron Age, it seems to have been mostly abandoned by the third century AD. An official policy implemented by the imperial administration to clear settlements close to the Wall cannot be ruled out. The local population may also have been vulnerable in occupying territory between the imperial army to the south and emerging Scottish power bases to the north. For the most part, however, the major consequence of the Roman presence to the south would have been economic in nature.

It is likely that there was prolonged contact between the inhabitants of unconquered Scotland and the provincial population. As we have seen, Hadrian's Wall contained crossings which facilitated movement across the frontier. An inscription from Colchester dating to the third Century AD attests to the presence of a visitor from Scotland:

> DEO MARTI MEDOCIO CAMPESIUM ET VICTORI(A)E ALEXANDRI PII FELICIS AUGUSTI NOS(TR)I DONUM LOSSIO VEDA DE SUO POSUIT NEPOS VEPOGENI CALEDO

> *'To the god Mars Medocius of the Campeses and to the Victory of our Emperor Alexander Pius Felix. Lossio Veda, descendant of Vepogenus, a Caledonian, set up this gift from his own funds'*[56]

The *Campeses* were divine mother figures who were particularly associated with horses and training grounds. Whilst the identity of Vepogenus is unclear, it seems likely that he must have been an individual of some repute, as Veda clearly takes pride in his association. Veda's presence in Colchester is unexplained. It is possible that he was a trader and therefore visited the settlement in order to sell his wares. Pottery originating from Scotland has been found at a number of sites on Hadrian's Wall, indicating that individuals from beyond the frontier did trade with the provincial population. Mercenaries may also have been drawn from across the frontier. A counterfeit mould for making illegitimate Roman coins was found at Brighouse Bay near the Solway Firth. The mould would have been used to create fake coins which were probably then placed into circulation among the frontier community. Roman Britain provided ample opportunity for economic exploitation.

The acceleration of Romanization across the province, with the ensuing spread of luxury items and exotic goods must have appealed to high status individuals in Scotland. Two hoards from Birnie near Elgin contained over 300 silver denarii, alongside evidence for the presence of Roman glassware and pottery. Some of these items may have been traded across the frontier, but they may also have been diplomatic gifts presented to important chieftains to maintain their loyalty to Rome. The use of subsidies to pacify and engage rulers whose territories neighboured provinces was an established Roman tactic. A hoard of almost 2000 silver denarii from Falkirk probably represents one such subsidy. Brooches appear to have been particularly valued by elites in Scotland. A particularly beautiful example of such a brooch comes from Erickstanebrae in Dumfriesshire. Originally worn on the heavy cloak of a soldier or provincial official, this golden fibula contains an inscription which references the emperor Diocletian, dating it to the late third or early fourth century AD. While it could have been lost by an imperial commander on campaign, it could also have been a prestigious gift presented to a local ruler. In return for payments or prestigious goods, the imperial administration would expect to receive mercenaries, political support or acquiescence from the tribes.

Traprain Law in East Lothian was a major hillfort associated with the powerful Votadini tribe during the Roman period. A major hoard of Roman silver recovered from the site indicates that the tribe had established contact with the imperial administration. Weighing around 20 kg, the hoard consists of over 200 fragments of silver objects. Originally, most of the objects belonged to a set of tableware which would have graced the table of a wealthy Roman aristocrat. However, the objects have been cut up so could no longer have been used for their original purpose. In essence, the objects were now raw materials to be melted down and utilized in whatever form their new owner saw fit. In all likelihood, the hoard was used as a payment by the provincial authorities to the ruler of the Votadini. The territory of the tribe, encompassing most of the eastern lowlands, made them a valuable buffer state to Rome in protecting the frontier from aggressive northern tribes. The hoard indicates the direction of imperial policy in safeguarding Roman Britain through using luxury goods to assure the goodwill of neighbouring tribes. Such a policy was less expensive and perhaps more effective than attempting to complete the conquest of Britain.[57]

DECLINE

The end of Roman Britain was the result of a long decline in the integrity and effectiveness of the imperial administration to respond to internal crises and external threats. The third century AD witnessed a profound crisis in the political stability of the empire as a whole. Between 235 and 284 AD, a total of over twenty individual rulers replaced each other in swift succession. This rapid turnover of emperors was a result of a number of factors, including external pressures from hostile tribes, lack of dynastic stability and the rise of an aggressive superpower in the form of Sassanid Persia in the east. Provincial army groups fought each other to elevate their generals to imperial power. The empire came staggeringly close to collapse, and it is something of a miracle that it survived due to a radical series of political reforms, including an imperial power sharing agreement, and a succession of competent emperors who steered the empire towards unity rather than fragmentation.

Britain was not immune to the convulsions striking the rest of the empire. Given its geographic location, the province was always potentially vulnerable in any imperial fragmentation. Around 260 AD Marcus Postumus, the commander of the Rhine army, broke away from the imperial regime and established a Gallic empire, including the provinces of Spain, Germany, Gaul and Britain. This separatist empire endured for fourteen years, even after the assassination of Postumus, until it was reincorporated into the wider empire. The precedent of Britain as part of a separate imperial entity could not be undone. In 286 AD, Carausius the commander of the Channel fleet seized control of Britain and northern Gaul, and proclaimed himself emperor. Britain was only recovered by imperial forces after an invasion in 296 AD. Usurpers would continue to appear in Britain during the late fourth and early fifth Centuries AD, acting as a distraction to the imperial authorities from more pressing matters.

The threat posed by governors in Britain to the security of the imperial regime prompted revised approaches to the political organisation of the province. In the third century AD, Britain was split into two separate provinces. Britannia Superior was governed from London, whilst Britannia Inferior was ruled from York. In the early fourth century, Britain was designated as a Diocese, under the command of the Praetorian Prefect of Gaul based at Trier. The British Diocese was subdivided into four separate provinces, namely Maxima Caesariensis governed from London, Britannia Prima governed from Cirencester, Flavia Caesariensis governed from Lincoln and Britannia Secunda governed from York. The purpose of these reforms was to minimise the political power of any individual governor in Britain, and therefore prevent any further fragmentation. It is debatable whether the lack of administrative unity may have hindered the opportunity to deal decisively with emerging external threats.

By the fourth century AD, Britain came under increasing military pressure from hostile tribes and seaborne raiders. The Picts of northern Scotland posed a considerable threat to the northern frontier. Raids were also conducted by Saxons from Holland and *Attacotti* and *Scotti* from Ireland. In an unprecedented assault in 367 AD, these tribes formed an alliance to coordinate their strike on Britain. Roman forces suffered horrific losses and Britain was only saved through a series of campaigns led by Count Theodosius. The construction of defensive walls around a number of towns in the third and fourth centuries AD is symptomatic of the vulnerability experienced by the provincial population during this period. It is noticeable that the British elite invested heavily in their country villas during the early fourth century AD. This is in stark contrast to elite investment in civic buildings within provincial towns, which appears to have decreased considerably during the same period. General instability would have impacted considerably on the British economy and encouraged urban decline. The countryside was not immune from the economic crash and a large number of villa estates were abandoned or fell into disrepair by 360 AD. The hostile tribes assaulting the provincial shores would accelerate the decline of the Roman occupation, but they would also remake Britain in a manner which could not be foreseen.

Chapter 6

After Rome

(410 – 1066 AD)

The period after the collapse of Roman power in Britain defies easy definition. Referred to as the 'Dark Ages' on account of the scarcity of reliable historical sources, it was an era of substantial and often violent change which laid the foundations for the political geography of Britain as we know it today. In preference to the 'Dark Ages', historians now refer to either sub-Roman Britain or the early Medieval period in order to define this period. Neither is wholly satisfactory. For our purposes, it is sufficient to dedicate this chapter to an examination of conditions in Britain between the end of the Roman occupation and the Norman invasion of 1066.

THE END OF EMPIRE

The demise of the Roman Britain is usually dated to 410. Conventional descriptions of the end of the Roman occupation often refer to the withdrawal of the legions symbolising the slipping of Britain away from the imperial grasp. This view is dangerously misleading and obscures events in Britain during the fifth century. There was no single withdrawal of Roman troops from Britain. Whilst the succession of usurpers in the late fourth century inevitably drained British military resources to wage campaigns in Gaul and other troops were withdrawn by legitimate rulers to shore up the imperial frontier in Germany, the army was never recalled as an entity from Britain. Instead, the control of the imperial administration over the former British province gradually faded away. The terminal date of 410 is assigned on the basis of a letter from the emperor Honorius, which purports to tell his British subjects to 'take precautions on their own behalf'. In other words, this letter indicates that Britain was no longer assured of the protection or resources of the empire and was therefore isolated from imperial control. Indeed, the historian Zosimus claims that the inhabitants of Britain were no longer subject to Roman law.[1] Doubt has been placed on the interpretation of

Honorius' letter with the suggestion that it may instead refer to the cities of *Bruttium* in Italy.[2] Nevertheless, it is clear that no emperor exerted authority over Britain after the first decade of the fourth century.

The absence of imperial control must have had a startling impact in Britain. This would particularly have been the case within military communities on the northern frontier. The Roman army had undergone a series of reforms during the later stages of its existence. By the fourth century AD, the army was divided in the main between mobile field units (*comitatenses*) and fixed frontier units (*limitanei*).[3] By the end of the century, there were probably around 5000 of the former and 12500 of the latter stationed in the Diocese. The *limitanei* based on the northern frontier would increasingly have been embedded within local society. The end of imperial authority over Britain left these troops in place, but disconnected from higher military command. In such circumstances, units would have had to fend for themselves requiring new relationships with local communities. Officers would no longer have been drawn from elsewhere across the empire, supplies could not be sourced from the continent and the flow of pay was abruptly halted. In short, a power vacuum would have been created.

The fort at Birdoswald was joined to Hadrian's Wall and stands in an imposing position overlooking the River Irthing. During the third century AD, the fort housed the first Aelian Cohort of Dacians from modern day Romania. The site was occupied at least into the fifth century AD. Towards the end of the fourth century, the northern granary collapsed and was not rebuilt. The end of the use of granaries at Birdoswald indicates a shift in supply chains for the fort. Without facilities for storing grain, the site must have been supplied regularly from a local source. A coin belonging to the emperor Theodosius (388 – 395 AD) was found within the rubble of the granary providing an indication of the date of its destruction. In the early fifth century, if not slightly before, the granary was built over by a large timber structure. At a later date, this was replaced by a large timber hall enclosing over 160 m^2. The location of the hall was deliberate. The view of the building was framed by the surviving western gateway and the main road through the fort was narrowed to make room for the structure. Smaller buildings close by presumably fulfilled a service function for the hall. The transition from stone granary to timber hall reveals a shift in the command structure of the military unit stationed at Birdoswald. Timber halls were used for feasting and communal activities, in stark contrast to the formal elements of a Roman headquarters building. The nature of command had evidently changed from bureaucratic unit commander to local warlord. It seems highly likely that the soldiers and officers based at Birdoswald adapted to the end of imperial rule by establishing their dominance over the local area. This dominance would have been continued by their descendants. Although still utilising the trappings of Roman military power through the surviving fort architecture, a new military structure was ascendant more akin to the relationship between a chieftain and his warriors.[4]

Life for the civilian population would have been similarly disorientating. A large proportion of the British population would have been on the move during the fifth century. The economic collapse of Roman Britain was mirrored by the decline of urbanisation. Without the means to repair them, baths, aqueducts and sewer systems would have fallen into disrepair. Access to exotic goods dwindled as trade suffered across the former imperial territories. In the absence of elite investment, public buildings decayed. New social groups would have formed as a response to the pressures of life in post-Roman Britain. Ironically, some of these groups reoccupied Iron Age sites. A significant number of hillforts were reused after the collapse of Roman rule. Cadbury Congresbury in Somerset was reoccupied during the second half of the fifth century. By 500 AD, the new inhabitants began to refortify the site for defensive purposes. Hillforts were no longer about status, but rather security. Excavations from the site have revealed that the fifth century inhabitants were using pottery looted from local cemeteries. In some cases, the pots were centuries old and originally held cremation burials.[5] This desperate search for usable pottery indicates the collapse of local markets and the fading of established trade routes.

BYZANTIUM

Britain was not completely isolated by the end of imperial rule. Trade connections with the Mediterranean endured with the Byzantine Empire, the eastern successor to Rome. Indeed, the largest assemblage of Byzantine pottery from north of the Mediterranean was discovered at Tintagel in north Cornwall. Most Byzantine pottery in Britain is found in the south-western peninsula of Devon and Cornwall. It mostly occurs on elite sites including the hillforts at South Cadbury and, later in its existence, Cadbury Congresbury. Access to Byzantine goods allowed emerging elites to demonstrate their status and power, much as Roman artefacts did after 43 AD. Tintagel occupies a spectacular position overlooking the sea. There is no definite proof that the site was occupied during the Iron Age, but was probably inhabited during the late Roman period. From the fifth to the seventh century, Tintagel served as a prosperous royal site. Most of the pottery from the site is Byzantine, with relatively small amounts of late Roman material. Of the Byzantine pottery, 75% comes from the Eastern

Mediterranean with the remainder from North Africa. This was not a trickle of trade which arrived accidentally. The volume of Byzantine pottery at Tintagel suggests that it arrived as a result of direct contact between the local ruler and the Byzantine Empire. It is possible that tin was the basis for this relationship, as it had been for Mediterranean interest in Cornwall since the Bronze Age. This would explain why Byzantine pottery is usually found in the south-west of Britain. The Byzantine Empire did have its own tin mines in Cappadocia, which suggests there may have been other motivations behind trade with Tintagel. It has been suggested that the Byzantine Empire may have been maintaining diplomatic relations with Cornish elites. Similar to high level political contact between Rome and Britain after Julius Caesar's raids, this arrangement was designed to protect imperial interests and potentially identify opportunities for military intervention. The Byzantine Empire was never in a position to consider annexing Britain but it may have been politically expedient for them to maintain this façade. Byzantine pottery is not limited to high status sites in Cornwall. It has been found in smaller quantities on settlements inhabited by less wealthy groups, such as that at Trethurgy. Whilst Byzantine pottery may have been available in local markets, it could also have been offered as gifts from leaders to their retainers. The use of exotic goods to reinforce social and political hierarchies is not without precedent.[6]

ARTHUR

No account of post-Roman Britain can ignore the problem of Arthur.[7] Despite being the most well-known British individual prior to the medieval period, his existence cannot be proven. The story of King Arthur and his knights is too well known to bear repetition here. This romantic version can be traced back to the account of Geoffrey of Monmouth writing in the twelfth century, long after Arthur's supposed time. Later medieval authors contributed to the narrative of King Arthur's chivalric court and his ill-fated romance with Guinevere. The historical evidence for Arthur, often stated to have reigned during the fifth or sixth centuries, is limited. The earliest source, written by Nennius in the ninth century, describes him as a *dux bellorum* or leader of battles, who won a series of notable battles over the invading Saxons. Scattered references in Welsh sources written during the ninth and tenth centuries also make reference to his existence. The poem *Y Gododdin* compares a noted warrior unfavourably with Arthur. This reference indicates that the poet expected his audience to be familiar with Arthur and his martial attributes. Another text, the *Annales Cambriae*, refers to Arthur's victory at the battle of Badon and his death alongside Medraut/Mordred at the battle of Camlann. These are the only texts which refer to a historical Arthur prior to the creation of his romantic image during the medieval period. It is noteworthy that the earliest account refers to Arthur not as a king, but as a warlord in the style of the late Roman period. There are a vast range of theories which attempt to clarify the existence of the historical Arthur. All are ultimately based on this limited range of source material. There is no archaeological evidence which supports the existence of Arthur.[8] A number of post-Roman sites are linked in folklore to the story of Arthur, including South Cadbury and Tintagel. No artefacts or inscriptions bear witness to the reign of a ruler with the same name. Great excitement was caused by the discovery of an inscribed stone at Tintagel which bore the name 'Artognou'. Tintagel is reputed to have been the birthplace of Arthur. Despite dating to the sixth century, the name inscribed on the stone has no connection to the legendary king. As we have already noted, the stories associated with Arthur owe much to existing British folklore and ritual, as demonstrated by the importance of his sword Excalibur and its return to a watery environment. The power of tales about Arthur consists of his identity as a legendary warrior who united his people against dangerous invaders. Arthur's importance therefore transcends his immediate historical context to bear wider significance for the people of Britain, particularly in times of danger. It is no coincidence that Winston Churchill chose to write about King Arthur in 'A History of the English-Speaking Peoples'. The current evidence for a historical Arthur does not allow his existence to be proven nor disproven.

THE COMING OF THE ANGLO-SAXONS

Arthurian tales of a noble leader defending his people against an aggressive foe reflect the historical context of the fifth and sixth centuries through the migration of external tribes into Britain. These population movements contributed to the later naming of some of the British nations, including England and Scotland. Historical accounts of the Anglo-Saxon invasion of Britain are provided by Gildas and Bede, writing in the sixth and eighth centuries respectively. In his provocatively entitled *Ruin of Britain*, Gildas describes the destruction wrought by foreign invaders. Towns were sacked and burned; priests and civilians alike were butchered in orgies of violence. Gildas gruesomely describes corpses littering the once busy streets looking as though they had been squeezed through a wine press. The once mighty towns of the Roman province were ruined. In essence, this was an apocalypse over the landscape of Britain. It is not difficult to see how tales of a mighty warrior who united his people and drove back the invaders gained power in these circumstances.

Bede provides a historical context for the arrival of Anglo-Saxon invaders in his *Ecclesiastical History of the English People*. According to Bede, Anglo-Saxon warriors were invited into Britain during the mid-fifth century by a king named Vortigern. He intended to use the mercenaries to secure his own territory and granted them land in return. Initially, the crews of three longships were settled in Britain. They were led by two brothers, Hengist and Horsa, the latter of whom was killed in battle. Hengist and Horsa were renowned in their homeland and came from noble stock who claimed descent from the god Woden. Once the vulnerability of Britain became clear many more of their compatriots joined the first mercenary force. Although offered land and money in return for their military service, the incomers rebelled against Vortigern and seized control of much of Britain. Bede carefully notes the origins and settlement patterns of the invading tribes, the Jutes, Angles and Saxons. The Jutes settled in Kent and around the Isle of Wight. The Angles, from whom the term English comes, settled in Mercia, Northumbria and other areas across England. The Saxons established themselves across southern Britain. From these historical sources, a standard picture of the Anglo-Saxon invasion has been formed. In the fifth and sixth centuries, invading tribal forces gradually took control over much of the landscape through violent conquest. The British population was forced into retreat and survived mostly in remote areas, such as Cornwall and Wales, where the Celtic character of Britain has endured. The territory controlled by the invaders became England. The British language, a type of Celtic ancestral to modern Welsh, was replaced across much of its previous range by the Old English spoken by the Anglo-Saxons, the ancestor of modern English. This established historical narrative has persisted for decades. It has even been argued that an apartheid system was established in Britain, with an Anglo-Saxon elite dominating the remaining British population.

Archaeological evidence can be used to support the historical evidence for the Anglo-Saxon invasion. The *Notitia Dignitatum* is a late Roman military document dating to the end of the fourth century. The document outlines the locations, titles and commands of imperial administrators and military officers across the empire, along with their geographic areas of authority. The *Notitia* is problematic, in that the offices described were not all contemporary, with notable differences between the eastern and western imperial territories. For our purposes, the interest of the *Notitia Dignitatum* lies in its inclusion of a military commander with the title *Comes Litoris Saxonici* or Count of the Saxon Shore. This command had authority over a number of military installations along the British coast from Norfolk to

Hampshire. The Count of the Saxon Shore may also have been responsible for similar installations further up the north coast and on the other side of the Channel. These installations presumably held troops protecting the coast from seaborne invaders. A number of Saxon Shore forts survive in some form. Three forts appear to have been constructed earlier than the others, probably during the early or mid-third century. These forts, at Brancaster, Caistor and Reculver, were constructed according to the usual design for Roman auxiliary bases with a playing card shape and earth rampart. The later group of forts, dating to the end of the third or early fourth centuries, were constructed using a different design which is unique in Roman Britain. These forts, such as those at Portchester and Pevensey, were built with massively thick walls up to 3.5 m in width and imposing bastions on the outer faces of the walls. This design is highly unusual in Britain and bears a resemblance to military architecture from the eastern provinces. These forts were specifically designed to be imposing, similar to later medieval castles.

The presence of incoming Anglo-Saxons has been detected through changes in burial practice, artefacts and new architectural features. Cremation cemeteries appear in the fifth and sixth centuries. Although cremation was used in Roman Britain, a renewed emphasis appears to have been placed on this method for disposing of the dead similar to that used in the Germanic homelands of the incoming tribes. The ashes of the deceased were buried in pots, sometimes alongside animal remains and grave goods. Inhumation remained popular in southern Britain, as it had during the late Roman period. However, corpses now tended to be buried without coffins but accompanied by a range of grave goods, in contrast to Roman burials. In some areas, burials were accompanied by weapons indicating an emphasis on status. Surprisingly, not all such inhumations were male. Women and children are also known to have been accompanied in the grave by swords. A number of artefacts have been identified as being of Germanic design, particularly different forms of brooches worn by men and women. These were presumably imported or created by Anglo-Saxons. Two distinct building types are believed to have been used by Anglo-Saxons on British settlement sites. Large timber halls, reminiscent of the great hall of Heorot immortalised in the epic poem Beowulf, were established in Britain during this period. *Grubenhaeuser* were developed in the Netherlands during the second century. These buildings were constructed over sunken pits which conveniently leave a distinct archaeological profile. Although it was originally assumed that these structures indicated that Anglo-Saxons lived in squalor, it is now thought that this sunken floor design provided a convenient space below floor level for storage and insulation.

Despite this relative wealth of evidence for the arrival of Anglo-Saxons in Britain, the nature and scale of their invasion is open to debate. Indeed, it can be argued that the traditional historical narrative of a violent conquest is deeply flawed. Whilst Gildas' lurid account of the destruction of Britain may be emotive, there is a lack of archaeological evidence to support this scenario. If Britain had been subject to a hostile invasion followed by a genocidal rampage, we would expect to find substantial supporting evidence in terms of mass graves, urban destruction and the abandonment of farming landscapes. None of this exists. On the contrary, a significant element of continuity in the British landscape pervades this era. Whilst Bede's account may seem more reliable on account of the detail he provides, there are still grounds for disquiet. Hengist and Horsa, for example, are names which translate as 'gelding' and 'horse'.[9] The existence of two brothers who essentially founded a new people evokes obvious comparison with Romulus, Remus and the legendary founding of Rome. Like Arthur, there existence can neither be proven nor disproven, but is certainly open to doubt.

The imposing features of the Saxon Shore forts seem to provide firm evidence for an emerging seaborne threat during the third century which would eventually engulf Britain. Yet all may not be as it seems. The *Notitia Dignitatum* does not clarify how the Count of the Saxon Shore came by his name. Most authorities assume that it represents the nature of the threat, i.e. the shore threatened by Saxon raiders. There is an alternative possibility. The ruse allegedly used by Vortigern in importing Germanic warriors to deal with his internal security problems was not innovative. Throughout the late Roman period, imperial authorities absorbed tribal groups into the empire to provide military support and protect the frontiers in exchange for land, money and privileges. Such groups were termed *foederati*. It is entirely possible that Anglo-Saxon groups were stationed in Britain during the later stages of the Roman occupation. Germanic-style brooches in Britain at the end of the Roman period may well have belonged to such troops. In this case, the Saxon Shore would not reflect the anticipated foe, but rather the troops based there. There are problems with the identification of Saxon Shore forts as coastal defences against raids from the Continent. Not all of the forts are positioned in strategic locations. Excavations at Portchester revealed a surprising lack of structures within the fort. Rather than the military command buildings and barracks we would expect in an active Roman base, the interior seems to have contained only temporary timber structures. It is therefore possible that the later Saxon Shore forts were constructed as storage depots whose imposing features were designed to discourage brigands rather than provide defence against invasion.[10]

Recent advances in genetic science offer an insight into the scale of the

Anglo-Saxon settlement in England. In an extreme view, the invading Anglo-Saxons destroyed most of the native British population either through genocide or the monopolisation of resources, such as food supplies and productive farmland. In this instance, the proportion of modern inhabitants of Britain who could trace descent to the native British population prior to the fifth century would be minimal. Although British females may have been absorbed into the Anglo-Saxon population, we would expect most male lines to have died out leaving no trace in our genetic heritage. This is not the case. A study conducted by Stephen Oppenheimer identified a low level of gene type matches between Britain and the Anglo-Saxon homelands, of around 5%.[11] This indicates neither a large scale population movement into Britain nor the replacement of the native population by the incomers. Whilst there are continuing issues with genetic analysis, including the emergence of new techniques and problems in securely dating population movements, it is clear that this evidence refutes the historical portrayal of a British genocide.

Place name analysis offers an insight into the hidden relics of our linguistic heritage. Few loan words from the native British language found their way into Old English. However, a number of place names do indicate a substantial level of communication between Anglo-Saxons and Britons during this period. The Old English terms *walh* and *cumbre* were used to denote the native British. Settlements with names such as Walsall, Walcot and Cumberwood, may therefore indicate that they continued to be inhabited by native speakers throughout much of the Anglo-Saxon period. Latin names also found their way into Old English place names. The Latin *vicus*, denoting a settlement outside of a Roman auxiliary fort, became *wic* in Old English leading to settlement names such as Wickham and Wycomb. Whilst not necessarily indicating the existence of auxiliary forts (as *wic* also means trading emporium), these sites may have appeared as Romanised settlements to Old English speakers. The use of Eccles as a place name is also noteworthy. Probably taken from the Latin *ecclesia*, it may have been absorbed into Old English to denote settlements which contained sacred sites. The analysis of place names is complex and it should not be assumed that these hints denote an archaeological reality. Nevertheless, there is a strong indication that Anglo-Saxons communicated and interacted with the native population. We would expect invaders intent on genocide not to pay close attention to existing settlement names or local sentiments. This was clearly not the case. Place names reflect a significant level of continuity between the Roman period and the following centuries.[12]

The arrival of Anglo-Saxon incomers is undisputed. Rising sea levels in the fifth century, alongside political turbulence in their homelands, may have prompted their migration to Britain. Yet we should discount the notion of an Anglo-Saxon invasion followed by the extermination of the native population. Genetic evidence indicates that the population movement into Britain was relatively small, perhaps less than 10,000 individuals in total. There was assimilation between the natives and incomers leading to the distinctive culture of Anglo-Saxon England. Given the impact which these incomers achieved, it is possible that they quickly formed an elite group either on their own accord or in alliance with pre-existing rulers.

English speaking areas in the late sixth and early seventh centuries witnessed the coalescence of powerful groups and their rulers into forms approaching kingdoms and kings as we would recognize them. These emerging royal houses sought to legitimize their authority through emphasising the historic longevity of their ruling dynasties, often falsely. Rulers in Kent, for example, claimed descent back to Hengist and Horsa and therefore ultimately to the god Woden. The historic landscape of Britain was exploited by kings through linking royal architecture to sites of ancient significance.

Yeavering in Northumberland is a perfect example of the manipulation of the landscape by emerging dynasties. By the early seventh century, Yeavering was a key royal site for the northern kingdom of Bernicia.[13] Yeavering is not a single site, but rather a hilly landscape dominated by Yeavering Bell which rises over 360 m over sea level. Archaeological evidence indicates that Yeavering was first visited by hunter-gatherers during the Mesolithic period who probably hunted deer on the hilltops. Neolithic people constructed at henge monument close by. During the Bronze Age, Yeavering was settled during the period of expansion into upland areas. There is substantial evidence for large scale woodland clearance during this period. The local Bronze Age community buried their dead beneath cairns and in a cemetery in the shadow of Yeavering Bell. Perhaps as early as the late Bronze Age Yeavering Bell was in use as a hillfort, one of the largest ever constructed in Northumberland. The hillfort was surrounded by a defensive perimeter stone wall standing up to 3 m in height. An area of 13.8 acres was enclosed. The hillfort was densely occupied when in use. In all, 125 separate hut platforms have been identified on the site. It is likely that Yeavering Bell was occupied on a seasonal basis. Winters would have been deeply inhospitable so the population probably moved to lowland settlements during harsh weather. The hillfort would have been of ceremonial importance for the community, as well as a refuge in times of crisis. Although the hillfort went out of use, Yeavering continued to be occupied during the Roman period. Roundhouses were built by local farmers surrounded by extensive field systems.

Yeavering's importance was reaffirmed in the sixth and seventh centuries with the creation of a royal hall and associated buildings (Fig 7). The royal complex included a number of unusual features including the Great Enclosure, 'theatre' and numerous burials. Bede mentions events at Yeavering around 627 AD. Bishop Paulinus visited Northumberland to convert the masses. Paulinus visited King Edwin and his queen at Yeavering where he stayed for a total of thirty-six days. Local people flocked to hear the bishop and receive religious instruction. According to Bede, large numbers of Northumbrians were baptised in the nearby River Glen. Yeavering was one of a series of royal residences established by the Bernician kings. It would have been visited several times a year by the royal party and their entourage, perhaps to hunt over the hills and fells close by.

The royal complex sits on a small hill dominated by the Yeavering Bell hillfort which looms menacingly overhead. The Great Hall would have been occupied by the king. It was where he assembled and feasted his retainers. Nearby a large structure known as the Great Enclosure was probably used as a giant stockyard. It probably housed cattle which supplied the king during his visits. These animals would have been gathered as a form of taxation from local communities. A full stockyard therefore displayed the power and authority of the king. The most unusual structure at Yeavering is variously described as a 'grandstand' or 'theatre'. It consists of tiered seating radiating from a single platform and post. Defying easy explanation, it has been interpreted as the location for royal speeches to an assembled community. Given the Christian context of Yeavering in the early seventh century, it may also have been used for sermons and ceremonies.

The royal complex did not sit in isolation from the historic past. On the contrary, it was conspicuously linked to earlier structures. The first burials of the post-Roman period were deliberately associated with a Bronze Age ring-ditch complex. The Neolithic henge was reused as a metal working area. It has been theorised that many of the Anglo-Saxon buildings on the site were aligned with earlier Bronze Age structures. The siting of a high status site below a large hillfort was not accidental. Rather it drew visible parallels through the continuity of power within the local landscape. The old British name for Yeavering was *Gefrin* (hill of the goats), with the royal complex designated as *Ad Gefrin* (at the hill of the goats). The connection to the presence of wild goats may echo ancient religious veneration of the hilltop mammal, perhaps connected to shamanism. An Anglo-Saxon burial on the site contained a goat's skull and a ceremonial staff which may have displayed a goat motif. The burial was aligned with the Great Hall. Northumbrian kings may have used an existing local ritual connection with goats to enhance their own standing, even after conversion to Christianity. Yeavering was twice destroyed by fire during the seventh century as a result of enemy action. It fell into disuse by 685 AD and was replaced by a new royal site at Milfield. The use of Yeavering by the Bernician kings demonstrates a conscious attempt to manipulate a historic landscape into creating the perception of longevity for an emerging elite.

SUTTON HOO

The conscious self-definition of royal dynasties during the seventh century is also reflected in their funerary practices. The royal burial at Sutton Hoo in Suffolk is unique in Britain as an Anglo-Saxon inhumation of unparalleled wealth and sophistication. The creation and promotion of identity and status in death is as important as in life. Ostentatious funeral ceremonies provide a opportunity for a dynasty to display its power, emphasise the legitimacy of the succession and bind the community together in a collaborative act of mourning. Sutton Hoo consists of a barrow cemetery overlooking the river Deben. The area was deforested during the Bronze Age and subsequently given over to farming in the following centuries. During the late sixth and seventh centuries it was used as a cemetery for high status individuals. Another cemetery close by served the local community. At least nineteen mounds have been identified on the site. The cemetery was used for both cremation burials and inhumations. A further thirty-nine inhumations dating from a slightly period were also discovered near to the mounds. Many of these burials showed signs of physical trauma and severe wounds, indicating that the site may have functioned as an execution cemetery after the elite burial ground fell into disuse. This would nevertheless suggest that the mounds were still associated with power and authority.[14]

The famous burial at Sutton Hoo was placed in Mound 1.[15] It took the form of a ship, with a burial chamber constructed within and a mound heaped over the top. This was an extremely labour intensive method of constructing a funerary monument. The ship was over 27 m in length and 4.5 m wide, with a depth of around 1.5 m. It originally the ship would have been crewed by forty oarsmen. Analysis of the ship indicates that it had undergone extensive repairs during its lifetime. The ship was therefore not specially constructed for the burial. On the contrary, it too was nearing the end of its natural life. The burial chamber, measuring 5.5 by 4.5 m housed the burial and associated grave goods. The use of a ship was clearly of great symbolic importance to the local community. It may indicate an ancestral link to the sea or a belief in a post-mortem sea journey. Ship burials are particularly associated with Scandinavia and may the format chosen for the Sutton Hoo burial may be the result of dynastic links across the sea. Interestingly a second mound was found to possess traces of a ship burial.

There is no doubt that the individual buried at Sutton Hoo possessed a warrior identity. A mail shirt and range of weapons, including six separate types of spear, accompanied him in death. As befitting a warrior, he was also equipped with a magnificent pattern welded sword, formed by the hammering of eight separate bundles of iron rods. This weapon would have been an object of admiration on account of the evidence craftsmanship involved in its creation. The scabbard and sword belt were lavishly decorated with garnet and gold fittings. The Sutton Hoo helmet is also a work of art. Formed from iron and equipped with a face mask, ear flaps and a neck guard, it gave the owner a new powerful identity. This form of helmet is probably a descendant of parade helmets used by the Roman army. Contemporary helmets of a similar nature have been found in high status burials in Sweden. The helmet is decorated with flowing interlacing motifs and scenes from Scandinavian and Germanic mythology. The shield deposited within the burial chamber also reflects Scandinavian influences. It is decorated with a bronze dragon and a bird of prey made from bronze and gold leaf.

Aside from the impressive collection of weapons and associated martial equipment, there are a number of artefacts which evidence the power and status of the deceased. Sixteen pieces of silver, probably originating from the eastern Mediterranean, were deposited. The largest consists of a great dish with a diameter of over 70 cm. The dish is marked by the stamps of the Byzantine emperor Anastastius I, who ruled at the end of the fifth and early sixth centuries. This artefact was therefore already a century old when it entered the burial mound. It contains images associated with imperial power including an eagle and two seated figures who probably represent Rome and Constantinople. Two silver spoons marked with the Greek '*Paulos*' and '*Saulos*' may have Christian significance, referencing the conversion of St Paul. A leather purse contained thirty-seven gold coins and three blanks. These coins all come from Merovingian Gaul and were produced between 575 and 625 AD. They do not represent a random sample as each coin was produced at a different royal mint. As a special collection, their presence in the burial mound may have been for a particular purpose. It has been suggested that the coins may have been provided to pay for the passage of the deceased to the otherworld, perhaps even to pay the ghostly oarsmen who would crew his ship. Two other objects may reflect the royal identity of the deceased. A massive whetstone topped by a bronze stag has been interpreted as a sceptre. Although sceptres are known from the Classical world, this form of artefact is unique in Anglo-Saxon Europe. Similarly a massive iron stand, rising to 1.7 m tall, has been identified as an item of royal regalia possibly used to display a banner.

The deceased person buried at Sutton Hoo was clearly an individual of high status, able to command the resources of his community and possessing links to Scandinavia and the Mediterranean.[16] No body was found during the excavation of the ship. This led archaeologists to initially assume that mound was a cenotaph constructed for an individual in the absence of a body. It is now certain that acidic soil conditions encouraged the decay of the skeleton leaving no trace of the corpse. Sutton Hoo lies in the kingdom of the East Angles. The East Anglian dynasty was founded by Wuffa *c.* 575 AD. His people assumed the name of the Wuffingas, and one of their kings is almost certain to have been buried at Sutton Hoo. The most likely candidate is Raedwald, who ruled *c.* 617 – 624 AD. The date of his death would correspond to the date suggested by the Sutton Hoo assemblage. Described by Bede as a somewhat reluctant convert to Christianity, this may explain the faint traces of Christian belief within the assemblage.

THE STAFFORDSHIRE HOARD

Hints of Christianity also pervade another spectacular find from this period. The Staffordshire hoard was discovered in Hammerwich near Lichfield. Although analysis of the hoard is still ongoing at the time of writing, most authorities date deposition to the seventh century. The hoard is the largest assemblage of gold and silver metalwork ever found in Anglo-Saxon Europe. It consists of over 3500 separate items of broken gold and silver. The hoard also contains 3500 cloisonné garnets. Although a range of different artefacts types were found, the overwhelming majority are associated with a military context. Silver foil pieces probably come from one or more helmets. Ninety-seven sword pommel caps form part of the hoard, although hundreds of swords are potentially represented in the full range of artefacts. A pectoral cross would originally have been worn ostentatiously on the chest of a clergyman or prominent Christian believer. Decorated in gold with a prominent central garnet, the cross appears to have been deliberately damaged. Another Christian cross, possibly used in processions or attached to a bible, was deliberately folded prior to deposition. Whilst this could be taken as evidence of anti-Christian sentiment, it could also represent a solution to a practical problem of transporting loot. A biblical inscription on a silver gilt strip also hints at engagement with Christianity. The strip may have been attached to a bible and refers to Numbers 10:35. Interestingly, this specific passage is martial in nature, imploring God to rise up and destroy the enemy. It seems rather fitting for the context and military nature of the hoard.

The unique nature of the Staffordshire hoard demands explanation.[17] Parallels have been drawn with the Sutton Hoo burial, but these finds come from radically different contexts. The Staffordshire hoard was categorically not a royal burial. Instead it bears witness to the military realities of life in Anglo-Saxon England. The hoard was discovered within the territory of the powerful Mercian kingdom, not far from the royal seat at Tamworth. Although no contemporary settlement has been found in the immediate proximity of the hoard site, the Roman Watling Street runs through the area and was probably still in use during this period. The quality of the hoard betrays considerable wealth. The garnets may even have originated in India or Sri Lanka. We cannot assume that there is an overt religious element to this collection. The Christian artefacts were probably a common feature of combat equipment during this period and need not represent a pagan backlash against conversion. It is noteworthy that most of the items represent decorative elements which could have been stripped from the fallen rather than complete weapons or armour. The hoard could therefore represent the spoils of war looted from the battlefield and covertly hidden whilst on the march for later retrieval. The redistribution of sword pommels would have been useful for rewarding retainers and therefore enforcing social and military hierarchies. As we have noted, hoarding in Britain was used for centuries as a means of appeasing or thanking the gods by putting items beyond use and into the hands of the deities. An alternative explanation for the presence of the hoard may be that it was deliberately dedicated to a god in thanks for victory in battle. Without the emergence of further evidence, we may never be sure of the real explanation for the deposition of the Staffordshire hoard.

MERCIA

By the late eighth century, the kingdom of Mercia had exerted its control over much of southern England and held sway as far north as the Humber.[18] Mercia was formed from a series of smaller tribal groups unified into a single kingdom. Their ruler Offa was *bretwalda*, a title with a complex meaning close to overlord or high king, symbolising an individual who ruled over a large area. The same title had earlier been attached to Raedwald of the East

Angles. Mercian kingship was itinerant meaning that the king ruled on the move as he travelled across the kingdom. This perpetual movement allowed Offa to affirm the loyalty of his supporters, exert his authority across the far reaches of his kingdom and menace potential foes. The Mercian expansion was powered by a series of military conquests backed by political and diplomatic pressure. Offa constructed fortified settlements or *burhs* as bulwarks against attack.[19]

In 787, Offa launched his most audacious military construction campaign. His plan was to construct a great dyke running from the Bristol Channel to the Irish Sea. Bishop Asser, writing a century later, notes that the purpose of the dyke was to separate Mercia and Wales from sea to sea. The ambitious scale of Offa's Dyke is difficult to comprehend. It demanded a complex programme of land clearance, surveying and personnel management. Labour for the project was probably provided by the Mercian population as a form of tribute, as well as military levies. Offa's Dyke is in fact a great linear monument in the form of a bank and ditch over 7 m deep and 20 m across. The top of the bank carried a timber palisade which in some parts was reinforced in stone. This was not a passive barrier, but a defensive fortification. Some scholars have even suggested that it contained watchtowers. A system of beacons, originally used to plot the course of construction, would have communicated warnings of attack and allowed a robust military response to have been prepared. Offa's Dyke protected Mercian territory from incursions by Welsh raiders. It also allowed the king to control the movement of traders and merchants across the frontier. The construction of this immense earthwork demonstrated the power of a king able to inscribe his authority across the landscape itself. When considering Offa's Dyke, it is hard to dismiss the suspicion that the king may also have been influenced by old tales of the operation of Hadrian's Wall. Offa would have been familiar with Bede's writings, which mention the Hadrianic frontier. Perhaps Offa was consciously emulating a monument imbued with the symbolism of imperial power and military might.[20]

RELIGION

The religious beliefs of the Anglo-Saxons prior to their conversion to Christianity are clouded in obscurity. It should not be assumed that native cults dating to the Iron Age, if not before, had died out. There is increasing evidence for profound continuity in religious belief in ancient Britain. Identifying specific belief systems of individual groups is complicated by a number of factors. In recent years, archaeologists have emphasised the importance of natural places for the religious beliefs of contemporary and historic societies.[21] Unfortunately, the veneration of natural features and phenomena leaves little archaeological trace, in contrast to a deliberately constructed sacred sanctuary. There are indications that Anglo-Saxons may have focussed their attentions on particular natural features. The royal site at Yeavering, for example, is dominated by the hill of Yeavering Bell which looms overhead and may have possessed religious significance. The significance of watery environments as a means of depositing offerings to the gods appears to have continued during their period. At Fiskerton in Lincolnshire artefacts continued to be deliberately deposited in the River Witham up until the fourteenth and fifteenth centuries. There is a particular concentration of weaponry and pins from around the eighth century indicating that ritual deposition was unabated during the Anglo-Saxon period. These offerings appear to have been associated with bridges and other crossing places. It is possible that they were offered in thanks to a local deity in thanks for a safe crossing.[22]

Bede, writing from a Christian perspective in the eighth century, noted that pagan cults focussed their attention on the worship of idols and animal sacrifices. He described the destruction of a temple at Goodmanham in East Yorkshire, which consisted of a central shrine surrounded by enclosures which contained idols venerated by visiting worshippers.[23] Idols such as these were probably wooden and therefore unlikely to survive. Christian groups were prone to destroying pagan idols and sanctuaries, as was the fate of the sacred site at Goodmanham, leaving little evidence for archaeologists to find. Traces do survive of the importance of animal sacrifice. A number of Anglo-Saxon inhumations around the Humber and Wash estuaries were discovered alongside associated horse remains, which may have been sacrificed during funerary rites. It has been estimated that up to 10% of the local buried population may have been accompanied by horses. Individual horse inhumations have also been found which suggests that their significance was not merely linked to mortuary practice. Horses were clearly objects of veneration by the local population.[24] Indeed, individual horse inhumations are not uncommon in the area. In light of these extraordinary burials, it is difficult not to trace a connection to the equine significance of the names of the alleged leaders of the Anglo-Saxon colonists, Hengist and Horsa.

Conversion to Christianity did not require the immediate rejection of pagan beliefs and methods of worship. On the contrary, there was a significant level of continuity between pagan and early Christian practices. Christianity persisted in some areas of southern Britain after the end of the Roman conquest. According to Gildas, the rulers of Wales and south-western Britain remained Christian. Ireland appears to have been converted to

Christianity by British missionaries during the fifth century. In 597, the ambitious Pope Gregory despatched a mission under Augustine to complete the conversion of Britain. Over the following decades, the rulers of a number of kingdoms became Christians. Conversion was therefore a gradual process rather than the sudden destruction of an alternative belief system. In a letter dated to 601 AD, Pope Gregory outlined a tentative approach to conversion which assimilated, rather than extinguished, pagan architecture and the religious calendar. Gregory noted that it is impossible to 'eradicate all errors from obstinate minds at one stroke'.[25] In other words, a pagan worshipper could not change their beliefs and ritual practices overnight. Gregory instructed that English pagan temples should not be obliterated. Although idols had to be destroyed, pagan sanctuaries could instead be stocked with altars and relics, and treated with holy water. Pagan festival days were absorbed into the Christian calendar, but replaced with a suitably Christian celebration such as a day of holy martyrs. Animal sacrifice could also not be prohibited, but rather than serving as offerings to pagan gods, they should instead provide meat for feast days. This use of existing religious architecture is problematic for archaeologists as it can prove difficult to distinguish between pagan and Christian religious groups. Raedwald, ruler of the East Angles and probable occupant of Sutton Hoo, underwent a partial conversion to Christianity. According to Bede, he incorporated the Christian god into his existing pantheon. Indeed, Raedwald maintained a temple where an altar of Christ stood next to one on which offerings were made to pagan deities.[26]

The early Christian church in Britain also emphasised its links to the Roman Empire. A number of churches were constructed within or close by substantial Roman sites. The church of Escomb in County Durham, established around 675, was constructed using stone from the nearby fort of Binchester. Whilst this provided an advantageous source of stone, it was also a way for the church to establish a connection with the indigenous heritage of the local area. The reuse of imperial inscriptions may have symbolically laid claim to the power and authority of the Roman imperial regime. The monastery at Jarrow, for example, contained two fragments of a larger inscription which may originally have come from a monument erected by the emperor Hadrian on the edge of the northern frontier. Such a link may have been particularly apt for a northern Christian outpost centuries later. The Christian community was clearly fascinated by the local Roman heritage. Bede preserves one of the earliest antiquarian descriptions of Hadrian's Wall within his *Ecclesiastical History of the British People*.

Bede was born in 673 and belonged to a family which earned its living off land owned by the monastery of Wearmouth. At the age of seven, he was offered to the abbot in order to complete his education. Bede later moved to

Fig 1: Stonehenge is perhaps the most iconic archaeological site in Britain, with a religious significance which has persisted from prehistory to the present day. (Credit: English Heritage Photo Library)

Fig 2: Despite the astonishing levels of preservation at the site, the meaning and function of Seahenge remains elusive. (Credit: English Heritage Photo Library)

Fig 3: The reconstructed gateway of the fort at Arbeia (South Shields) monumentalises the strength of the Roman army in northern Britain. (Photo by author)

Fig 4: Feeding the legions and auxilia was a monumental task requiring the construction of specialist granaries to store grain. (Photo by author)

Fig 5: The temple of Antenociticus at Benwell was used by officers and soldiers stationed at the local fort. (Photo by author)

Fig 6: The settlement at Chysauster provides an insight into rural communities who were relatively unchanged by the Roman conquest. (Credit: English Heritage Photo Library)

Fig 7: The royal site of Yeavering utilised the existing sacred and political landscape to emphasise the power, status and legitimacy of its residents. (Credit: Peter Dunn, English Heritage Graphics Team)

Fig 8: Hereford Cathedral is home to the *Mappa Mundi* which depicts the medieval worldview through a rich mixture of mythology, geography and theology. (Photo by author)

Fig 9: The motte at Cambridge represents the only visible remains of the Norman castle.(Photo by author)

Fig 10: Clifford's Tower preserves part of the medieval castle which ensured that the city played a leading role in northern England. (Photo by author)

Fig 11: The original gatehouse at Ludlow Castle mimicked elite Anglo-Saxon architecture and was consequently ill suited for defence. (Photo by author)

Fig 12: From one approach route, Stokesay mimics the appearance of a fortified defensive site rather than an elite residence. (Photo by author)

Fig 13: The great hall at Stokesay Castle would have impressed visitors with the wealth and sophistication of the owner. (Photo by author)

Fig 14: Knowlton is a startling example of continuity in the use of sacred landscapes over centuries, in this case a church constructed within a Neolithic henge. (Credit: English Heritage Photo Library)

Fig 15: Ely Cathedral rises majestically over the surrounding low lying land, therefore exploiting the landscape to focus attention on the building. (Photo by author)

Fig 16: Durham Cathedral served as a pilgrimage site associated with Bede and Saint Cuthbert. (Photo by author)

Fig 17: Ludlow Castle dominates surrounding transport routes, including the river Teme. (Photo by author)

Fig 18: The impressive Iron Age earthworks of Caynham Camp in Shropshire may have been reused during the Civil War period. (Photo by author)

Fig 19: Pillboxes are a common reminder of how close Britain came to invasion during the twentieth century. (Photo by author)

Fig 20: The ROC nuclear bunker at York was designed to monitor the aftermath of a nuclear attack. (Photo by author)

Fig 21: The Sage at Gateshead is a spectacular example of urban regeneration as a result of the decline in heavy industry. (Photo by author)

the sister monastery at Jarrow which would be his home for the rest of his life. The founder of the monasteries at Wearmouth and Jarrow was a Northumbrian nobleman named Benedict Biscop. He undertook a series of visits to Rome during the mid-seventh century which had a profound effect upon his worldview and religious beliefs. Returning to Northumbria, Benedict convinced King Ecgfrith to grant him up to seventy hides of land for the foundation of a monastic community at the mouth of the River Wear. Building at Wearmouth began in 673 and involved the recruitment of specialist craftsmen from Gaul. Around 681, King Ecgfrith donated a further forty hides of land for a monastery overlooking the River Tyne. This new monastic house, dedicated to St Paul, would complement the monastery dedicated to St Peter at Wearmouth. Although geographically separated, the two monasteries were closely linked. Bede describes them as one monastery in two location, related as the head is to the body. From 688, the two monastic houses were united under a single abbot. The community at Jarrow was established by a small group of between seventeen to twenty-two monks from Wearmouth. A later source records how the community grew to over 600 monks possessing lands which could provide for 150 families by contemporary reckoning. The monastic community of Jarrow and Wearmouth was famed as a centre of scholarship, exemplified by Bede's works. It was also renowned for its stonemasons. In 710, the King of the Picts asked the abbot to provide him with skilled craftsmen to construct a stone church.

The monastery sat on the south bank of the River Tyne, close to the tributary River Don, in an area of marshy ground.[27] Indeed, the local population were known in Bede's day as marsh dwellers. A number of religious houses in north eastern England were constructed close to major water courses during this period, perhaps for transport and trade links. The relatively isolated location of Jarrow, close to a large area of tidal mudflats, may have provided opportunities for monks to seek solitude and retreat from the larger monastic community. The monastery consisted of two separate churches, one of which may have served the local community. These churches were eventually joined through the creation of a large tower between the ninth and twelfth centuries. Two other large buildings probably provided accommodation and workspace for the monks. As such, the monastery was substantially different from later medieval monastic complexes. A separate guesthouse was situated close to the river and was lavishly decorated. It probably served important visitors seeing the abbot on official business. The modern St Paul's Church in Jarrow preserves elements of the smaller monastic church within its chancel. The monastery at Jarrow declined after the eighth century, although it remained a place of pilgrimage for Christians wishing to visit the home of Bede. The site was revitalised during the eleventh century and the monastery reconstructed in the contemporary Benedictine style.

SCOTLAND

The process of unification between disparate groups and factions into more formal kingdoms was also experienced in Scotland during this period.[28] The region was inhabited by five different peoples, the Picts, Dál Riata, Britons, Anglo-Saxons and later Vikings. The Picts were a construct of Roman authors to define the people living north of the Forth-Clyde isthmus. The term is first noted in the third century and means 'painted ones', perhaps a reflection of the use of woad to colour their bodies. It is difficult to assess whether these were in fact a united group during the Roman occupation of the rest of Britain. Nevertheless, by the end of the Roman period the Picts were capable of exerting considerable pressure on the imperial frontier. The Picts were united into a single grouping by the end of the seventh century. The Picts remain curiously enigmatic because of the lack of reliable evidence we possess for their history and social structures. Pictish symbols, a form of writing which remains undeciphered, has been a source of particular fascination for historians and archaeologists alike. There are at least fifty distinct symbols used by the Picts. Some of these represent easily identifiable fauna, but many are more abstract in design. They were used widely at least until the seventh century and have been found inscribed on undressed stone, rocks and cave walls. They have even been found in association with Christian art. The meaning of these symbols and their use is unclear. The ambiguity of their appearance in conjunction with Christian images may suggest that they represent a Pictish language rather than possessing any deeper ritual significance.

The Dál Riata occupied the west of modern Scotland, particularly the region around Argyll and Bute. They were Gaelic speakers and are also referred to as the Scotti (from where the name Scotland comes from, although this term didn't really exist until the thirteenth Century). The Dál Riata are reputed to have been connected to the Dál Riata tribe from Antrim in Ireland, indeed it has been claimed that the population in Argyll and Bute may have originated in a migration from Ireland. However, there is no archaeological evidence to support such a population movement. Migrant communities from Ireland did establish themselves elsewhere in Britain during this period. The Deísi from southern Ireland migrated to Dyfed in Wales at the end of the fourth century.[29] Literary sources preserve the story of their flight from Ireland. Ogham script used in the homeland of the Deísi is also found in south-west Wales. Local placenames also preserve Irish traces. Unfortunately, the migration of the Irish Dál Riata is not supported by a similar wealth of evidence.

Increasingly complex social groupings in northern Britain are reflected in the architecture and organisation of high status sites. The fort at Dunadd was used as a royal site by the Dál Riata. Situated at one end of the spectacular Kilmartin Valley, the site was originally constructed as an Iron Age hillfort. A defensive site was re-established during the late fourth or fifth centuries. Enclosing walls and a lower enclosure were added during the following two centuries. Dunadd was strongly associated with royal rule. Indeed, royal proclamations continued to be made at the site up to 1506. Two carved footprints carved into the stone near the monumental entrance alongside a bowl cut into the rock were probably used in kingly rituals. The siting of the fort at Dunadd may have taken into consideration factors other than its strategic location. The Kilmartin Valley was an area of ritual importance throughout the Neolithic and Bronze Age. Similar to the inhabitants of Yeavering, the Dál Riata may have been attempting to link their royal rule to existing belief structures. Artefacts recovered from the site indicate that Dunadd was connected to prime trading routes. The site has yielded one of the largest quantities of imported pottery in Britain during this period. Some of these artefacts may have been transferred to sites of lesser status in the local area to reinforce existing hierarchies. Artefacts transported considerable distances to Dunadd include metalwork from Ireland, tin from Cornwall, pottery from Gaul and a glass *tessera* from Italy.

Christianity arrived in Scotland in 563 through Columba, an Irish missionary intent on converting the native population. The population of northern Britain was therefore exposed initially to Irish rather than mainland European Christianity during the conversion period. Columba established a monastery at Iona in the Inner Hebrides. The monastery swiftly grew in size to eventually enclose up to 20 acres. Iona became a leading religious centre and played a critical role in the conversion of communities in Scotland and northern England. It was also important as a place of learning connected to other religious houses across Europe. Iona was composed of a number of separate buildings including a church, cells for monks, guest houses, library and barns to support agricultural activity. It can be argued that the gathering strength of Christianity across Scotland contributed to the gradual unification of scattered groups and communities into a single kingdom.

The term 'Alba' used to denote a unified kingdom encompassing much of modern Scotland first appears around 900. The first king is reputed to have been Domnall mac Custantín. From this date, the rulers of Alba were noted in the *Anglo-Saxon Chronicle* meaning that they had achieved wide recognition as leaders of a political entity. The establishment of the kingdom of Alba witnessed the emergence of a Scottish identity which would continue to grow over the following centuries. It should be stressed that Alba did not control all of the area we classify as modern Scotland. Viking settlements persisted in Shetland and Orkney. Mixed Gaelic-Norse communities thrived in the Hebrides and along the Western seaboard.

VIKINGS

The term 'Vikings' invokes images of violent destruction and pillaging by seaborne raiders. Over the last few decades, our archaeological view of Vikings has changed considerably in part due to a series of spectacular excavations which have revised our view of life in Viking Age Britain.[30] The term 'Viking' appears to have come from a Norse verb used to describe the action of a warrior or pirate who went raiding. It was therefore not an ethnic description, but rather denoted those who went on seaborne raids. The *Anglo-Saxon Chronicle* uses the term to refer only to small raiding parties rather than large armies. Instead, the British appear to have described the incomers as *Dani* (Danes) or *Nordmanni* (Northmen). Viking groups were therefore ethnically diverse and included individuals from Norway, Denmark and Sweden. These were later supplemented by Norse settlers from Ireland, Scotland, Iceland and elsewhere.

In 793, Scandinavian raiders attacked the monastery at Lindisfarne, one of the great Christian centres of eighth century British Christianity. The impact of this raid was as significant as a modern terrorist attack. The raiders had clearly been attracted by the wealth of the institution and inability of its inhabitants to defend themselves adequately, but there were also religious undertones to the attack. According to contemporary Christian writers, the Vikings drowned some of the monks in the sea which was perhaps deliberately intended as a perverse form of baptism. The altars were desecrated in the search for hidden treasure. Although the Lindisfarne raid is usually interpreted as the earliest Viking attack on England, there may have been an earlier raid on a royal estate belonging to Beorhtric, king of Wessex, close to Portchester in Dorset. The exact date of the raid at the end of the eighth century is unclear, but it resulted in the deaths of the king's men. In the years following the Lindisfarne raid, attacks on religious sites in Britain intensified. Communities at Jarrow, Tynemouth, Hartness and along the western coast of Scotland were targeted by Viking raiders. In 850 a Danish army wintered in Britain for the first time, indicating a dramatic shift in Viking intentions. The following year, 350 ships sailed up the River Thames and attacked Canterbury and London. The presence of Viking armies in Britain marked an escalation in violence and the political impact of Scandinavian incomers. In 865, a Danish *micel here* or 'Great Army' arrived in East Anglia with the intention of seizing control of the Anglo-Saxon kingdoms. The Great Army seized York and placed a puppet ruler over Northumbria. Over the following years, the army exerted its control over Mercia and East Anglia.

The danger posed by marauding Viking groups is reflected in the fortification of towns across Mercia and Wessex. The *burhs*, or fortified towns, were first created in Mercia during the reign of King Offa, particularly between 780 and 790. The Mercian *burhs* share common attributes in defending riverside towns from Viking attack. Most are associated with major river crossings and therefore were designed to protect Mercia from riverine penetration. Examples can be seen at Gloucester, Chester, Tamworth and Hereford. Some of these sites took advantage of existing Roman remains for protection or building materials. The Roman walls of Chester, once a great legionary fortress of XX Valeria Victrix, were still intact by the end of the ninth century when a Viking force was besieged within it by a local levy. The legionary defences appear to have been reinforced with timber supports and extended to the River Dee. At Hereford, located at a strategically vital crossing point of the River Wye, gravel and clay banks enclosed the town and minster down to the riverside. In the early tenth century these walls were reconstructed in stone and an additional fighting platform supplemented the formidable defences.

The *burhs* of Wessex are associated with Alfred the Great (849 – 899), the king who led the resistance to the Great Army. Stories abound of the courage, resourcefulness and piety of Alfred, including the famous tale of the fugitive king being scolded by one of his subjects whilst in hiding in the marshes of Athelney. To protect his kingdom from Viking incursions, Alfred planned a network of *burhs* which would ensure that no part of his territory was further than 32 km from a fortified location. Archaeologists now suspect that many of these *burhs* already existed prior to Alfred's reign and this defensive network may form part of the legend which surrounds the king of Wessex as one of the greatest British leaders. The *Burghal Hidage*, created in the early tenth century, records a total of thirty *burhs* within the kingdom of Wessex. Similar to the burhs of Mercia, many of the sites in Wessex utilised Roman fortifications such as Chichester, Exeter and Portchester. *Burhs* on virgin sites often emulated the defences of Roman forts. Other burhs exploited naturally defensible features, particularly promontory locations. The Iron Age hillfort of South Cadbury, reoccupied in the fifth century in the chaos after the end of the Roman occupation, was again utilised as a defensive *burh* to meet the emerging threat. New defences generally consisted of a clay or turf rampart crested by a timber palisade. Ditches were usually cut in front of the rampart to impede any direct attack. *Burhs* did not just offer a tactical advantage the Anglo-Saxon kingdoms. They also brought economic benefits. The confidence imbued by formidable defences close to important trade and transport routes attracted merchants and traders, ensuring that many *burhs* became important commercial centres.

REPTON

In 873 the Great Army over-wintered at Repton in Derbyshire. The site was deliberately chosen for its propaganda value. Repton was one of the most important religious houses in Mercia and, moreover, a burial place of Mercian kings. The occupation therefore offered the army an opportunity to demonstrate its dominance over one of the sacred centres of Mercia. Certainly, they showed little respect for the sanctity of their surroundings. In order to defend their position, the Danes constructed a large D-shaped enclosure and utilised the church as a fortified entrance point. The cutting of the ditch, which ran down to the banks of the River Trent, required the desecration of the churchyard and the removal of burials. Substantial damage was done to the fabric of the church, either through accidents or deliberate vandalism.

Besides fortifying Repton, the Great Army also buried their dead.[31] These burials provide an insight into life in the Great Army. One burial in close proximity to the church consists of an individual who died in combat. Scientific analysis demonstrates that he originated in Denmark. The deceased received a number of mortal wounds. His eye and skull had been pierced by a sword or spear thrust. His leg received a sharp blow which almost severed the limb and probably removed his genitals. After death, the unfortunate victim appears to have been disembowelled. He was buried in a decidedly ritualistic manner. A silver Thor's hammer was hung around his neck. A boar's tusk was deposited in place of his penis. The wing of a jackdaw was also placed in his grave. This may have served as a replacement for the wing of a raven, associated with the god Odin. The boar's tusk and jackdaw's wing probably had magical significance, in reanimating his missing body parts. The close proximity of his grave to the Christian church, unlike the other Viking burials at Repton, may indicate a deliberate attempt to utilize the religious power of Christianity. The circumstances of this violent death remain unclear. It is tempting to see him as a casualty of the battle to seize Repton. Yet his death could also be the result of internal feuding within the

Norse camp. Analysis of tooth enamel from skeletons at Repton indicates that the army contained Swedes as well as Danes. In a multi-national force restricted to a single camp over the long hard winter, it is highly likely that fights erupted on occasion. Another intriguing burial was placed in the old mausoleum which lay outside the camp enclosure. A single male was buried in a stone coffin with weapons, coins and associated grave goods. Yet around his coffin was placed the bones of over 260 individuals. These skeletons were disarticulated, meaning that they have been removed from elsewhere. It seems highly likely that these were the bones of the Mercian dead removed from the churchyard and reinterred around the grave of the deceased Viking. Even in death, the Great Army exerted their dominance over the local population.

THE ORKNEYS & SHETLAND

The Viking colonisation of the Northern Isles is difficult to trace from a historical perspective, although Norse settlers are likely to have arrived by the end of the eighth century. However, it is significant that the names of major settlements, farms and natural features in Orkney and Shetland are overwhelmingly Scandinavian in origin. This fact has been taken as evidence for genocide conducted by incoming Norse settlers in exterminating the local population. Genetic analysis conducted by the BBC and a team from University College London established that, of those who could trace their ancestry locally for at least three generations, 60% of the male population of Orkney and Shetland possessed DNA of Norwegian origin.[32] This figure dramatically increased when the sample was limited to males who could trace their family tree in Orkney or Shetland for several centuries to between 60 and 100%. These proportions are suggestive of a violent conquest by incoming Norse males. Analysis of mitochondrial DNA, which traces female lines of descent, established that around 66% of the population of Orkney possessed female ancestors from Scandinavia. This indicates that Norse settlers brought their wives and female relatives with them to the new territories. A comparative genetic analysis of the inhabitants of the northern and western isles examining both male and female lines of descent identified key variations in Scandinavian ancestry. Some 44% of the population of Shetland possessed Scandinavian ancestry compared to 30% on Orkney and 15% on the Outer Hebrides. Whilst a number of variables may affect these results, including more recent migration, the findings indicate variation in the scale of Norse colonisation. Whilst the native population of Orkney and Shetland may not have been exterminated by the incomers, it is almost certain that Norse settlers established themselves in positions of power.

One of the most interesting Norse sites on Shetland is the settlement at Jarlshof on Sumburgh Head. The area had been settled since prehistoric times on account of its fertile soils and access to the sea. Norse settlers established a farmstead in the ninth century, close to the ruins of an old broch which may have still be defensible and provided a source of building stone. The farmstead was a long rectangular building with a floor space of over 100 m^2. Jarlshof is an exposed location vulnerable to harsh weather conditions. Two opposing doors minimized the impact of the wind on those entering or leaving the building. The stone walls were supplemented with an earth core. The farmstead was divided into a living area and kitchen. The former contained wooden living platforms for the inhabitants to sleep on. The kitchen contained both a hearth and oven. Surrounding buildings probably functioned as barns and agricultural outhouses. The occupants of Jarlshof were amply supplied with utilitarian goods, including metalwork from Scotland and Ireland, bone pins and sandstone whetstones. A series of graffiti artworks scratched on slate and sandstone were also discovered in the farmstead. Intriguingly, two rough profile portraits of a young male closely resemble figures on a Pictish symbol stone from the Brough of Birsay on Orkney. It is therefore possible that these pieces of graffiti were scratched by a Pict kept as a slave on the Norse farmstead, a surviving remnant of the local indigenous population.

DANELAW

Between 886 and 890, Alfred the Great agreed a treaty with Guthrum, leader of the Great Army, which essentially partitioned the territories of 'all the English race and all the people which is in East Anglia'. The treaty carefully defined the territory allotted to Norse settlers describing a boundary which ran along the Thames and Lea rivers to Bedford, and then along the River Ouse and the Roman Watling Street. The inclusion of the latter is particularly evocative of how Roman features were still used to define the geography of England. The area to the north of the boundary was known as the Danelaw. The actual extent of Norse settlement within the Danelaw is elusive.[33] A study of twelfth century charters has revealed that 60% of Lincolnshire farmers, 40% of East Anglian farmers and 50% of farmers in the northern Danelaw possessed names of Scandinavian origin. Furthermore, the Domesday Book records that around 50% of personal names recorded in Cheshire were of Scandinavian origin, which included individuals who possessed 30% of manors in Cheshire. Reliance on personal names to trace ethnic origin can prove untrustworthy. Scandinavian place-names may prove more reliable. As may be expected, there are relatively few Scandinavian place-names outside of the Danelaw, whilst 744 have been identified in Yorkshire. There are significant regional variations. In Cheshire, most Scandinavian place-names belong to the Wirral. Further north in Lancashire, Scandinavian place-names congregate around the coastal strip, possible evidence for Norse farmers operating on reclaimed salt marsh. Even within the Danelaw some areas, such as Northumberland and Durham, display a noticeable absence of Scandinavian place-names. The most common form of Scandinavian settlement name ends in *–by* (meaning farmstead), such as Kirby and Selby and 850 examples have been identified across the Danelaw. This stands in contrast to place-names ending in *–ton* (farmstead in Old English) such as Beeston. However, in some areas the English form became a hybrid through being integrated with a Norse personal name, such as Grimston. Place names ending in *–thorp*, such as Bishopsthorpe, also betray a Scandinavian presence and are often assumed to represent settlements established on outlying or inferior land. Caution is required in using place-name evidence to indicate a Norse settlement. It may instead represent the renaming of a local settlement by an incoming Scandinavian lord. Nevertheless, place-names are suggestive of the wider cultural impact of the creation of the Danelaw.

YORK

The commercial and political centre of the Danelaw was the city of York (Jorvik).[34] The city was first captured by Viking forces in 866, when puppet rulers were installed to allow the conquerors to pursue their onslaught of the southern kingdoms. A decade later Viking rulers assumed control of the city and would rule over it until the expulsion of Eric Bloodaxe in 954. A historical source indicates that the population of York in the seventh Century was around 30,000 people. The Domesday Book records that the city contained 1800 building plots. The Viking rulers of York utilized and extended the Roman defences of the city to enclose a large area, including the riverside, down to the Rivers Ouse and Fosse. Defensive timber bridges were probably constructed across the two rivers. Many of the streets of the modern city appear to have been established during this period. This is reflected in street names ending in –gate (relatively common in York) which comes from the Norse word meaning ‘street’. The famous Shambles, originally a street of butchers, is referred to in the Domesday Book as being in existence by the reign of Edward the Confessor in the mid-eleventh century. It is not clear whether the evolution of York was part of a managed urban plan. It seems more likely that the city evolved organically. Most of the building plots excavated over the last few decades possess a standard width of 5.5 m, which may indicate some form of control over urban planning. A number of churches were established in York during the Viking period. A large cathedral church was located somewhere in the region of the modern York Minster, although its precise location remains unidentified. The foundation stone of the Church of St Mary on Castlegate, dating to the tenth or eleventh centuries, states that the church was contructed by two individuals named Grim and Aese, indicating Scandinavian ancestry. Interestingly, the inscription itself is carved in a mixture of Old English and Latin indicating a degree of linguistic assimilation. The riverside would have been a particularly busy area, packed with trading vessels from across the Viking world. One area was still known as 'Dublin Stones' in the medieval period, indicating the spot where ships from the Viking city of Dublin would moor. Excavations at a number of Viking period sites in the city, including the famous Coppergate dig, have demonstrated the range of goods which flowed into York. These include quernstones from the Rhine, schist sharpening stones from Norway and silk from Byzantium. More intriguing are Islamic coins from modern Uzbekistan and a cowrie shell from the Red Sea. Industry in the city included metal, glass and leather workers. York was clearly not a city living in shadow of an occupying force, but rather a thriving commercial centre buoyed by the trading contacts of the Viking world.

The period between the end of the Roman occupation and the Norman conquest of 1066 was a formative period in the archaeological history of Britain. It was not a dark period of isolation and barbarity, but rather an age where Britain was subject to new influences from the homelands of the Anglo-Saxons and Norse incomers. Even the creation of the Danelaw, which appeared to sacrifice large swathes of English territory to Scandinavian hegemony, played a significant role in the formation of an English kingdom. Alfred's descendants pursued the reconquest of Norse territory which would be completed by the mid-tenth century, paving the way for a unified kingdom of English territory ruled over, in the short term at least, by a single dynasty. Across the modern nations of England, Scotland and Wales, this period witnessed a gradual process of political unification through emerging kingdoms and cultural diversity influenced by European migrants and the continuing rise of Christianity.

Chapter 7

The Medieval Period

(1066 – 1485 AD)

In Hereford Cathedral can be found the largest map from the Medieval world still in existence (Fig 8). The *Mappa Mundi* was inscribed on a single sheet of vellum around the year 1300. It has been miraculously preserved, allowing the contemporary visitor to view it as the original scribe intended. The scribe 'Richard of Haldingham and Lafford' has left his mark on the map. It provides an unparalleled insight into the worldview of the British at the end of the thirteenth century. The *Mappa Mundi*'s depiction of the world is an intriguing fusion of geography, mythology and theology. Strange mythical beasts, including mysterious dog headed men, lurk on the edges of the known world. Given the context of the *Mappa Mundi*, it is unsurprising that it depicts a Christian view of global geography. The centre of the map is dominated by Jerusalem, the centre point of medieval Christianity and a continuing flashpoint for religious tension. Paradise, in the form of the Garden of Eden, is depicted around the edge of the earth. Other locations from Biblical geography include Noah's Ark, Sodom and Gomorrah.

Britain and Ireland are depicted in the north-western corner of the *Mappa Mundi*. The geography of Britain is depicted in considerable detail reflecting the personal experiences of the scribe. A large number of important settlements are illustrated on the *Mappa Mundi*. Important settlements are indicated at Winchester, Canterbury and Ely. The latter shows the spire of the cathedral rising over the fens. The illustration of London reveals the Tower of London, constructed by William the Conqueror, looming menacingly over the Thames. Fortifications play a vital role in the topography of Britain as revealed on the *Mappa Mundi*. Important castles are shown in critical border areas, including Conwy, Caernarvon, Chester and Berwick. To a certain extent, the *Mappa Mundi* depicts a landscape defined through castles and other fortifications. This was in stark contrast to the earlier periods of British history.

Yet the *Mappa Mundi* was not solely a medieval creation. It reveals a world view which was informed by the knowledge and imagination of

Classical Greece and Rome. Some of the mythical beasts illustrated on the map were taken directly from some of the greatest works of Classical mythology, including the sea monsters Scylla and Charybdis from Homer's *Odyssey*. On the edge of the map closest to Britain can be seen an even more impressive figure from the Classical world in the form of the emperor Augustus, who reigned from 31 BC to 14 AD. Augustus was the first Roman emperor and the adopted son of Julius Caesar. Unlike his adopted father, Augustus never set foot in Britain although he expressed his interest in mounting an invasion on several occasions. The emperor is depicted in the form of an important pope. Accompanying text indicates that Augustus ordered this survey of the known world, a subtle reference to the Roman census which prompted Mary and Joseph to visit Bethlehem. The prominent inclusion of Augustus on the *Mappa Mundi* demonstrates that medieval Britain was as much a product of the past as it was of the present. The British worldview continued to be enriched by its contacts with continental Europe and the memory of historic events and figures.[1]

THE NORMANS

The beginning of the medieval period is conventionally dated to the victory of William the Conqueror over the forces of Harold Godwinson at Hastings in 1066. The political geography of Britain on the eve of the Norman Conquest can be conveniently divided between England, Scotland and Wales, although these terms were not necessarily in common usage. The actions of Alfred the Great and his descendants in dealing with the Scandinavian masters of the Danelaw had encouraged the gradual growth of a united English kingdom ruled, for the most part, by a single royal dynasty. The inhabitant of Scottish territory did not possess as strong a national identity as the kingdom to the south. Only by the early fourteenth century did a clearly defined Scottish identity appear beneath a single Scottish king. For much of the period under discussion, Scottish territory was peopled by a number of different ethnic groups, including Norse communities in Caithness and the Hebrides, and Cumbrians in the southern lowlands. High status Norman incomers would also play an increasing role in local politics. Wales (a term taken from the Latin *Wallenses* meaning borderers) was marked by continuing political division and conflict formed by the rivalries of a series of minor kingdoms including Gwynedd and Powys. This lack of political unity, as well as the challenging topography of Wales, proved problematic for the Norman invaders. As a result, they were inclined to rely on a series of powerful lords holding territories along the Welsh borders or Marches to control the population of Wales through violence and terror.[2]

Our understanding of the Norman impact on England in particular is enriched through the Domesday survey. The name Domesday, which first appears in the twelfth century, reflects the exacting detail of the survey through comparison with the Christian Day of Judgement. The survey was conducted in 1086, two decades after the initial invasion. The impetus for the systematic recording and valuation of most of England came directly from William the Conqueror. There are three possible motives behind the Domesday Survey. First, it allowed the king to obtain a clear assessment of tax contributions at a local level. This was invaluable in maintaining the economic stability of the new kingdom. Second, by examining the resources of all landowners in England, it provided the king with a useful resource in calculating the military resources he could command. It may be significant that the survey was begun barely a year after a threatened invasion from Scandinavia. Third, the Domesday survey had legal implications relating to the ownership of land. This would have been a particularly controversial topic in the decades following the Norman Conquest and a subject of large numbers of legal disputes. The records of the Domesday survey essentially provided new landowners with a level of legitimacy for the prior acquisition of land.

It is difficult to overestimate the scale of the task involved in undertaking the Domesday survey.[3] All of England was surveyed with the exception of areas north of the River Tees which were not completely under full Norman control at this date. London was also omitted from the Domesday survey. The city suffered a catastrophic fire in 1086 which may have prevented its inclusion. The rest of England was divided into at least seven circuits, each of which was assigned a group of royal commissioners who oversaw the gathering of data. Initially, local nobles and officials were responsible for the collation of information. The initial findings were then scrutinized by the royal commissioners who assembled juries of English and Norman individuals. Fortunately a copy of the questions posed by the royal commissioners has survived in a document from Ely. Amongst the information gathered was the names of respective landowners in 1066 and 1086, value of the land and the number of male workers. The process was so accurate that the writer of the *Anglo-Saxon Chronicle* complained that not a single farm animal escaped being recorded. The local surveys were collated and entered into a single text named Great Domesday which is remarkably almost wholly the work of a single scribe. Unfortunately, this text is not complete as work seems to have been suddenly halted, perhaps as a result of the death of William in 1087. Additional records for Essex, Norfolk and

Suffolk can be found in a supplementary text created earlier in the survey process known as Little Domesday.

English society at the end of the eleventh century was predominantly rural in nature. The Domesday survey records around 270,000 heads of household living in the countryside. The vast majority of rural dwellers were *villeins* or peasants who worked for their local lord but also retained their own land on the common fields around their settlement.[4] The royal commissioners were not interested in the sizes of families, as they had little bearing on taxes, military levies of land ownership. Assessing the overall population size therefore relies upon using reasonable estimates. Calculating the urban population poses additional difficulties. The urban survey is notoriously incomplete as the sizeable settlements of London and Winchester were both excluded. London alone may have supported a population of around 25,000 individuals. Estimate of the total urban population in 1086 vary, but it is not unreasonable to suspect that it may have numbered around 125,000. The whole of England may have held a total population of 2 million, depending on the accuracy of our estimates for family size and the populations of unrecorded areas.[5]

In stark terms, the Domesday survey records the impact of the Norman Conquest on landownership across the English countryside. By 1086, out of the 180 largest landowners in the kingdom, only two were of English origin. Lower down the scale, there were other English landowners, mainly those who claimed descent from the family of Edward the Confessor or those who served the new king in some capacity. After the initial invasion, William had moved swiftly to seize land belonging to those who had opposed him. This decision had political and military motivations. Unlike previous invasions, the Norman Conquest was not accompanied by a wholesale population movement. It has been estimated that only around 8,000 Normans established themselves within their newly conquered kingdom. Most Norman incomers maintained territories in both Normandy and England. This led to a dual sense of identity in which Normandy was prioritized over England down to 1204 when Normandy itself was conquered. The damage inflicted during the conquest was also recorded in the survey. This was particularly the case in Yorkshire. During 1069 – 1070, William launched a major punitive campaign memorialized as the 'Harrying of the North' in response to a series of northern insurgencies. The Domesday survey describes 33% of Yorkshire as waste, presumably as a result of Norman reprisals years earlier, which involved the calculated destruction of agricultural infrastructure and resources.[6]

CASTLES

The Norman victory was assured and consolidated in large part by their custom of constructing castles. By 1100, Norman lords had established around 500 castles in England. The first of these was hastily constructed at Hastings soon after they landed. According to the twelfth century historian Orderic Vitalis, the Norman Conquest was achieved through the absence of castles created by the English. In conjunction with their use of heavy cavalry, the creation of castles gave the Normans a distinct military advantage over their enemies. Castles are widely seen as classic examples of medieval architecture. Fine examples continue to dominate local landscapes in the present day. Yet there is considerable disagreement between modern scholars as to the purpose and nature of castles in the medieval period. Deriving from the Latin *castrum* meaning armed camp, castles are often assumed to have served a purely military function. In this regard, they provided a fortified stronghold able to withstand sieges and providing accommodation for nobles, their retainers and troops. This conventional view is no longer sustainable in light of considerable archaeological investigation of the subject over recent decades. As we shall see, the term castle is applied to a range of structures embodying considerable variety in design, size and structure. Whilst some did possess a military function, the key similarity between these structures is their function as a high status residence.[7]

The first Norman castles to be established in Britain were constructed before the invasion. In 1051, according to the *Anglo-Saxon Chronicle*, Norman supporters of Edward the Confessor hastily constructed a series of castles during a period of political crisis. In doing so, they demonstrated the Norman propensity for constructing castles and their primary function as defensive structures in times of war. Five castles are believed to have been established in 1051. Four were built in Herefordshire and a single castle was constructed in Essex. Although their occupation was short lived, they served as a precursor of the rise of castle building after 1066. The eleventh and twelfth centuries witnessed the rapid construction of castles across Britain. The majority of Norman castles used the motte and bailey design. This consisted of a mound topped by a tower (motte) and a lower enclosure providing accommodation, store buildings and a chapel (bailey) (Fig 9). The use of the motte provided an element of surveillance over the surrounding landscape. It also provided a visual demonstration of Norman status and power. The Normans also utilized a ring-work design for some of their castles, consisting of an enclosure surrounded by a fence and ditch. Norman castles were established in rural and urban areas. Of the thirty-six castles constructed by William the Conqueror, no fewer than twenty-four were situated close to urban centres. Contrary to popular opinion castles were not always located on high ground. Often they were positioned in river valleys and other lowland areas where they could control road transport networks and navigable river systems.

One of the castles built by William the Conqueror was established at York in 1068. William recognized the importance of the city in controlling the north of his kingdom. The castle took the form of a motte and bailey. The original motte is now crowned by Clifford's Tower (Fig 10). Despite possessing a garrison of some 500 men, the castle was attacked by a force of Northumbrian rebels the following year. Returning to the city to rout the rebels, William constructed a second motte across the River Ouse. Even this renewed programme of fortification was in vain. In autumn 1070 a coalition of Danes and Northumbrians raided York. The Norman troops desperately torched the houses closest to the castles to prevent them from being used as source for material to bridge the surrounding ditches. Unfortunately this plan was unsuccessful and the castles were burned. William reconstructed the castles on both banks of the River Ouse upon securing the city. Although both used the motte and bailey design, one in fact had two baileys. By the twelfth century, York Castle served as a notable royal stronghold and played a key role during negotiations with Scottish rulers. In 1190, the castle was the site of a massacre of the Jewish population of York. A mob motivated by a desire to renege on their debts and religious hatred besieged Jewish families in the castle. Unable to escape, the Jewish families committed suicide or were slaughtered by the mob. Around 150 individuals were killed during the persecution. Considerable rebuilding was required after the siege. In 1246, Henry III ordered the reconstruction of the castle in stone. The king realized the strategic importance of York during periods of hostility with Scotland. The project encompassed the construction of Clifford's Tower and the strengthening of the inner bailey. Construction required considerable logistical management, including the acquisition of lead from Derbyshire. Repairs and additions were ongoing throughout the early fourteenth century, including the refurbishment of one of the gate towers and the creation of a new exchequer building. Flooding has been a consistent problem in York into modern times caused by the presence of the Rivers Ouse and Foss. The castle was not immune to inclement water levels. In 1315 a section of the surrounding wall collapsed due to flooding. Considerable subsidence was noted at the end of the fourteenth century, when attempts appear to have been made to strengthen the banks of the Foss and therefore protect the castle from further flooding. The adverse environmental conditions ensured that considerable investment was required over time to ensure that the castle continued to be fit for purpose. Although Clifford's Tower remains something of a shell, it gives a fine example of the visual power of mottes and towers in dominating their surroundings.

Despite the novelty of castles in the early medieval period, in some respects their construction demonstrated a considerable level of continuity with the past. In the final stages of the Anglo-Saxon period, elite residences often took the form of rural *burhs*. These residences usually consisted of a wooden hall and associated outbuildings. They were often surrounded by a ditch and fence ring work enclosure, similar to some of the early Norman castles in England. Although not specifically defensive in purpose, rural *burhs* used their architecture to display the high status of their inhabitants. A considerable number of early castles were constructed on the sites of earlier elite residences, including Goltho (Lincolnshire) and Trowbridge (Wiltshire). Archaeologists have also noted the frequent conjunction of early castles and churches in close proximity to each other. Such associations may be linked to the existence of an earlier rural *burh* on the site, which was replaced by a castle. Norman architecture was also used to evoke high status Anglo-Saxon sites. The castle at Exeter was constructed in 1068 after a serious revolt. The gate tower utilized a startling Anglo-Saxon design emulating a rural *burh*.[8] The original gatehouse at Ludlow Castle also used Anglo-Saxon architecture (Fig 11). Individuals approaching the castle would have been struck by its resemblance to Anglo-Saxon elite residences. These similarities were a conscious attempt to link incoming Norman lords and their residences to earlier displays of status and power.

Norman attempts to display continuity with power and authority in the past were not limited to Anglo-Saxons. On the contrary, it can be argued that there relationship with Roman history was of greater significance. Aside from the motte and bailey, Normans also introduced the *donjon* or stone keep to Britain. The White Tower in London incorporated some of the Roman city walls within its design. The second *donjon* has aroused considerable interest as it was positioned at Colchester, an area of limited strategic importance to the Normans. However, the castle was constructed on the site of the imperial temple to Claudius erected after the Roman conquest.[9] This striking reuse of an area rich in imperial symbolism was a deliberate attempt to link the Norman Conquest to that of Rome. An earlier chapel was preserved close to the castle which appears to have been associated with Cunobelin and the foundation of Colchester. It is possible that the Norman conquerors were consciously emulating the behaviour of Roman invaders over 1000 years before. Other Norman castles were also connected to earlier Roman sites. The first castle to be built by the invaders was on the site of a Roman fort at Pevensey. Although the location may have offered tactical benefits, it was also ripe in symbolism. The castle at Chepstow incorporated an audience chamber in the imperial style and reused Roman stones from the nearby town of Caerwent. The castle at Newcastle was built on the site of the *principia* or headquarters building of the Roman fort. In doing so it evoked the military power and imperial authority of the Roman past.

WELSH CASTLES

In the thirteenth century, castles formed a key element of the English subjugation of Wales under Edward I. The kingdom of Gwynedd became increasingly powerful during the mid-thirteenth century and exerted its influence over surrounding areas. Gradually the Welsh people came to support a single leader in the form of Llwelyn ap Gruffudd. Llwelyn's status is shown by the title of Prince of Wales he received from the English king. Relations between the Welsh prince and Edward I deteriorated to such an extent that the English king launched a military campaign into Wales in 1276. The purpose of this campaign was to bring Llwelyn to heel. After accomplishing his objectives, Edward set about constructing a series of castles to consolidate his hold over Wales at Rhuddlan, Flint, Aberystwyth and Bulith. These castles were considerable construction projects and required substantial investment in English time, money and labour. The construction of the castle at Rhuddlan involved straightening the curves of the River Clwyd to allow vessels to navigate the watercourse and supply the castle. Edward's commitment to establishing new castles demonstrated his intention to maintain firm control over Wales.

In 1283, a serious revolt broke out in Wales which resulted in a hard fought English victory and the death of Llwelyn. Edward's response was the construction of three new castles at Harlech, Conwy and Caernarfon. These new fortifications symbolized Edward's military control over Wales in physical form.[10] The locations of the castles were carefully chosen for strategic purposes. All were sited next to the sea. This ensured that they could be easily resupplied and prevented them from being encircled and overrun by Welsh rebels. The castles were not built on virgin sites. On the contrary, they were constructed on existing important sites whose destruction displayed English military might and political resolve. Conwy was the location of an important Cistercian abbey which served as the burial ground of Llwelyn's family line. Its replacement by an English fortification held great symbolic power. Each castle was located no more than a day's march from its nearest neighbour, facilitating the rapid movement of reinforcements during times of war. At Conwy and Caernarfon the king ordered the construction of new planned towns. These settlements supported the operations of the castles.

They also had a political role in demonstrating the economic and social benefits of English rule. Inhabited by English colonists, they bear a close resemblance to colonies imposed by the Roman imperial administration in the provinces.

Arguably the most spectacular of Edward's castles is at Caernarfon.[11] The castle does far more than provide an English stronghold, it also evokes a powerful imaginary past. A number of features at Caernarfon arouse interest. The gatehouse is ornamental in design and includes a decorative statue of the king. Entrance to the castle is via five sets of doors and six separate portcullises. These features go far beyond providing a secure entry point and should instead be seen as processional or ceremonial elements. They promote a sense of drama in keeping with the medieval model of the Arthurian world. Edward was keenly interested in the romantic vision of Arthur and his court. He viewed the bodies alleged to belong to Arthur and Guinevere unearthed at Glastonbury, constructed a round table at Winchester Castle and re-enacted the Arthurian royal court at an event on the Lleyn peninsula. Edward's enthusiasm for Arthur is also reflected in his attachment to the concept of Roman imperial power. Caernarfon unusually displays plain (not whitewashed) walls featuring prominent stone banding. The castle also possesses polygonal towers. In medieval thought Arthur was believed to have been the grandson of the emperor Constantine. The physical appearance of Caernarfon is strikingly similar to Constantinople. Moreover Caernarfon's main tower displays stone carvings of imperial eagles. It may also be significant that Caernarfon was the site of the Roman fort of Segontium. The design of Caernarfon demonstrates Edward's intention to link his rule to Roman imperial power and the imagined reign of King Arthur. The importance of the latter for Edward's worldview may lie in his legendary role as the king who united Britain.

APPROACHING CASTLES

Castles express the power, authority and influence of their occupants.[12] This can be communicated through their size, design or location. Castles occur not in isolation, but within complex landscapes where their importance is signified through their interaction with other features, such as settlements, transport routes and sacred sites. Two castles in particular demonstrate the importance of understanding castles within their wider landscapes, namely Ruthin in Denbighshire and Castle Acre in Norfolk.

Ruthin Castle was created by Edward I during his initial campaign in Wales. The castle was established in a prominent position on a sandstone ridge overlooking River Clwyd. This facilitated surveillance over the surrounding landscape. The red sandstone used to construct the castle made it visually striking. A new settlement was founded close to the castle and other local features associated with the site included a garden, park and mill. The position of Ruthin Castle was particularly important for visitors approaching the area from England. The raised position of the castle allowed it to be seen for miles around. Visitors would first have passed the local gallows, a potent symbol of the authority of the local lord. They would then have crossed the town and viewed the bustling market place. Leaving the town behind them, the visitors would have passed through the park with views over orchards belonging to the local lord before reaching the castle gatehouse. This planned route emphasized the economic, legal and political power of the local lord. Their influence consisted not just of controlling the castle but also the population of the local landscape.[13]

Castle Acre was first established during the Norman period. The castle overlooks two major transport routes in the forms of the River Nar and a Roman road. Interestingly, the route of the Roman road appears to have been deliberately manipulated through a diversion to enhance the approach to Castle Acre. This diversion encouraged visitors to appreciate a number of features associated with the castle and its lord. Castle Acre can be seen as forming a single component of three individual sites fused together to form an impressive image for the approaching visitor. The first feature viewed on the approach to the castle was the Castle Acre Priory. The association of castles with religious buildings is a particular feature of Norman England demonstrating the piety of the incumbent lord. As previously noted, the relationship between high status residential and religious sites was also reasonably common in the Anglo-Saxon period. After the Priory, the visitor next viewed the local town, whose presence emphasised the authority of the lord over the civilian population. Castle Acre therefore sits within a complex landscape which was deliberately manipulated to enhance the impression it created.[14]

STOKESAY CASTLE

Stokesay Castle in Shropshire demonstrates the ambiguous nature of many castles beyond the major sites we usually associate with the term. Indeed, it is debatable whether Stokesay should in fact be described as a castle on account of its role as a fortified manor house. Stokesay Castle is located in the picturesque valley of the River Onny. Although situated on slightly rising ground, it can by no means be described as being located on a hilltop position.

On the contrary, it is overlooked by the rising sides of the valley. Stokesay was constructed in the 1280s by Lawrence de Ludlow, a wealthy wool merchant from nearby Ludlow. The construction of Stokesay were designed to display Lawrence's wealth and success.

In terms of understanding the site as a castle, the most important feature consists of the south tower. Stokesay is located close to the main route from Shrewsbury to Ludlow and would have been conspicuous to travellers making their way between the two important settlements. When approaching from the south, the tower appears almost to stand in isolation, with the other buildings less visible. The tower contains prominent arrow slits alongside its existing windows. From a southern perspective, the tower displays two projecting lobes (Fig 12). This image is strikingly similar to the contemporary Welsh castles built by Edward I, including Rhuddlan and Harlech. There is a suggestion that the stones of the tower may have originally been banded which would also provide a visual connection to Edward's Welsh castles. The moat which originally surrounded the castle would have emphasized the martial nature of this aspect.

The other buildings of Stokesay Castle belie this warlike image presented to passing travellers. Established within a compound surrounded by the moat, the approach to the site was originally via a causeway which passed surrounding ornamental ponds. For any discerning visitor was gained access to the castle, the great hall would have been particularly impressive due to its size and sophistication (Fig 13). The splendid timber cruck roof still survives. Originally, the hall would have provided dining space for Lawrence de Ludlow's household. A timber staircase provided access to upper rooms. One of these was floored with decorative tiles which also featured in Lawrence's Ludlow townhouse. Next to the great hall stood the solar block, which provided private apartments for Lawrence's family. The south tower was built slightly later than the solar block and may reflect Lawrence's growing status. It was consciously designed to impress visitors, especially those conducting business. By this stage Lawrence was involved in providing commercial and financial services for the king and regional nobles.

Despite its external features, Stokesay was definitively not a defensive structure. The south tower was an isolated feature. The arrow slits in the tower were compromised by the windows embedded within it. Whilst the moat would prove a challenge to hostile forces, the site could not withstand a siege. The position of the site is dictated by the need to be seen rather than defence. Yet some features of the site would have been useful in providing protection against thieves, who would have formed a potential problem given Lawrence de Ludlow's evident status and wealth. The moat and fortified tower would have provided a useful deterrent to opportunistic thieves. In summary,

Stokesay provides an alternative perspective on the use of castles in contrast to the contemporary fortified sites constructed by Edward I in Wales.

TOWTON

Conflict archaeology is not limited to the study of fortifications. From the medieval period onwards, the prevalence of historical sources allows the location of battlefields to be identified in some instances. Battlefield sites can be investigated archaeologically through excavation or, more commonly, less intrusive methods such as metal detecting or field walking. Landscape surveys can also be valuable in analysing the topography of a particular conflict. The analysis of battlefield sites may allow scholars to check the reliability of historical accounts, which can often be skewed by political propaganda or the confusion of war. Conflict archaeology offers opportunities to explore aspects of warfare beyond the normal realm of military history, including medicine, military society and even religion. The challenge of studying the archaeology of battlefields lies in finding remains linked to warfare. For obvious reasons, physical structures are rare. Metal weapons or munitions can be traced through metal detecting and can be used to trace movements on the battlefield. Mass graves are particularly difficult to find, although one spectacular discovery from Yorkshire offers an insight into the horrific violence of medieval conflict.

The medieval period witnessed a period of intense warfare during the Wars of the Roses which began in 1455. The conflict raged between supporters of the Houses of York and Lancaster. One of the most important battles of the Wars of the Roses took place at Towton on 29 March 1461. The battle resulted in a notable Yorkist victory which led to the rise to power of King Edward IV. Contemporary accounts refer to Towton as one of the most savage battles of the conflict. Combat is alleged to have lasted for a total of ten hours and fighting even continued during a heavy snowstorm. William Shakespeare described the battle as a tumultuous fight between elemental forces, such was the savagery and size of the armies. Historical sources claim that a total of 28,000 soldiers were killed at Towton. Whilst this number seems incredibly large, a number of independent sources refer to the same figure, lending credence to substantial fatalities. Many of the deaths seem to have occurred during the Lancastrian rout at the end of the battle, as fleeing soldiers attempted to cross a local river and drowned or were cut down by pursuing Yorkist troops.

Many of the dead at Towton were buried in a series of mass graves, some of which may have been marked by tumuli. Archaeologists have excavated one mass grave which has yielded a remarkable level of detail about the physical realities of medieval combat.[15] The mass grave was formed by a single pit measuring 3.25 m x 2 m. Identifying the number of individuals within a mass grave is difficult as bones become jumbled and displaced. A key technique for assessing the number of individuals is to identify the number of unique bones such as the cranium or pelvis. This becomes complicated as bones become fragmented and therefore archaeologists can only identify the minimum number of individuals within a specific assemblage. Skeletal analysis of the Towton grave indicates a minimum of thirty-eight individuals were interred. All of the deceased were male and aged between 16 and 50. There is considerable diversity in the age, stature and physique of the skeletons. Radiocarbon dating indicates a high probability that the mass grave is associated with the battle at Towton, rather than as a result of plague or other serious epidemic. The bodies were laid in the pit in a manner which became gradually more haphazard probably because the gravediggers were eager to finish the task swiftly. If contemporary accounts of severe snowstorm are accurate, this may explain their haste.

Twelve of the individuals buried at Towton betrayed evidence for earlier fractures which had partially or fully healed. This history of violence indicates the harshness of military life in the medieval period. 96% of the visible wounds were inflicted on the craniofacial area or the rear of the skull. There is a clear emphasis on head wounds and facial mutilation. Only a single individual escaped injury to his skull, instead being killed by a slashing blow to his spine. Injuries to arms and hands reflect desperate attempts to shield themselves from slashing weapons. Analysis of one skeleton, designated as Towton 25, has allowed archaeologists to reconstruct the chronology of his wounds. Aged between 36 and 45 years old, this individual already carried a severe fracture perhaps sustained in an earlier fight. His first wounds at Towton came in the form of five slashing wounds to the skull. These were caused by a right handed opponent wielding a sword or similar weapon. The lethal blow was inflicted on the back of his skull. A slashing cut impacted with such force that it caused substantial brain trauma. This injury would have felled Towton 25. However, two further wounds were inflicted probably after death. One of these was a slashing cut to his face.

Skeletal analysis of the Towton mass grave allows us to reconstruct the fates of these men. In the past, it has been suggested that the viciousness of their injuries indicates that they were captured and tortured by the enemy. However, there is little evidence to suggest that they were physically restrained. It seems more likely that their deaths were a result of combat. Only two wounds can possibly be attributed to projectiles. Archery formed a component of the early stages of medieval combat so the occupants of the

Towton mass grave probably perished at a later phase in the battle. The prevalence of head wounds suggests that these men were not wearing helmets when they were killed. The absence of helmets could be explained if they had been discarded during a rout. It can therefore be argued that the individuals interred within the mass grave were massacred during the flight of Lancastrians at the end of the battle. The violence of their wounds reflects the desperate struggle for survival in their final moments.

MONASTERIES

The Norman Conquest not only began the process of integrating castles into the landscape, but also revitalized religious houses. Before 1066, less than fifty monasteries were operating in Britain. By the end of the medieval period over 2000 religious houses had been founded. The connection between the promotion of castles and monasteries was not coincidental. Indeed, they were often founded in close proximity to each other, thus demonstrating aristocratic wealth and power. The endowment of religious houses was a popular aspect of Norman culture which was easily transplanted to the new kingdom. William the Conqueror was especially renowned for his generous patronage of religious houses in Normandy. In a world of bloodshed and sin, religious philanthropy offered the possibility of redemption and salvation. Financing a monastery through a donation of money or land would go some way to redressing the sins of bloodshed and murder inherent within a military lifestyle. Some knights chose to become monks themselves towards the end of their lives as a means of assuaging their guilt. The nobility therefore had good reason to associate themselves with religious houses.

Some religious buildings constructed under the Normans nevertheless represented an element of continuity in the use of the landscape. Knowlton Church in Dorset was constructed during the twelfth century to serve the local community. The area was used as a hunting park throughout the medieval period. Intriguingly, the church was situated within a prehistoric ritual landscape. Knowlton sits within Cranborne Chase, a terrain filled with notable Neolithic and Bronze Age monuments. The church itself was sited within the centre of a Neolithic henge (Fig 14). A large barrow stands in close proximity to the site. The Dorset cursus also runs close to the church. The juxtaposition of the Christian church and pagan henge indicates a conscious attempt to display continuity in the religious significance of the site. The henge was not obliterated as it easily could have been, but rather preserved an integral element of the church complex.

The concept of monasticism is closely intertwined with the Christian faith.[16] Isolation from a world which was seen as inherently evil and filled with sin became a respected Christian practice by the fourth century. Initially, this involved hermits seeking a solitary life of contemplation in isolated places such as the deserts of Syria and Egypt. This form of monasticism is termed eremitic, where withdrawal from the world promotes closeness to the divine. A second form of monasticism, termed coenobitic, instead takes the form of a religious community where monks live, eat and worship together. The community was still expected to separate itself from the wider world to avoid temptation and seek to be as self-sufficient as possible. This form of monasticism was popular in Britain. One of the most popular works on the organisation of monastic communities was the rule of St Benedict, created by Benedict of Nursia in the early sixth century.

The early monastic houses established after 1066 were Benedictine (following the rule of St Benedict) or Cluniac (following the model of the great French monastery at Cluny) in nature. The distribution of Anglo-Saxon monasteries had been limited to southern England. The Norman influx ensured that new institutions would be found across Britain. Discontent with the piety of Benedictine communities prompted the rise of new monastic orders. Augustinian houses constructed during the twelfth and thirteenth centuries focussed on greater engagement with the wider community. At the other extreme, Cistercian monasteries sought greater austerity and isolation in their interpretation of the rule of St Benedict. The Cistercians founded their monasteries in remote locations across Britain, beginning in Waverley, Sussex, in 1128. To avoid distractions and concentrate on their interaction with the divine, Cistercian monasteries also housed lay brothers whose role was to attend to the daily tasks required in supplying and maintaining the community, leaving the monks to worship. The great expansion in monastic communities across Britain petered out by 1200. New forms of religious philanthropy gained greater prominence. This reflected a renewed emphasis on personal religion within, rather than isolated from, the wider world. This perspective had political connotations in the context of the Crusades. The giving of alms to the poor became increasingly popular and could arguably be seen as an activity closer to the teachings of Jesus as recorded in the Bible than supporting a monastic community. New religious houses continued to be built in the form of friaries. Dominican and Franciscan friars were dedicated to serving the needs of the community through serving the poor in a pastoral role. For this reason, friaries were located close to urban centres although often on poor land. Friars eschewed the trappings of wealth and status, preferring to live in abject poverty like the people they served. This was a radical contrast to the remoteness of other monastic communities. The structure and layout of religious houses reflected the religious order which they served. For example, Cistercian monasteries are associated with substantial accommodation quarters serving the lay brothers distinct from the residential areas occupied by monks. Friaries were constructed in urban areas and contained elements within their layout which facilitated preaching to the public.[17]

The key factor in choosing the location of new monasteries was the provision of water. This was essential, not only for drinking, but also for cleansing. Monasteries are therefore usually found close to water sources such as rivers, streams or springs. As we have noted, some monasteries were deliberately sited in remote locations to distance their occupants from the temptations of the secular world. As a thriving community, the monastery required a suitable hinterland to supply it with food and other provisions. This could be provided through agricultural land owned by the monastery and farmed by monks, lay brothers or tenant farmers. Alternatively, the monks could engage with local markets. The agricultural outputs of some monastic houses were substantial. By the end of the thirteenth century, the Cistercian monks at Melrose possessed a flock of sheep which exceeded 12,000 animals.[18] The layout of monasteries tended to conform to a general pattern which nevertheless allowed for individual variations due to the vagaries of the local landscape. The most important elements of the monastery were the church and cloister. The church was used for worship on a daily basis and included the high altar and seating for the community. Monastic churches were usually rectangular or cruciform in shape. The cloister was important was the hub of the community, where monks would have processed through on the way to complete their duties and rituals. This role was facilitated by the covered walkway. A number of buildings were connected to the cloister. The chapter house hosted daily meetings of the religious community. The refectory served as the dining area for the monks and the dormitory provided their accommodation. Other buildings would have supported the daily running of the institution in the form of kitchens, workshops and barns. Individual farms at a distance from the monastery may have been worked by lay brothers or tenant farmers.

DURHAM CATHEDRAL

The religious landscape of medieval Britain was divided into dioceses under nominated bishops. Each diocese was centralized on a cathedral within an urban area. Medieval cathedrals were organised in two distinct categories. Monastic cathedrals housed a community of monks. Secular cathedrals were led by a dean who headed a chapter of canons. The location of cathedrals within urban locations has left an indelible impact on the landscape of Britain to this day. Ely Cathedral dominates the surrounding Fenlands (Fig 15). Indeed they can be classed as some of the most striking buildings within the modern cityscape. York Minster crowns the skyline of the city. It should be remembered that cathedrals represent considerable investment in resources, money and labour. Durham Cathedral is a particularly spectacular example (Fig 16).[19] Perched on a wooded hillside overlooking the River Wear, it dominates its surroundings and is claimed to be the finest example of Norman architecture in Britain. The location of the cathedral was deliberate. It was built in the site of an earlier Anglo-Saxon church, known as the white church, which was placed on an easily defensible location. The religious community claimed descent from the monastery at Lindisfarne and therefore had prior experience of Viking raids. It is hard to imagine the level of engineering excellence required to construct such an edifice. Durham Cathedral was built between 1093 and 1133. It housed the shrine of St Cuthbert and the bodies of St Oswald and the Venerable Bede. Its association with the former ensured that it was a favoured destination for medieval pilgrims. The cathedral was monastic in nature and supported a community of Benedictine monks. Durham was strategically important for the Norman regime as it oversaw the tempestuous northern regions. The cathedral was therefore constructed within the precinct of Durham castle. The latter, which now houses part of the university, was established under William the Conqueror. Responsibility for maintaining order and security in the north of England rested with the Prince-Bishops of Durham who occupied the castle. Durham Cathedral was therefore not simply a religious building but rather part of a larger complex of structures imbued with political meaning. The castle and cathedral therefore asserted a political statement emphasising Norman dominance over northern England.

Durham Cathedral is a key example of Romanesque architecture. This style flourished during the eleventh and twelfth centuries and was named for its resemblance to the architecture of Rome. The exceptional level of preservation within the structure of the cathedral allows archaeologists to glimpse the architectural style applied by the Normans. Analysis of the fabric informs our understanding of the construction of large stone buildings during the early medieval period. The cathedral preserves the earliest surviving large stone vault in the world, incorporating the use of the pointed arch. Durham Cathedral also contains the earliest known example of the use of stone ribbed vaulting. Stone ribs allow the weight of the ceiling to be transferred to the walls of the structure, thereby minimising the possibility of structural problems during the lifetime of the building. This innovation allowed the cathedral to reach a considerable height and appear almost to soar to the heavens. Some elements of Durham Cathedral bear a close resemblance to one of the most important buildings in the Christian world. This was the old St Peter's Basilica in Rome (to distinguish it from the basilica visible today), the construction of which began under the emperor Constantine during the early fourth century. The religious importance of the basilica lay in its location on the alleged site of the tomb of St Peter. The dimensions of the nave at Durham closely match those of the old St Peter's Basilica. Moreover, the spiral columns which can be seen within the cathedral evoke those surrounding St Peter's Shrine. In emulating some of the architectural features of the basilica, the cathedral claims a connection to one of the holiest Christian sites. It may be pure coincidence that the emperor Constantine was originally elevated to imperial power at nearby York.

ST ADRIAN'S PRIORY

The Isle of May is located in the Firth of Forth in Scotland and housed the Priory of St Adrian. The priory housed a small community of Benedictine monks which probably never exceeded ten individuals. Saint Adrian was an inhabitant of the original monastery on the island who was killed, along with many of his fellow monks, during a savage Viking raid in 875. The island was abandoned by its religious community after the Viking attack and left barren for centuries. In the mid-twelfth century the island was granted to Reading Abbey by King David I. Under the auspices of Reading Abbey, a new religious community was founded based around the shrine of St Adrian. The site became a focus for pilgrims and the shrine continued to be maintained even after the priory was moved to another island during the fourteenth century. The priory took the form of a group of four buildings arranged around an open area. The church was rectangular design. The eastern range contained the dormitory where the monks slept and their refectory occupied the southern range. One of the other buildings may have housed guest quarters for visiting pilgrims and important guests.

The Isle of May is a relatively exposed location which must have proved challenging in sustaining even a small religious community. Certainly, crops could not have been cultivated on the site. A small number of sheep and cattle may have been farmed on the island. Most of the food for the religious community must have taken the form of fish and seabirds. Produce may also have been transported across from the mainland. Recent excavations have concentrated on analysing the remains of the human population in the cemetery. Surprisingly, this burial ground was not organized as a series of individual graves dug in an individual manner. Rather, the graves were deposited beneath a burial cairn formed from local beach stones. This form of grave architecture is extremely unusual in a Christian context and is usually associated with pre-Christian pagan burials. The continuity of this burial practice suggests that it had ritual significance. This may be linked to the burials of the original victims of the Viking raid in 875. One male individual was interred close to the church during the fifteenth century. Intriguingly he was buried with a scallop shell placed in his mouth. The scallop was associated with St James and the pilgrimage to Santiago de Compostela in Spain. The shell was used as a symbol by pilgrims who had completed the journey. St James was particularly popular in Scotland due to his association with the Stewart dynasty. It is possible that this particular individual was a pilgrim who undertaken a pilgrimage to Santiago de Compostela in honour of St James and later perished whilst on pilgrimage to the shrine of St Adrian on the Isle of May. His life story demonstrates the piety of individuals during the medieval period and the mobility which such faith encouraged.[20]

LONDON

As we have seen, London functioned as the provincial capital for most of the Roman occupation. However, during the Anglo-Saxon period the city lost out to rival settlements. Certainly during the tenth century, Winchester possessed a greater claim to being the royal capital of England. Significant remodelling in London appears to have taken place around 900. A new series of streets were laid out with a particular focus on the area around the quayside. From the origins of the city, London's importance was dictated by its role in facilitating trade and commerce through the River Thames. Emphasis on the river frontage demonstrated the importance of this area in the economic life of the city. Within a century London was firmly reconnected to trading networks encompassing France, Germany and the Low Countries which appear to have been temporarily suspended during the preceding centuries. These international trading links reinvigorated the city. Later kings placed increasing importance on London and it is noteworthy that Edward the Confessor rebuilt Westminster Abbey. This building was chosen as the venue for William the Conqueror's coronation in 1066. The construction of the Tower of London by the Norman king in 1067, one of only two stone keeps in Britain built under his rule, demonstrates the perceived importance of the city to the incomers.

The eleventh century witnessed rapid growth in London as the city sprawled across the former Roman urban boundary.[21] Indeed, at the peak of the urban sprawl the limits of the city were similar to those of the present day. London's expansion was fuelled by the economic boom provided by commercial links with the continent and supported by the fact that there were no rival urban centres within close proximity. In 1100 London possessed no fewer than 110 parish churches, providing an indication of the size of the city. A century later, there were 18 major religious houses operating within the city. By 1300 this total had risen to 33 individual institutions. Development projects within the city focussed in particular on the area around the quayside. Investment in facilitating effective logistical support and storage space would inevitably reap economic benefits. From 1100 the river frontage was consolidated and gradually expanded into the Thames during the following centuries. Embankments of timber and stone were used to reclaim land from the river, thus increasing the space available for riverside activities. Impressive construction projects continued throughout the medieval period including the creation of ostentatious buildings such as the Guildhall and Leadenhall in the fifteenth century. Traces of the imperial past of the city were still present within the urban fabric. London Bridge was remodelled in stone during the twelfth century but remained on the site of the original Roman crossing. The first Guildhall was constructed on the site of the Roman amphitheatre. Aside from the practical benefits of reusing Roman sites, such activity carried a subtle reminder of the past importance of the city and its previous dominance as an urban centre over the rest of Britain.

Estimates of the population of London at the beginning of the twelfth century tend to suggest around 20,000 individuals living within the city. By 1300 the population had probably quadrupled, although some estimates place the population as high as 100,000 individuals. The outbreaks of plague in the fourteenth century inevitably had a broad impact on population levels, probably more so than later epidemics. A significant proportion of the city's population was not of British origin. From the eleventh century there is substantial evidence for the presence of merchants and traders from Rouen, Flanders and Germany living in London on a permanent basis. Initial attempts to confine foreign merchants to areas around the riverside were gradually relaxed allowing them to live throughout the city. The presence of a thriving and prosperous migrant community created a multicultural environment which had a significant impact on the nature and economy of the city.

Royal interest in the city of London was motivated by three key factors. The wealth of the merchant and aristocratic classes made them an invaluable financial resource in times of economic crisis through providing economic support in the form of taxes or loans. The proximity of the population of London to the abbey and palace of Westminster ensured that they played a vital role in royal ceremonies and processions. Finally, the political elite of London provided the king with valuable advice and counsel, as well as forming a necessary conduit to the city populace. In the early stages of the medieval period, kingship was usually highly mobile in nature as the ruler progressed around his kingdom in order to meet his nobles, deal with local issues and, most importantly, to be seen by his subjects. Gradually London became increasingly to be seen as the centre of royal power. The reign of Henry III (1234 – 1272) was particularly important in this regard, as the king focussed on the Palace of Westminster as the seat of the bureaucracy associated with his legal and economic obligations. Edward I continued this trend by summoning his retainers to meet with him at Westminster. Although later kings would summon parliaments to meet at other cities, the function of the Palace of Westminster as the centre of the royal bureaucracy made it an attractive seat for the king to meet with his nobles and advisors. The presence of the court brought great benefits to the city of London in terms of its infrastructure and reputation across the western world. This symbiotic relationship ensured that London became the epicentre and hub of the political geography of England.

LUDLOW

The medieval period witnessed substantial growth in urban development. The twelfth and early thirteenth centuries in particular saw the establishment of up to 500 new towns. This growth, often encouraged for political and strategic purposes, was accompanied by numerous economic benefits. Ludlow in Shropshire offers a prime example of a new market town which flourished during the medieval period.[22] The name Ludlow is probably derived from two separate terms. Lud refers to the loud waters of the River Teme which roar past the town. Hlau comes from the tumulus, probably of Bronze Age origin, which originally stood in the graveyard of the parish church until it was removed at the close of the twelfth century. The connection between a sacred Bronze Age site and a Christian church indicates continuity in religious belief associated with a specific location. The site of modern Ludlow was not occupied prior to the medieval period. Two ancient trackways did cross the area. The Clun-Clee ridgeway was in use from the Mesolithic period judging by the presence of microliths along its course. Artefacts from the Neolithic and Bronze Age have also been found in association with the ridgeway. A second trackway, possibly dating to the Roman period, crossed the Rivers Corve and Teme close to Ludlow. A substantial Iron Age hillfort was constructed only 3 km from Ludlow. The name of the nearby village, Caynham, betrays the Anglo-Saxon origins of the settlement. The area of modern Ludlow known as Linney references an Anglo-Saxon term for dry land, indicating the area may have been used for the growing of flax close to the River Teme.

In 1086, the site of Ludlow lay within the parish of Stanton. According to the Domesday survey, Stanton possessed twenty-two hides or units of land under the plough and was the most productive manor in southern Shropshire. The population of the parish can be estimated at around 700 individuals. Economic activity was not limited to agriculture. The Domesday survey also recorded the presence of blacksmiths and mills. In the aftermath of the Norman Conquest, this area had been granted by William the Conqueror to one of his closest lieutenants, William FitzOsbern, who controlled most of Herefordshire. In turn, FitzOsbern granted tenancy of a number of his manors to Walter de Lacy I, a Norman knight who accompanied the king to England. After FitzOsbern's death, his son led an ill-advised rebellion against the king in 1075. As a result, William redistributed the FitzOsbern to loyal Norman knights. Walter de Lacy was the prime beneficiary, receiving 163 manors which made him one of the most important Norman lords to hold land in the Welsh Marches. The king was eager to ensure that loyal and competent barons were in place to protect the frontier with Wales.

A castle was constructed at Ludlow around 1088.[23] Construction may be linked to the rebellion of Walter de Lacy's son against William II. Nevertheless, the castle occupied a strategic position controlling local transport routes and overlooking the River Teme (Fig 17). The original castle was built of stone and took the form of a large enclosure with an imposing tower. The site was probably approached by a bridge. The walls were protected by at least four projecting towers. The Norman section of the castle now forms the inner bailey. At around the same time, a small settlement grew immediately next to the castle in an area now known as Dinham. This settlement was probably occupied by individuals who serviced the castle and its inhabitants. A defensive ditch later became the line for the thirteenth century town wall.

Historical sources indicate that Ludlow possessed its own identity by 1138. The growth of the town during this period has been categorized within four key stages. The first phase consisted of the development of a high street market place running down from the castle. The parish church and graveyard (incorporating the earlier tumulus) were located at the end of the high street. This ensured that the marketplace was framed by the castle and church respectively. The second phase increased the size of the town within a t-shaped plan through linear expansion beyond the marketplace. This development possibly followed an existing transport route. The third phase witnessed the laying out of streets from the marketplace down to the River Teme. Finally, the town was expanded on to the flood plain formerly used for the growing of flax and the infilling of the marketplace with permanent stalls and shop units.

In 1199, the growth of Ludlow was reflected in the reconstruction and expansion of the parish church of St Laurence to 80% of its modern size. A tax assessment of 1377 demonstrates that Ludlow supported a population of 1172 adults, making it the third largest provincial town in England. Although half the size of Shrewsbury, it still ranked as larger than towns such as Southampton and Derby. This expansion required the removal of the Bronze Age tumulus from the church grounds. Medieval Ludlow was known to conform to the laws of Breteuil, the Norman town of FitzOsbern. This required that the town be divided into burgage plots, which were rectangular plots of land held by settlers who paid the local lord an annual rent of twelve pence. The burgage system persisted into the seventeenth century. Analysis of the townscape indicates that medieval Ludlow held more than 500 burgage plots.

By the thirteenth century, Ludlow was a bustling and prosperous market town famed for its connection to the wool trade and cloth production. At least nine mills were operational on the nearby Corve and Teme Rivers. In 1200, the town possessed two schools, one of which was a grammar school. Three chapels were founded during the twelfth century, with more religious houses added later. These included the Austin and Carmelite friaries. Town walls were constructed by 1260, when a tax was levied for their upkeep. The walls provided protection during a time of threat from Wales, whilst the series of gates allowed economic control over goods entering and leaving the town. The Gough Map, produced in the fourteenth century, depicts Ludlow as an important settlement. The church tower can clearly be seen, as can the castle and imposing town walls with projecting towers. In the space of a few centuries, Ludlow had grown from the area around a single tumulus to a thriving market town.

CLIMATE CHANGE IN THE MEDIEVAL PERIOD

In recent years, archaeologists and scientists have focussed increasingly on evidence for climate change in the past and the effects which this has had on economics, agriculture and society. The years between 900 and 1300 have been identified as an area of relatively mild climate in Europe and the North Atlantic region. This period is described as the Medieval Warm Period or Medieval Climatic Optimum.[24] Historical records indicate that severe winters were reduced in their frequency and nature. Glaciers were significantly reduced exposing more land to human exploitation. The benefits of these milder conditions are best demonstrated by the Scandinavian colonisation of Greenland. The peak climatic conditions of the Medieval Warm Period varied across the North Atlantic region. In Britain, the most favourable period seems to have occurred between 1150 and 1350. The primary benefit of this milder climate was through agricultural productivity. It is likely that farming was expanded onto higher ground. Harvest yields are likely to have been significantly enhanced. There is even evidence that grapes were grown in Britain during the Medieval Warm Period.

Not all climate change events during the medieval period were advantageous or sustained. This has been most clearly illustrated during a major excavation at Spitalfields cemetery in London.[25] The site was connected to the largest medieval hospital in the city known as St Mary Spital. Burials were interred at the site from the early twelfth through to the sixteenth centuries. Over 10,000 graves were excavated during the project providing an insight into the lives of the inhabitants of medieval London. As may be expected from such a large site, most of the graves were carefully and systematically laid out to use the land effectively and prevent later disturbance. However, this approach was not consistent across the cemetery. One hundred and forty pits containing group or mass burials were encountered during the excavation. The discovery of mass graves from the medieval period is normally linked to fatalities from the Black Death of 1348. Yet sophisticated radiocarbon dating techniques revealed that the graves belonged to the mid-thirteenth century. This result is inconsistent with plague victims. Close analysis of the burials revealed two distinct categories of mass graves reflecting two catastrophic events. The first group held up to twenty bodies and may be linked to a notorious famine which struck London in 1252. The second group of mass burials were larger in size and contained up to forty bodies. These graves may be linked to a major volcanic eruption which took place in 1258. Widespread geological evidence in the form of ice cores and ash sediment attests to the severity of the eruption. The location of the volcano remains to be identified. Nevertheless the impact of the eruption is evidence in historical accounts. The eruption spewed material into the atmosphere which limited the amount of heat and light reaching the earth. Contemporary sources record a severe drop in temperature leading to the failing of crops, death of livestock and widespread famine. It is likely that the larger mass graves of Spitalfields contain the remains of those who perished in the aftermath of the eruption.

During the ninth and tenth centuries, large scale changes are evident in land usage across rural areas of Britain. Through a gradual process, isolated farms coalesced into village communities. This shift in settlement patterns had a profound impact on rural society. Each village hosted a manorial court which provided a forum for the resolution of disputes and maintained the wellbeing of the community. Norman landowners in the aftermath of the Conquest appear to have encouraged the development of new settlements in order to simplify their administrative burdens. After all, villagers were far easier to govern than individual farmsteads.

The landscape of the medieval countryside around these new villages was characterized by the development of open fields. This was a system of land ownership which required communal collaboration by local farmers. The open field system facilitated the management of associated farmland by the community as a whole and promoted sustainable farming practices. It also left a lasting mark on British countryside which persists to this day. In its earliest form during the Anglo-Saxon period, each village probably possessed two open fields surrounding the settlement. This is reflected in the prevalence of early field names linked to opposing points of the compass. Through the increase of farmland available to the community through woodland clearance or land management, many villages increased the total number of open fields up to four.

Although there were probably regional or localized variations in the operation of the open fields system, we possess a good understanding of how it was managed. Each field was divided into strips. Every farmer in the village would possess at least one strip in each field. The ownership of strips could be allocated randomly or in a systematic manner. Strips were bundled into furlongs on which the same crops would be grown. This enabled farmers to collaborate according to demand. Livestock would graze on the open fields outside of the growing season. The open fields system brought particular benefits in terms of the quality and fertility of the soil. The farming community would decide on an annual basis which field should be left bare or fallow. This tradition of not exploiting a single field each year ensured that soil nutrients would not be exhausted. As each farmer possessed land in each field, no individual would be unduly discriminated against. Oversight of the management of the open fields rested with the manorial court which had the power to punish individuals who tried to sow crops in a field designated as fallow. In any given year, between 25 – 50% of farming land within the village would be uncultivated depending on the number of open fields.

The prolonged cultivation of medieval fields has left a visual trace in features known as ridge and furrow which can still be seen on modern farmland. Ridge and furrow features appear as undulations in the ground caused by the action of repeated ploughing of a particular field. Ploughing turned the soil and gradually caused the creation of a distinct groove or furrow in the ground. These can be up to 15m in length. The creation of ridge and furrow features was a deliberate act to provide suitable drainage, particularly in areas with heavy soils or a history of flooding. The furrow acted as a drain drawing water away from the raised bed of earth provided by the ridge. The use of ridge and furrow as an effective drainage technique was not limited to the medieval period. Indeed, anecdotal evidence suggests that it was practised during the Second World War.[26] In the modern period, great swathes of countryside displaying ridge and furrow features have been lost due to intensive ploughing or shifts in land use. Nevertheless, good examples do remain particularly in the northern regions of England.

The open field system is not simply a relic of a bygone age. On the contrary, it is still used effectively within one English rural community at Laxton in Nottinghamshire.[27] Laxton has maintained the open fields system since at least the medieval period, although the amount of farmland available within the open fields has decreased significantly. Currently the village possesses 195 hectares of land divided into three open fields. These are subdivided into 164 individual strips. A manorial court of local farmers still oversees the system and decides which fields should be left fallow on an annual basis. Whilst the return of open fields on a broader scale is incompatible with modern farming practices, it is obvious that the system provided numerous social benefits for rural villages. It promoted the cohesion of a farming community and encouraged collaboration in order to maintain sustainable approaches to agriculture.

Not all rural land was governed in such a collegial manner. The medieval period witnessed the widespread development of parks across lowland areas of Britain. Whilst we nowadays associate parks with areas for public recreation, they were originally areas of enclosed woodland for raising and hunting deer maintained by the nobility. Hunting allowed kings and nobles to demonstrate their martial prowess in a peaceful environment. However, it is questionable how much hunting could be accomplished in heavily wooded parks. The origin of parks can be traced to the ancient Persian Empire. There is no clear evidence for the creation of deer parks in Britain prior to the Norman Conquest. They were particularly common from the twelfth century onwards. One reason for the popularity of deer parks can be found in the introduction of Fallow Deer which proved easier to manage than native species, such as Roe and Red Deer. Woodland parks provided a plentiful supply of venison as well as timber which could be sold on at profit. It has been suggested that there were around 3200 deer parks in England alone by 1300. This may equate to roughly 2% of the English landscape. The Welsh terrain limited the creation of woodland deer parks, although some were established to the west of the Marches. Medieval deer parks have also been identified in southern and eastern Scotland. Most of the evidence for the identification of such sites has been gathered from land ownership records.[28]

WHARRAM PERCY

Some of the most enigmatic remains of medieval Britain take the form of deserted medieval villages (DMVs). These sites often take the form of mysterious earthworks and rarely leave any trace above ground level. Indeed, many DMVs have left no trace beyond their inclusion on old maps and manorial records. There are over 3000 DMVs in Britain, the majority of which were abandoned by the end of the medieval period. Although often difficult to analyse in depth without a rigorous programme of excavations, DMVs offer an unparalleled opportunity to explore rural life in medieval Britain. Traditionally the desertion of these villages has been attributed to the ravages of the Black Death which first arrived in Britain in 1348 and resurfaced on a number of occasions through to the seventeenth century. In this analysis outbreaks of the Black Death either wiped out entire settlements or took such a toll that they were no longer economically viable. In recent years scholars have moved away from tracing the existence of DMVs to outbreaks of the Black Death. Instead, they are now attributed to a broader range of factors including changes in agricultural practice, economic pressures and the increasing attractions of urban life.

The most well-known and intensely studied DMV in Britain is Wharram Percy near Malton in Yorkshire.[29] Wharram Percy was subject to an intensive series of archaeological investigations in the twentieth century which enabled archaeologists to trace the growth and decline of the settlement. Today the village consists of the remains of St Martin's Church and extensive earthworks which preserve some of the layout of the original village. The area was occupied from the Neolithic period, although the village reached its zenith in the twelfth to the fourteenth centuries. The area was first inhabited during the Neolithic and Bronze Age periods on account of flints recovered locally. Early settlers were probably attracted by the water supply provided by the stream or beck originating from a series of local springs. This water source would have been used to support grazing animals. By the Iron Age at least two farms had been established at Wharram Percy. At least one of these displayed considerable status through the provision of defensive ditches. By the later Roman period, five farms were operating on the site of the later village. Anglo-Saxon occupation has been identified in the form of two *Grubenhäuser* built on the edge of the village area sometime during the sixth century. Over the following centuries, a village gradually coalesced in the site as opposed to isolated farmsteads.

In the late fourteenth century, the village consisted of thirty houses arranged in two Rows or lines. The first Row consisted of twenty houses along the edge of the hillside. The remainder were located in a single Row along the valley floor. Each plot consisted of a toft (house and associated outbuildings) and croft (associated patch of arable land). Excavations have revealed that the majority of the village houses during the medieval period consisted of longhouses. The longhouse consisted of three distinct areas. The first consisted of a space which may have been used as sleeping quarters or alternatively as a dairy. The main living space was equipped with a hearth for cooking and as the centrepiece of social activities within the house. The final area was used for agricultural purposes, including potential living space for animals. The longhouses were built using a cruck building design. This meant that the roof was supported by robust internal supports whilst the chalk walls appear flimsy and unsubstantial. This means that the houses were stronger structures than they appear archeologically. The waste from the longhouses appears to have been transferred to a midden and then reused as fertiliser on the fields. Each villager would have farmed land on the three large open fields surrounding the village. Each field was divided into unhedged strips of land known as selions. Excavation of the longhouses provided evidence for the daily lives of the villagers. Activities linked to spinning and weaving were identified through finds such as spinning whorls, needles and thimbles. Wooden chests for the secure storage of valuables were noted in some houses. Social life was represented through bone flutes and dice. Perhaps surprisingly, pottery was discovered which had been produced as far away as France and the Mediterranean.

According to the Domesday survey of 1086, Wharram Percy consisted of nine ploughing units. Eight of these were the property of the king with the reminder held by an individual named Chilbert in return for military service. An abbreviation in the text seems to indicate that the village technically had two manors. Archaeologists have identified two manor houses in Wharram Percy. The first, in the south of the village, was established in the twelfth century and probably remained in use into the early thirteenth century. It consisted of a two storied stone building providing private accommodation for the lord and his family. Other buildings would have formed part of the same compound including a hall for receiving villagers and guests. In the mid-thirteenth century, the south manor was demolished and replaced by longhouses. A new manor was constructed in the north of the village. This was a far more impressive series of structures including a hall with dais for the lord, living area for his family, large barn for sheep or grain and a grain drying kiln. A driveway for moving cattle out to the open fields was established. Two stockyards provided animals with further access to grazing areas. The compound may even have contained a private garden for the lord and his family. Interestingly, the north manor was established on the site of a substantial elite Iron Age residence. This area within the village may have been associated with high status for over a thousand years.

The other substantial building at Wharram Percy was the Church of St Martin. The excavation provided archaeologists with a rare chance to examine a parish church in considerable detail. The church was first constructed in the tenth century as a timber building. In the following century, a small stone church was established. This probably functioned as a private church used by the lord and his family. In the twelfth century, a large two celled church including a nave and small tower. This was utilized by whole community as a place of worship. Over the following centuries the church was gradually expanded to include a north aisle, porch and chapel. In the fifteenth century, the local lord added an additional storey to the tower emblazoned with his coat of arms. The churchyard holds the graves of over 1000 villagers. Grave slabs reveal the presence of Anglo-Saxon lords and medieval men at arms in the service of the local lord. Close to the church was a mill and later fish pond.

The abandonment of Wharram Percy cannot be connected to outbreaks of the Black Death. The disease did strike the village. Walter de Heslerton, lord of the manor, died of the plague in 1349. Yet a survey in 1368 revealed that thirty houses were occupied in Wharram Percy. Gradual depopulation may be indicated by the occupation of only sixteen households by 1458. The last record of villagers inhabiting Wharram Percy belongs to 1517. After this date the village appears to have been abandoned and given over to sheep. In 1543 1180 sheep were grazing on the site. The shift from village to sheep pasture suggests that the end of Wharram Percy was economically motivated. The booming wool and cloth trade probably tempted the local lord to replace his human tenants with a sheep flock.

THE DEATH OF A KING

Perhaps the most spectacular archaeological discovery in Britain in recent years has been the unearthing of the probable skeleton of King Richard III in Leicester. Richard III is a divisive historical figure. For centuries, he has been depicted as a cruel and ruthless monarch. This owes much to Shakespeare's portrayal of the king. In the modern world his qualities and deeds remain a source of controversy and attract both his supporters and detractors. The Richard III Society has been particularly instrumental in encouraging a more considered approach to the king, his reign and legacy. The Society also played a leading role in the archaeological investigation which unearthed the royal grave.

Richard III died during the battle of Bosworth Field on 22 August 1485. His death ended the Wars of the Roses and also signalled the end of the medieval period and beginning of the Tudor dynasty under King Henry VII. The historical sources allow us to reconstruct the fate of Richard's corpse. After the battle it was transported to Leicester by the new king. Henry's purpose in moving the corpse was to expose it to public view. This macabre display demonstrated both the end of the war and his victory over his enemies. There could be no hope for Richard's supporters that the king had evaded death to fight another day. After three days the body of the late king was interred in the church of the Franciscan friary (otherwise known as Grey Friars). Ten years later, perhaps after his personal animosity had abated, Henry VII ordered the grave to be capped by an alabaster tomb.

The archaeological investigation was primarily designed to identify and record the principal buildings of the Franciscan friary.[30] Locating the grave of a single historical figure is notoriously problematic. It relies heavily on the accuracy of contemporary historical sources and requires the stripping away of folklore and hearsay. Grey Friars was formally dissolved in 1538. In the following years, it is likely that the buildings were ransacked. One seventeenth century source claimed that Richard's corpse was exhumed during the dissolution and the bones flung into the River Soar. Archaeologists held little hope of locating the royal grave.

Initial excavations identified several buildings within the friary complex, which was founded between 1224 and 1230. A chapter house and associated cloister walk had been heavily robbed for building materials. The chapter house encompassed around 50 m^2 and would have been the location of daily meetings of the religious community. The surviving fabric of these structures was of poor quality reflecting the poverty of the religious order. Further excavations revealed the church building. A number of graves were identified and copper alloy letters which had probably been removed from tomb inscriptions. Surprisingly, the eastern end of the church was constructed or faced in brick, making it one of the earliest medieval buildings in Leicestershire to have used brick. Although the church building had been heavily damaged during and after the dissolution, the graves themselves were undisturbed.

One grave in particular appeared promising to the excavators. Placed in the south-west corner of the church building, it did not occupy an imposing position. Although church buildings were used for the inhumations of high status individuals, they would have had limited public access preventing the grave from becoming a site of pilgrimage or focus for resistance by his former supporters. Excavation indicated a body which had been buried in great haste with little respect. In contrast to the other graves beneath the church building, the grave cut was too short. For this reason, the skeleton was twisted to fit and the head propped up on the corner of the grave. This indicates that the gravediggers were working hastily. This may have been due to the advanced decomposition of the corpse.

The skeleton displayed the marks of a violent death. Its hands were crossed at the wrist. Although this arrangement was common in medieval England, it was not normal practice in Leicester. It is therefore possible that the corpse's hands were tied. The corpse was buried without a shroud, coffin or clothing. Ten separate wounds were clearly visible on the skeleton. Obviously these do not include wounds which did not penetrate to the bone. Eight of the wounds were inflicted on the skull, and included two fatal sword blows to the back of the head. The top of the skull may have been pierced by short weapon resembling a dagger. The emphasis on wounds to the skull is similar to the patterning of wounds at Towton. The positioning of a number of the wounds suggests that they were inflicted whilst the individual was not wearing armour, including cuts to the ribs and buttock. It is entirely possible that some of these wounds were inflicted after death when the corpse was stripped. Such signs of 'overkill' are not unusual in warfare, when heightened emotions prompt warriors to inflict violence on deceased enemies either through sheer fury or to claim some form of personal glory.

Does the skeleton belong to Richard III? A range of evidence suggests that it does. Radiocarbon dating indicates a high probability that the deceased died between 1456 and 1530. The skeleton belongs to a male aged somewhere between his late 20s or late 30s, consistent with Richard's death at the age of 32. The individual enjoyed a diet rich in seafood, which is indicative of high status. Moreover, the skeleton indicates that the individual suffered from severe idiopathic adolescent-onset scoliosis, a debilitating condition which may have led to visible physical symptoms. Contemporary historical sources make reference to Richard's physical symptoms, although the validity of some of these accounts is still a matter of considerable debate. Historians have identified two living descendants of Anne of York, sister of Richard III. Mitochondrial DNA allows the female line of descent to be traced. Comparison of the mitochondrial DNA of the living descendants of

Richard's family and the skeleton indicate a close match. Although not direct descendants of the king, this result is sufficiently convincing. Furthermore, this DNA type is considered rare in Europe providing circumstantial evidence for the royal identity of the skeleton. Although further analysis is required to conclusively identify the skeleton as that of Richard III, it seems more than likely on the basis of the current evidence that the identification is indeed correct.

Chapter 8

The Post-Medieval Period

(1485 – 1901 AD)

The Chapel of the Guild of the Holy Cross in Stratford upon Avon was decorated in the fifteenth century with a series of elaborate wall paintings imbued with great religious significance. These images provide a startling insight into the Christian worldview at the end of the medieval period. Topics addressed in the paintings include the Dance of Death, Saint George and the Dragon, local saints and the murder of Thomas Becket. The overriding theme of the design scheme was the inevitability of death and the pressing need to prepare for Judgement. This iconography embroidered the architecture of the chapel with key concepts of the Christian faith. Yet in 1563 the Corporation of Stratford ordered the images to be covered in whitewash and hidden from sight. The complex imagery of Christian theology was to be replaced literally with a blank canvas. The decision to cover the wall paintings was not taken lightly. Indeed the Corporation had little choice but to conform and demonstrate its allegiance to the Church of England. Yet the task cannot have been lightly accomplished. We can easily imagine that it must have been undertaken with heavy hearts by the men selected by the Corporation to whitewash the walls. This may be reflected in the fact that the images were only lightly covered rather than permanently obliterated, perhaps with the hope that they would soon be uncovered. In overseeing the task, the Corporation appointed their Chamberlain who faithfully recorded payments made for defacing the images in the financial accounts. The Chamberlain was a man of good standing who had made his fortune as a glover and would eventually rise to become High Bailiff of the Corporation. Within a few months of the whitewashing of the Chapel, the Chamberlain's wife would give birth to a son. His name was William and he became the greatest playwright the world has ever known.[1]

The story of John Shakespeare and the whitewashing of the chapel provides a tantalising glimpse of the realities of life during the early modern period. It was a time of great change in religion, politics, industry and society. These titanic shifts are reflected in the diversity of the archaeological record.

Yet the parameters of the post-medieval period are notoriously difficult to clearly identify, as indeed they are for any artificially delineated 'age'. Perhaps controversially, I have chosen to extend the period until the close of the Victorian era in 1901. Whilst many scholars separate the Industrial Revolution from the early modern period, in fact these radical advances in technology and engineering can be viewed within a broader period of change which altered life in Britain forever. The challenge which John Shakespeare faced in adjusting to the new religious environment of post Reformation England was similar to those of his descendants in learning to live with a British landscape covered in extensive mills, railways and mines.

THE DISSOLUTION OF THE MONASTERIES

In 1534 Henry VIII became head of the Church of England. His rejection of the authority of the Pope was motivated by personal and political factors, but ultimately was aligned with the wider Reformation sweeping Europe during this period. From an archaeological perspective, the major impact of Henry's religious choices lies in his decision to dissolve the monastic institutions under his control. This heralded a profound shift in the religious landscape of Britain. Much that has been lost can never be reconstructed, particularly the icons, statues and other artworks removed under the king's orders. Whilst the visible impact of the Dissolution can be easily traced in ruined monastic buildings, it is also startlingly clear in the missing stained glass windows and empty statue bases of religious houses which survived. The damage inflicted by the Dissolution permeated every level of religious life in Britain.

The Dissolution of the monasteries was carefully orchestrated by commissioners acting on behalf of the king. The initial targets were the smaller monastic houses. In 1536, 243 monastic houses worth less than £200 per annum were closed. Over the following four years the remaining monasteries were dissolved. It is important to note that this purge did not merely entail the closure of buildings, but also the disintegration of monastic estates. A wide range of communities were adversely affected by the closures, including the tenant farmers on monastic lands. The loss of monastic institutions also deprived local communities of the pastoral support provided by their inhabitants, including hospitality to travellers and charitable hand outs for the poor. The closure of monasteries could be a swift process, often accomplished at night. Aside from the removal of precious artefacts, a key priority was the removal of building roofs to prevent their rehabilitation at a later date. Monastic estates were sold off to wealthy individuals poised to profit from the closures. Many sites became wealthy residences of the elite classes. Longleat, now home to a famous safari park, owes its origins to the closure of an Augustinian priory and the construction of a mansion after 1572. The lands around former monasteries were ideal for the laying out of formal gardens, which were in great demand by the nouveau riche of Tudor England. Agricultural land owned by former monasteries was often divided into new farm estates, some of which were purchased or managed by former monastic officials.

Yet the Dissolution also provided new opportunities for religious institutions. Eight cathedral priories became secular cathedrals. A few large monasteries were preserved through conversion into new cathedrals in the decade after the start of the Dissolution, including Chester and Gloucester. At a number of monastic institutions, chapels which had formally been used for worship by lay people were retained. Examples of such survivals can be found at Furness and Rievaulx. The Dissolution could not completely recast traditional forms of belief. Saintly shrines proved a particular target for destruction. When royal officials opened the Shrine of St Cuthbert at Durham, they discovered that the body of the saint was miraculously complete. The body was reburied and remains a place of pilgrimage and worship to this day.[2]

THE MARY ROSE

Henry VIII is commonly regarded as the founding father of the Royal Navy. Whilst this description is not completely factually accurate, it does reflect Henry's use of naval force to repel the threat of invasion from France. In the summer of 1545 a French fleet of up to 300 vessels carried an invasion force of some 30,000 men across the English Channel. On 19 July 1545, the royal fleet sought to engage the French armada in the Solent, a narrow channel which runs between the Isle of Wight and the mainland. One of the most heavily armed ships in the English fleet was the Mary Rose, which had been in service for thirty-five years. As the two opposing fleets drew towards each other, the Mary Rose swung around. A freak blast of wind caught the ship which heeled over and rapidly sank. Anti-boarding netting strewn over the top deck prevented the majority of those on board from escaping to safety. From a nominal crew of 415, only thirty men survived the wreck. Among the dead were the captain Roger Grenville and Vice Admiral Sir George Carew.

Despite early salvage attempts, the Mary Rose lay on the seabed until the twentieth century. Preservation was aided by anaerobic conditions and the angle at which the wreck lay on the seabed. The raising of the wreck in 1982 attracted an international television audience and popularized British marine archaeology. The causes of the sinking of Mary Rose have been subject to debate since July 1545. Contemporary French sources predictably claimed responsibility for sinking the pride of the royal fleet. Yet the wreck shows no sign of hostile assault. Other possible explanations have included gross indiscipline amongst the crew. One historical source notes that the lower gun ports had not been closed prior to the sinking. There is also evidence that the Mary Rose was dangerously overloaded with equipment and crew. In 1540, the Mary Rose carried 81 heavy guns. This number may have increased over the following five years. Some authorities claim that the Mary Rose was carrying as many as 700 individuals at the time it sank, although this number may be an overestimate. It can therefore be theorised that the overloading of the ship, failure to close the lower gun ports and a freak gust of wind combined to cause the ship to sink as it sailed to engage the French.

Excavation of the Mary Rose has illuminated the lives of the crew: 179 separate individuals have been associated with the wreck. All are male and represent a cross section of ages. Close analysis of the skeletal remains have allowed the occupations of some individuals to be tentatively identified. The Mary Rose sank at a time of change in the armaments of naval vessels. The crew contained both archers and gun crew and 137 longbows and 3500 arrows were discovered on the ship. Arm guards worn by archers on the Mary Rose were decorated with Tudor roses and pomegranates.[3] The latter was a symbol associated with Catherine of Aragon and may betray the presence of an elite archer unit on board. Some of the skeletons display traces of prolonged involvement with archery through changes to the arm bones and spine. A number of individuals had probably served at sea for a considerable portion of lives. This is indicated by evidence of back strain and heavily muscled ankles and feet suggesting long periods spent in unstable environments. A chest discovered on the Mary Rose contained a quantity of gold and silver coins. A skeleton found close by belonged to an individual who suffered from Perthes disease which would have caused profound physical impairment. The presence of such an individual on a fighting ship during wartime is anomalous, but could be explained by his role as purser or treasurer of the vessel.[4] Recent research has concentrated on the origins of Mary Rose crew members. The findings have been surprising. Analysis of oxygen isotopes in the dental enamel of crew members indicates that between 33% and 60% of those sampled originated on the European mainland south of Britain. It has been suggested that these foreign individuals may have been mercenaries or even Spanish prisoners pressed into military service aboard Henry's fleet. Language problems arising from a multinational crew may have contributed to the disastrous sinking of the ship.[5]

TUDOR ROYAL PALACES

Popular perceptions of the Tudor period often concentrate on the intrigues of court, whether Henry VIII's romantic dalliances or the political manoeuvres of Elizabeth I's courtiers. The importance of the royal court during the Tudor period is reflected in the number of royal palaces retained by the dynasty. Throughout the medieval period, kingship was itinerant in nature meaning that the monarch was often mobile throughout his kingdom. This allowed the king to interact with his nobles and increase his visibility to his subjects. During the Tudor period, monarchs still enjoyed a degree of mobility through formal royal progresses, which involved travelling around houses belonging to the Crown and important nobles. Monarchs also moved between their own palaces around the Thames outside of formal progresses. These moves were often dictated by the need to avoid inclement weather conditions or outbreaks of disease in the capital. In the early part of his reign, Henry VIII displayed a particular passion for hunting and his travels often reflected his sporting pursuits.

Hampton Court Palace is perhaps the most well-known Tudor royal residence. The site was first in use during the thirteenth century, when the area was an agricultural estate owned by the Knights Hospitaller of St John Jerusalem. Hampton lay in close proximity to two royal estates and, as a result, over time it came increasingly to serve as overflow accommodation for parties visiting the royal properties. This association with the royal court intensified in 1494 when the estate was rented by an influential courtier, Giles Daubeney, who became Chamberlain to Henry VII. The king is known to have stayed at the estate. The following tenant, Cardinal Wolsey, invested heavily in Hampton in order to make it fit for purpose as a temporary residence of the royal court, when required. Under Wolsey's stewardship, the site became an ostentatious palace capable of hosting international delegations. Guest suites were provided for Henry VIII, his queen and offspring. An additional forty guest quarters were also constructed, each of which was provided with its own lavatory. A grand chapel served to emphasize Wolsey's religious status. It is clear that Wolsey's manipulation of the architecture and layout of Hampton Court was designed to endear him to the king. Unfortunately, this was insufficient to prevent Wolsey from falling disastrously from grace. It has even been argued that the ostentatious nature of Hampton Court may have incurred the jealousy of the king, and certainly contributed to hostility from Wolsey's political rivals. In 1528 Hampton Court Palace was seized by Henry VIII to serve as one of his official residences. Under Henry VIII, the palace arguably reached its high point as a royal residence. The king invested in renovating Hampton Court to cater to his needs, particularly in terms of entertainment and recreational facilities. A large hunting park was established in which the king and his retainers could pursue game. This was particularly valued by Henry after a series of near misses had put paid to his jousting career. Tennis courts and bowling alleys provided additional diversions from the taxing demands of royal business. A Great Hall served as a venue for elaborate feasts. Even a grand lavatory served to demonstrate the power and wealth of the king, through hosting twenty-eight individuals in a single sitting. Hampton Court Palace was not solely dedicated to pleasure. It continued to serve as a prestigious venue in hosting international parties. In 1546, for example, the site catered for an important French ambassadorial delegation visiting the king on matters of state. Including both French and English parties, a total of over 1500 individuals feasted in the palace on six consecutive days. In this way, the architecture of Hampton Court Palace was used to conspicuously display the wealth, influence and power of the monarch, and therefore represented the physical embodiment of royal status.[6]

THE CHANGING RURAL LANDSCAPE

The agricultural landscape of modern Britain is characterized by fields of regular shape (though varying in size) surrounded by some form of enclosure under the ownership of a single individual or family. This stands in stark contrast to the great open fields held under communal ownership during the medieval period. The change in layout of much of the British agricultural landscape was a result of the Enclosure Acts which became particularly common during the eighteenth century. In essence, enclosure meant the concentration of land into fields under single ownership through the breaking up of open fields. Rising prices of agricultural products prompted the search for greater farming efficiency. Open fields always left some land unused in the form of boundaries between different strips of land. Single fields increased the area of land available for exploitation. Enclosure began during the sixteenth century through the mutual consent of landowners. The process became more formalized through Parliamentary regulation during the eighteenth century and was increasingly common during the second half of the century. It has been calculated that around 20% of the surface area of England was subject to Enclosure Acts between 1750 and 1830.[7]

The process of enclosure was facilitated by the political influence of large landowners who often sought to profit from the redistribution of land. During the eighteenth century, owners of 75% of village land had to consent for enclosure to be considered. This consent took the form of a petition presented to Parliament. A commission would scutinise the application and, if agreeable, appointed three commissioners to oversee the formal enclosure process. These commissioners examined the ownership of land within the village and drew a map illustrating the new distribution of fields. Enclosure maps, often held by public record offices and local archives, remain a detailed source for land ownership during village enclosures. The designation of land ownership resulted in the eviction of farmers who could not prove their entitlement and the poor families who relied on the common pastures. This led to migration from rural areas to urban centres. As an Act of Enclosure was required for each village, this was a lengthy and time consuming process. As a result, a General Enclosure Act passed in 1801 allowed any village to enclose its fields as long as consent had been obtained from owners of 75% of the associated land.

The enclosures resulted in profound changes to the rural landscape. To maintain the integrity of new fields, they were surrounded by hedges of hawthorn or, in upland areas, dry stone walls. Hedges required careful maintenance through the practice of 'laying' which gradually thickened the composition of the barrier. In some instances a shallow ditch was dug alongside the hedge. Trees were occasionally planted with the hedgerows, though these proved controversial in areas where foxhunting was a popular pastime as they proved dangerous obstacles when the hunt was in pursuit of its quarry. The clearance of previously neglected areas of vegetation due to enclosure prompted the creation of artificial fox dens. The layout of a new village landscape by the enclosure commissioners offered an opportunity for the creation of new roads to allow access to far fields and neighbouring settlements. These can often be identified on maps due to their straight and purposeful routes unlike earlier roads which often deviated around large open fields. Over time, the clustering of fields belonging to individual farmers in distinct locations led to the construction of new farms away from village centres. It is therefore arguable that the process of enclosure had a profound impact on the social fabric of rural villages.

The early modern period also witnessed dramatic changes in land use in wetland areas, particularly in the Fens. Small schemes of wetland drainage can be traced back to the Roman occupation. During the thirteenth century, a great earthwork was constructed along the wash to protect the land from the encroachment of the sea. Running for almost a hundred kilometres, it was believed to be a reconstruction of an earlier Roman bank. From the sixteenth century, the attractive profits arising from agricultural produce encouraged landowners to maximize the amount of fertile land under their ownership. An Act of Parliament passed in 1600 allowed large landowners to overrule other interested parties in draining fenland areas. As a result, a complex system of dykes, drains and changes to existing watercourses was employed to drain the Fens of East Anglia.[8]

THE ARCHAEOLOGY OF SHAKESPEARE

The life of William Shakespeare has intrigued biographers and historians for centuries. The documentary record pertaining to Shakespeare has been exhausted and, in the absence of new source discoveries, it is likely that archaeology has the best chance of providing new evidence of the life and times of the enigmatic playwright. Visitors to Stratford upon Avon can visit some of the residences associated with Shakespeare, including his birthplace. Recent archaeological investigations have focussed on New Place, the home owned by Shakespeare from 1597 until the time of his death in 1616. New Place was a substantial residence which was the second largest home in Stratford at the time of its construction. Contemporary sources suggest that New Place had at least ten rooms. It was also unusual for its time in using a substantial amount of brick within the fabric of the house. New Place also contained a large garden up to 55 m in length which was used by Shakespeare to cultivate two orchards. Clearly New Place was of significance to Shakespeare as he chose to retire there from London in 1610.[9]

Aside from his domestic life in Stratford, Shakespeare's world revolved around the theatres of London where his great plays were staged, and in which Shakespeare himself performed as an actor. The first theatres frequented by Shakespeare were the Theatre and Curtain in Shoreditch which opened in the 1570s. Recent excavations at the Curtain have uncovered evidence of theatre life during the age of Shakespeare. Elizabethan theatres tended to have a uniform design being polygonal in shape with a central yard containing the stage. The central yard allowed space for audience members to stand close to the action. Wooden seating was available in the galleries overlooking the stage. Seating cost extra and pottery boxes discovered during the excavation were probably used to collect the admission fee. They would have been smashed open at the end of performances to gather the money, rather like modern piggy banks. Interestingly, one of the floor sections in the Curtain was surfaced with sheep knucklebones instead of brick. Clearly the entrepreneurial owners of the theatre were using cheap waste materials from the butchery trade in the fabric of the building.[10]

In the winter of 1598, Shakespeare and his close associates the Burbages became estranged with the landlord of the area on which the Theatre was constructed. As a response, the Burbages moved the Theatre south of the River Thames to Southwark. Their new venue was named the Globe.[11]

Southwark offered numerous benefits for the theatrical trade including favourable taxes. The area was filled with entertainment venues from brothels to bear baiting establishments. This was a perfect environment for a profession which always sailed close to being disreputable. A number of theatres were constructed in close proximity to each other on the south bank of the Thames, including the Swan, the Rose and the Globe. In 1591, Shakespeare's play Henry VI Part 1 was performed at the Rose and brought the audience to tears at a time of growing tension with France. Excavations have revealed that the Rose was a fourteen sided structure prior to its closure in 1605. The Globe burnt down during a performance of Shakespeare's Henry VIII in 1613. The blaze was attributed to the thatched roofing catching light when a cannon was fired on stage. The theatre was reconstructed as a twenty-sided structure with a tiled roof to prevent further fires. Artefacts discovered at the Globe include some which may have been used by the players themselves, such as mock weapons for staged fights. There is also significant evidence for snacks served during performances such as grapes, figs and plums. In this sense, archaeology reveals the social context of Shakespeare's performances.[12]

CIVIL WAR ARCHAEOLOGY

The post-medieval period is rich in the archaeology of conflict. Although this field has only been widely exploited within the last few decades, it is clear that the archaeological investigation of sites associated with warfare and defence allows scholars to compare both the terrain and remains with the historical record. The English Civil War forms part of a series of related conflicts widely united as the Wars of the Three Kingdoms which lasted roughly from 1641 through to 1652. This decade witnessed prolonged periods of violence across Britain which left an enduring landmark on the landscape and archaeological record. Conservative estimates suggest that around 84,000 individuals died violently during this period. An additional 127,000 people may have died indirectly as a result of conflict, for example through disease and deprivation.[13] Aside from the human cost of the war, substantial damage was inflicted on cities, towns and rural landscapes. The English Civil War was essentially a clash of ideologies between Royalists and Parliamentarians which played out on a highly localized level. Much of the violence was articulated through the seizure of particular localities in order to control particular territories. This strategy ensures that the archaeology of the English Civil War and associated conflicts is highly diverse and widespread across Britain.

The pace of the conflict and frequent uncertainty over the political loyalties of particular individuals and factions ensured that haste was often required in the consolidation of defensive positions. Urban centres were a particular focus for campaigns. A number of larger cities retained perimeter walls which dated from the Roman or medieval periods. Although often in need of repair, these ancient walls often formed the basis for new defences. Examples of major settlements whose walls were utilized during the war include Exeter, Bristol and Chester. Old walls required patching up and adapting for new military technologies, particularly the rise of artillery power as a dominant force on the battlefield. Gloucester is a prime example of the utilisation of an existing defensive perimeter. The medieval walls were substantially strengthened and reinforced in preparation for hostile assault. A large defensive ditch was dug to hinder approaches to the settlement. In places, the ditch measured up to 20 m in width and almost 4 m in depth.[14] Earthworks were frequently constructed to support the walls and increase the strength of the defensive perimeter. They were particularly useful for strengthening gateways, which were highly vulnerable to artillery barrage. As a rule, earth was more widely used as a material for defensive works during this period than stone. The reason for this is obvious. Earth is cheap, easy to manoeuvre and can be used in haste. It requires little skill to construct a defensive barrier of earth, in contrast to one of stone. Earthworks were used widely in areas which lacked pre-existing stone walls. Their existence can frequently be traced in the landscape today, including a notable example at Hyde Park in London.[15] While new defensive perimeters inevitably caused disruption in the daily life of major settlements, other consequences may not leave visible traces in the archaeological record. This includes the demolition of housing for building materials, social changes due to the arrival of military garrisons and the spread of disease during sieges. In these instances, historical sources may illuminate the archaeological record.

It is unsurprising that, in the race to achieve a tactical advantage over the enemy, existing sites of strategic importance were revitalized during the war. This was particularly the case with castles, many of which were refortified and garrisoned. It is important to note, however, that this continuity in use of certain sites also encompassed a significant change in how they were used. Castles were no longer used predominantly as a means of displaying status and wealth. On the contrary, they now served an immediate military purpose. This is reinforced by the deliberate destruction of a number of castles to prevent them from being used by the enemy. In 1649, for example, Parliament ordered that Montgomery Castle be destroyed for this purpose. Beeston Castle in Cheshire occupies a striking hilltop position overlooking the surrounding countryside. It conforms to the romantic view of a medieval castle. From a strategic position, Beeston dominates the local area and oversees the movement of troops and materials through the surrounding countryside. During the Civil War, the castle was reoccupied and a substantial programme of repairs was undertaken in improving the fabric of the structures on the site. Gun ports were added to the walls of the castle. Floor levels were lowered in some areas to increase the space available for storage in preparation for a siege. Further additions included a large timber gate and earthworks outside the perimeter. In 1646, Beeston Castle was put beyond use by order of Parliament.[16]

Castles were not the only historic sites to have received a new lease of life as a result of the conflict. Existing earthworks tempted local commanders into using them as fortified positions. The Neolithic henge at Maumbury Rings near Dorchester was one ancient site which served a military function. The Iron Age hillfort at Caynham outside Ludlow may have served as a siege camp in preparation for an attack on the town (Fig 18). Manor houses and country homes were also a focus for garrisons in order to control the surrounding countryside. In the absence of existing defences, earthworks were hastily thrown up to defend isolated residences.

The archaeology of the English Civil War has by no means been exhausted. A number of areas would repay further intensive investigation. Analysis of the topography and remains of battlefields encourages evaluation of associated historical accounts. The heavy use of musket and pistol balls during this conflict has prompted the use of metal detectors in surveying battlefields. Mapping of recovered artefacts allows the dispositions of opposing forces to be identified. Such a study can be complex. The site of the battle of Naseby, which took place in June 1645, has yielded 1000 musket balls within an area measuring only 5 km^2. The use of mines during sieges also deserves to be examined in more detail. This could provide a wealth of information about the understanding of seventeenth century military engineers in the calculated use of explosives for undermining defences.

THE JACOBITE THREAT

Between 1688 and 1746, adherents to the Jacobite cause posed a particular threat to the security of Britain. Although nowadays associated with romantic images of the Highlands of Scotland, Jacobites could be found across the lowlands of Scotland and in England. The Jacobite threat can be traced to the so-called 'Glorious Revolution' of 1688, when Prince William of Orange and his wife Mary ousted the reigning monarch King James VII. The old king fled into exile in France and thus began the enthralling image of a king over the water. Jacobites were adherents of the old king who were committed to restoring the Stuart dynasty in place of the incoming Hanoverians. Attempts to suppress the Jacobite cause focussed on controlling the landscape of Scotland through the use of innovative military engineering. This trend began in 1650 with the invasion of Scotland by Oliver Cromwell. Accompanied by a force of 35,000 troops, Cromwell attempted to control the population through force of arms. Yet he did not rely on traditional seats of power in the form of castles. Instead, Cromwell constructed a new style of artillery fort or citadel with project bastions which facilitated the use of artillery guns. Citadels were constructed at Ayr, Perth, Leith, Inverness and Inverlochy. The appearance of these artillery forts demonstrated a strategic attempt to dominate the Scottish landscape.

The first Jacobite action occurred immediately after the Glorious Revolution when forces loyal to the new regime besieged Edinburgh Castle in 1689. Despite only being garrisoned by around 120 men, the castle withstood siege for three months before surrendering. Inevitably the garrison was weakened by disease and deprivation. A mass grave discovered within the castle contained the remains of fifteen males who probably died during the siege. In an attempt to discourage further Jacobite trouble a new citadel was constructed at Fort William in the western Highlands. This fort was laid out in a pentagon design using the construction of earthworks to form a defensive perimeter. Loch Linnhe provided protection through limiting the number of approaches to the fort. An abortive uprising in 1708, aided by the French, prompted the replacement of the earth ramparts with stone and the addition of new barracks. Further defensive works were undertaken at Edinburgh and Stirling castles, demonstrating that medieval sites still had a role to play in securing Scotland.

Despite the creation of Fort William the Jacobite threat persisted. A major rising in 1715 was crushed by Crown forces. Yet the following year, economic pressures required a reduction in the number of large guns serving the military in the north. Renewed emphasis was placed on facilitating the movement of troops through Scotland in order to respond to emerging trouble spots. The first free standing barracks in Britain was constructed at Berwick to provide an entry point into Scotland. The Berwick barracks housed 600 soldiers and thirty-six officers. Accommodation was cramped with eight men living in each room and inadequate toilet facilities. Barracks were also constructed at four sites in the Highlands, namely Bernera, Inversnaid, Kiliwhimen and Ruthven. Each location was of strategic importance, usually in guarding an important transport route. The barracks adhered to a standard design of two blocks facing each other across an open square surrounded by a perimeter wall. Musket loops provided an opportunity to repel an infantry attack, although the barracks were vulnerable to sustained artillery fire. The barracks housed between 120 and 360 men. Constructed in hostile areas, the construction teams feared kidnap or assassination. Despite their impressive size and innovative design, contemporary military officers doubted their effectiveness.

In 1724 Major General Wade was appointed to conduct a survey of the state of the Highlands with particular regard to their security. Wade produced a report which was overwhelmingly negative and indicated a clear danger of further rebellions. In response, Wade was appointed as Commander in Chief of all military forces in the north of Britain with a broad remit to secure the Highlands. Wade realized that the rapid movement of troops was essential in combating future outbreaks of violence. To this end, he developed a new road network up to 400 km in length. Wade's strategy consciously mimicked that of the Roman army. Indeed, on an inscription on the Tay Bridge at Aberfeldy, he boasted over extending the military occupation of Scotland over 250 miles beyond the Roman frontier. Furthermore, a Board of Ordnance map drawn up in 1731 recording the disposition of clans during the 1715 revolt highlight the Roman fort at Ardoch as though drawing a conscious comparison with contemporary security measures.[17] Wade concentrated his road building programme on four key routes: Fort William to Inverness, Dunkeld to Inverness, Crieff to Dalnacardoch and Dalwhinnie to Fort Augustus. Roads were constructed to a set design with a width of between 3 and 5 m. A foundation for the road was formed by large boulders, topped with smaller stones and gravel. This robust design ensured that they could carry artillery pieces and wagons, as well as army units. Wade also oversaw the creation of two new military bases at Fort George near Inverness and Fort Augustus near Kiliwhimen. Fort George occupied the site of a medieval castle which had been reused as a citadel by Cromwell. The new design incorporated a late medieval tower house and provided accommodation for 400 soldiers. Fort Augustus was intended to serve as the headquarters of the northern Hanoverian army and included four imposing bastions linked by curtain walls. The defences of the royal castles at Dumbarton and Edinburgh were also reviewed.

The last great Jacobite rebellion broke out in 1745 under the leadership of Prince Charles Edward Stuart (popularly known as Bonnie Prince Charlie). Despite early successes which saw the Jacobites reach as far south as Derby, the rebels were forced back to Scotland and were ultimately defeated at the battle of Culloden in 1746. Wade's defensive measures proved less than successful during the rebellion. Most of the Highland forts and barracks were severely undermanned and could play no part in suppressing the revolt. The road network may have facilitated the movement of Jacobite forces. Fort George surrendered to the Jacobites in 1746 and Fort Augustus was badly damaged by an explosion in its gunpowder magazine. After Culloden, significant rebuilding took place at Fort Augustus and Fort William. Fort

George was relocated to a site overlooking the Moray Firth. The new site was designed to intimidate potential foes. It held 1600 soldiers and covered seventeen hectares. Requiring a labour force of over 1000 men to build, the fort was a physical statement of the Crown's intent to subdue Scotland. The power magazine held 2500 barrels of gunpowder. Between 1740 and 1767 the road network was expanded by almost 1500 km. A new approach was taken to garrisoning the Highlands. Large numbers of outposts were established which housed small numbers of troops. The purpose of these bases was to support wide ranging patrols to police the Highlands. Arguably, the end of the Jacobite threat can be attributed to substantial investment in military forts, outposts and roads.[18]

CAUSES OF THE INDUSTRIAL REVOLUTION

The social, cultural and economic environment which fostered the Industrial Revolution defies easy analysis. There was no single overriding factor which ensured that great technological advances were made in Britain in the late eighteenth century. Certainly, these innovations are of global historical significance. Many of the inventors, entrepreneurs and businessmen who shaped the period are now household names, such as George Stephenson, Richard Trevithick and Richard Arkwright. Yet the Industrial Revolution owes its origins neither to a single individual nor invention. Instead, it was a result of a thriving innovation ecosystem which supported and rewarded new ideas and technologies. For this reason, a series of complex factors contributed to an era of rapid technological change, including the patent system, networking opportunities offered by influential literary and philosophical societies in major towns and cities, and the growth of an experienced artisan class.[19] It is important to note that the Industrial Revolution did not provoke a complete break with the past. Traditional agricultural practices continued in use. Indeed, early factories show great similarities with contemporary farms through their typical layout of sheds arranged around an open yard.[20] The impact of the Industrial Revolution extended far beyond the economic spheres into how ordinary people dressed, worked and played.

COAL

In essence, the Industrial Revolution transformed the potential sources of fuel available to the population of Britain. In doing so, it nurtured the growth of industry beyond its traditional heartlands. Traditional sources of power imposed severe restrictions on industrial growth. Wood was widely used as a fuel. However, its exploitation could lead to disastrous ecological consequences and it could only be transported short distances. Hence industrial premises had to be located close to forests. Likewise, industrial buildings relying on water power required ready access to suitable watercourses. Contrary to popular opinion, watermills did not decline immediately as a result of the Industrial Revolution. Indeed they increased in number from 70,000 to 120,000 between 1760 and 1820.[21] Wind power also served as an important resource during this period, particularly for grinding grain. The location of windmills was dictated by the occurrence of regular winds close to suitable agricultural land, such as the Fylde coast in Lancashire.[22]

The exploitation of coal offered an alternative fuel source with the potential to unlock industrial potential in areas without the benefits of forests or watermills. By 1870 over 93% of British industry was powered by steam.[23] The desire to improve the efficiency of coal mining was central to many of the innovations produced during this period. Early steam engines were used to resolve the issue of flooded mining works by powering drainage programmes, not only for mining coal but also tin and copper in Cornwall. The first Newcomen steam engine was in use in 1712. Three years later, mines near Whitehaven were the deepest in the world thanks to the ability of Newcomen steam engines to drain water down to almost 250 m below ground level.[24] Whilst coal mining was inevitably a dangerous profession, technical innovations did improve the safety of miners, not least the safety lamps devised by Humphrey Davy and George Stephenson in 1815.

The increase in coal production during the eighteenth and nineteenth centuries was prodigious. In 1700 the output of British coal mines was around three million tons. By 1830 output had reached 75 million tons and increased to 115 million tons by 1871.[25] This astonishing growth was supported by the entrepreneurial activities of inventors and businessmen. Many wealthy landowners exploited coal seams on their estates. Intensive industrial exploitation of the coalfields had a substantial and long lasting impact on the British landscape. Typical mines consisted of shafts sunk into the ground with buildings clustered around the pit head, including engine houses. Coal was transported from the mine to railways, canals or ports via dedicated wagonways. The considerable logistical systems around the transport of coal also left a noticeable trace in the archaeological record. On the major rivers of north eastern England, coal was transferred from wagons onto ships through the use of wooden staithes. Some of these staithes are still visible and provide a poignant reminder of the importance of sea transport for the coal industry. Giant slag heaps formed from the detritus of the coal industry proved to be a dangerous addition to the landscape due to their unsettled disposition. In 1966, a spoil tip at Aberfan in Wales collapsed and killed 144 local people. Other noticeable archaeological remnants of the coal industry include the houses provided for miners and their families. Many communities came into existence due to the discovery of new coal seams. Accommodation for mining families was therefore essential for the sustainability of the industry. Distinctive miners' houses, often arrange in neat terraces, remain prominent in a large number of towns and villages in Britain, including Cramlington in Northumberland.

RAILWAYS

The development of the railway network evolved through a symbiotic relationship with the coal industry. Efficient transportation systems boosted the productivity of individual mines. As early as 1701, the creation of wagonways transporting coal from Gibside colliery near Gateshead to the River Tyne led to an increase in production from 20,000 to 70,000 tons over a two year period.[26] Early coal transports were drawn by horses. The invention of steam engines promised a more efficient logistical system, if they could be transferred from a static environment to provide locomotion. In 1801 Richard Trevithick demonstrated that steam engines could be placed within a vehicle by driving 'Puffing Billy' for a kilometre up Camborne Hill. Trevithick's success encouraged other railway pioneers in their own efforts, resulting in George Stephenson's locomotives. Parliament approved the construction of the first railway, running between Stockton and Darlington, in 1821. The first intercity railway running between Liverpool and Manchester opened in 1830. The railway network expanded through the entrepreneurial activities of railway innovators and the willingness of Parliament to support new ventures. The explosion in railway growth during this period is staggering. In 1838 500 miles of railway were in use. Within a decade this had grown to 5000 miles and double further by 1860. By 1880, the railway had supplanted sea travel as the main conduit for the transportation of coal.[27] Aside from moving coal from mines to market, locomotives also consumed a large volume of coal.

The creation of railways had a profound impact on the landscape. They required the use of complex surveying techniques to identify the best routes across the terrain. Aside from the laying of tracks, labourers or navvies dug cuttings and tunnels. Bridges and viaducts were used to surmount otherwise unnavigable obstacles. The viaduct approaching London Bridge station contained no less than 878 arches.[28] Some lines had sufficient impact to completely change panoramas across the landscape. The Great Western Railway, for instance, changed contemporary views of the fashionable resort of Bath.[29] The line from Exeter to Taunton created by Isambard Kingdom Brunel passed perilously close to the seashore and ensured that some of the picturesque beaches along its route were no longer accessible to the general public. A substantial logistical infrastructure was required to facilitate the movement of goods by rail. The colossal Great Northern Railway warehouse opened in Manchester at the end of the nineteenth century. Five storeys high, the structure allowed the exchange of goods between the rail, road and canal networks through a series of hydraulic lifts which moved wagons between different levels.[30] The teams of labourers who constructed the railways required temporary accommodation as they worked along the routes of new lines. Excavations on the site of the Risehill camp on the Settle to Carlisle railway, occupied during the 1870s, have uncovered traces of prefabricated huts raised above ground level. Cinders and coal were mixed to provide a secure surface for paths in an area prone to heavy rainfall. Whilst the lives of railway labourers were clearly hard, they seem to have made conscious attempts to construct decent temporary residences for themselves. Contrary to popular perceptions of drunken navvies drowning their sorrows in copious amounts of ale, there was relatively little evidence for alcohol consumption on the site. Investigation of local census returns indicates that the opening of the line had a positive impact on local agriculture, through facilitating the movement of livestock to distant markets.[31]

COTTON

Logistical efficiency was also important for the cotton trade, in which north western England played a pivotal role. Almost 300 settlements in Lancashire, Yorkshire and Cheshire were economically reliant on cotton by the end of the eighteenth century.[32] A series of technological innovations during the later eighteenth century revolutionized the textile industry, including Crompton's mule, Cartwright's power loom and Arkwright's spinning frame. This encouraged rapid growth in raw cotton imports for processing. In the 1750s, 2.8 million pounds of cotton were imported annually. By 1820 this volume had risen to 173 million pounds. Prior to 1914, cotton import levels reached 1.8 billion pounds.[33] For much of its existence, British involvement in the cotton trade was synonymous with human slavery. European ships transported African slaves to plantations in America and the West Indies. In exchange, goods such as cotton, sugar and coffee were shipped to British ports. For this reason, the archaeology of the cotton trade in Britain can be viewed as an extension of the global archaeology of slavery. Supporting the increase in the cotton trade was a vast industrial infrastructure including warehouses and mills. By 1861 452,000 individuals worked in some capacity in the cotton industry.[34] Although many mills were located next to watercourses, steam engines allowed them to be situated in more urban locations. This was advantageous in recruiting a suitable workforce. Although mills varied considerably in size and layout during this period, they often shared a series of common features. Several stories high, mills contained large open rooms to hold the associated machinery. Surrounding walls prevented intrusions from thieves or vandals. The latter were a particular threat during periods of political turbulence. Lavatories for the workers were usually clustered round the staircases. A tower bell or clock oversaw the delineation of shifts. Artificial lights increased the productivity of mills by allowing them to operate during the hours of darkness if required.[35] Early observers often expressed surprise that the mills were active at night. Conditions in the mills were notoriously dangerous. Cramped conditions in working some of the machines encouraged the recruitment of children who could work within narrow spaces.

MANCHESTER: URBAN GROWTH DURING THE INDUSTRIAL REVOLUTION

The Industrial Revolution had a profound and long lasting impact on the urban landscape of Britain. The growth of commercial and industrial centres encouraged migration from the countryside into emerging towns and cities. This population movement was facilitated by the growth of efficient transport networks and the economic boom prompted by technological innovations. The city of Manchester in northern England is a prime example of a settlement which witnessed rapid population and economic growth during this period. Many authorities claim Manchester to be the first industrial city in the world. On close examination, it is clear that Manchester was well placed to take advantage of the benefits offered by the Industrial Revolution. The city sits close to three important rivers, namely the Irk, Irwell and Medlock allowing access to river traffic. North-western England had an established reputation for the textile industry dating back several centuries. In part, this was due to the geographic and climatic conditions of Lancashire and Cheshire. Proximity to the Lancashire and Yorkshire coalfields was also important in supporting the industrial growth of Manchester. The port of Liverpool was of international significance for the cotton trade, particularly through its links with America and the West Indies. Transport links with the thriving port, strengthened through the creation of railways and canals, allowed Manchester to become a commercial hub for the cotton trade in northern England.

The rapid growth of Manchester is startling. In 1650, it was a relatively small market town indistinguishable from others across Britain. Within a century the town had significantly grown in size and housed a population of 23,000 individuals. Manchester's growth was directly linked to its ascension as a commercial centre for the cotton trade. Whilst much of the manual labour at this stage was undertaken by workers in their own homes in the surrounding countryside, Manchester housed commercial properties and warehouses supporting the trade. Gradually, textile manufacturing moved into Manchester itself. In 1782 Richard Arkwright built his mill within the town, powered by water and steam. Over thirty mills were constructed in Manchester over the following two decades. In 1801 the population of Manchester reached 70,000 and doubled again by 1830.[36] By the middle of the nineteenth century, the town contained a large number of industrial buildings including mills, print works and dye works. The Bridgewater Canal connected Manchester to Liverpool in 1776. Further canals connected industrial complexes across the town facilitating the movement of goods. Aside from the mills and works, numerous warehouses, offices and commercial premises were constructed during the nineteenth century. A single street in 1815 contained a total of fifty-seven warehouses, many of which were private houses rented out for commercial purposes whilst their inhabitants moved to the suburbs, containing over 100 companies linked to the cotton trade.[37] The establishment of mills and warehouses prompted the growth of support industries, particularly metalworking to maintain industrial machinery. It is noteworthy that in 1841 only 18% of the population were directly employed in the cotton industry. The commercial growth of Manchester was reflected in the growing fortunes of the local business elite. Houses for wealthy residents were built in the suburbs of the city, some of which were based on residences in London. The award of city status in the mid-nineteenth century encouraged the construction of elegant public buildings to emphasize the civic pride of Manchester.

Inevitably the rapid population growth within the city had unpleasant consequence for its poorest and most vulnerable residents whose living conditions were seriously undermined. Migration into the city created a demand for cheap accommodation which was answered by the spread of cheap, poor quality housing and insanitary living conditions. Our understanding of social history in Manchester during this period owes much to the pioneering work of Frederich Engels who lived in Manchester during the mid-nineteenth century. Driven by a passionate social conscience and horror at what he discovered, Engels documented his explorations of the most deprived areas. He noted the squalid housing, cramped space and squalid conditions of an area known as 'Little Ireland', a group of terraced streets close to the River Medlock. Migrant families from Ireland, drawn by the temptations of employment in local industrial complexes, lived up to twenty per house in back-to-back terraces.[38] Archaeological excavations across the city have supported Engel's observations about living conditions during this period of rapid industrial growth. A house excavated on Loom Street measured less than 16 m^2 in area.[39] It is frightening to consider that this structure may have housed up to twenty individuals. Nevertheless modern views of harsh landlords imposing squalid housing upon the poor during the nineteenth century are not completely accurate. Indeed, conditions began to improve for the working class in Manchester through the century, motivated in part by accounts by individuals like Engels and a growing social conscience concerning the plight of the less fortunate in society. It is probably no coincidence that the city also played a leading role in the creation of radical political movements. In 1897, the council opened its first housing block catering for needs of the working class. Victoria Buildings contained 283 separate flats with shared facilities and demonstrated a genuine civic concern to improve housing within the city.

Although the growth and development of Manchester during the Industrial Revolution is exceptional for its scale and success, it mirrors the rise of a number of settlements during this period. Technological innovation allowed manual labour in the cotton trade to be relocated from workers' cottages to urban mills. The growth of canals and railways promoted the movement of goods at an unprecedented rate. The location of Manchester within the landscape allowed the settlement to capitalize on these factors and channel them into an explosion in growth. A similar, though less spectacular, trend in urban growth can be traced at Huddersfield in Yorkshire where the traditional occupation of textile working in individual homes shifted to larger mills in the Colne Valley and prompted the growth of the town.

SHEFFIELD STEEL

The Industrial Revolution can be characterized as a series of interlacing industrial and technological innovations. The rapid growth of emerging transport networks linked to new manufacturing techniques to create economic growth on an unprecedented scale. The Industrial Revolution cannot be represented as linear growth but rather a complex nexus of relationships. The production of steel was vital for the spread of railways as it served as an important material in the construction of locomotives and rails. Steel was also needed for the manufacture of cutlery, tools, machinery and armaments. Sheffield in Yorkshire became the centre of the steel industry in Britain. Its role in steel production was formidable. Producing 200 tons of steel in 1840, this output had risen to 20,000 tons two decades later. Reasonable estimates suggest that the city was responsible for 40% of Europe's steel and produced up to 80% of cutlery on a global scale.[40]

The explosion in steel manufacturing in Sheffield is reflected in the archaeology of the city. A series of excavations have examined the premises of John Watts & Company, a major steel firm specialising in the manufacturing of cutlery during the nineteenth and twentieth centuries. In 1872, the company purchased an industrial unit close to Lambert Street. Their new premises were located in an area associated with squalid living conditions. Indeed the workshop was bordered by an array of cramped housing occupied by unskilled labourers. Within four decades the workshop had grown significantly in size. It had been transformed into a sprawling factory occupying surrounding buildings and the former sites of working class housing. The company also diversified its product range, venturing to sell new lines including pens, pocket knives and razors. The rapid spatial growth of John Watts & Company is a microcosm of the rise of a single industry during this period.[41]

CANALS

The ability to convey goods to market is a critical factor in the success of any business enterprise. Much industrial growth during this period was driven by the discovery and implementation of new transport networks, initially canals and later railways. Canals allowed goods to be moved far more efficiently than the old road network. Although canals had been dug in Britain during the Roman and medieval periods, the watershed moment for their importance in the Britain landscape came in 1759 when construction of the Bridgewater Canal began to link coal mines at Worsley with Manchester. The transportation of coal was thus fundamental to the spread of the canal network. Of 165 Canal Acts passed between 1758 and 1801, 90 recorded the carriage of coal as their main interest.[42] This more efficient process for transporting coal allowed industrial centres to be established in areas at a distance from the coalfields.

The construction of canals required considerable engineering skills to plot suitable routes and deal with topographic obstacles. The development of tunnels and bridges allowed engineers to identify practical solutions which would later be useful for the spread of railways. Canals also had an impact on urban settlement. This is most clear at Stourport-on-Severn, which grew at the confluence of the River Severn with the Staffordshire and Worcestershire Canal. Prior to the construction of the canal, only an inn and a few houses occupied the site. Yet the coming of the canal led to the construction of the town to serve as a bustling inland port. The canal opened in 1771. Within two decades Stourport-on-Severn had acquired 1300 residents and a number of industrial works, including yards for boat building. It remains a unique example of a settlement founded on the growth of the canal network.[43]

BLACKPOOL

The Industrial Revolution prompted changes in leisure practices by working class communities. In some ways, these may have been a natural reaction to the stresses and strains of manual employment in industry. The benefits of a steady income may also have been a contributing factor. In northern England, for example, the prevalence of pigeon lofts in some areas can be linked to coal mining, as miners sought outdoor pastimes during time away from the pits. Many northern towns facilitated 'Wakes Weeks', where communities went on holiday for a week. The origins of Wakes Weeks are obscure, but factory owners appear to have had difficulty in restricting their occurrence. Communal holidays must have enhanced the social cohesion of industrial workforces. Over time, the enforced closure of mills and factories offered an opportunity for machine maintenance. Often the destinations of such holidays were specific resorts such as Southport and Scarborough. The growth of railways encouraged leisure travel and innovative rail companies took full advantage by providing cheap fairs and tempting advertising for coastal resorts.

Blackpool owes much of its growth to the Industrial Revolution. When Queen Victoria came to the throne in 1837, the population was recorded as being only 710 individuals. By the time of her death in 1901 it had grown to around 48,000. This spectacular growth can be attributed to the economic benefits of living and working in a thriving seaside resort. Close proximity to the mill towns of Lancashire ensured that there was a ready audience for the benefits of bathing in the Irish Sea. Transport links were essential to Blackpool's success. The Liverpool-Barrow steamship called regularly at the resort from 1838 onwards. In 1846 a branch line connecting Blackpool with the Preston and Wyre railway opened. The growing number of tourists visiting the resort prompted a rapid increase in the provision of accommodation for holidaymakers, much of which was located in streets running from the Promenade. In 1861 there were over 180 hotels and boarding houses catering for visitors, although many operated only on a seasonal basis.[44] A series of attractions tempted holidaymakers to part from their hard earned wages. The North Pier opened in 1863 and gradually developed from a walking platform into an entertainment complex, as well as allowing passengers to board visiting steamers. Five years later the Theatre Royal opened. Construction of the Winter Gardens complex commenced in 1875, and provided an attraction which could be enjoyed regardless of the inclement Lancashire weather. The Promenade remained a focus for visitors and the first electric tramline in Britain was opened along it in 1885. The Pleasure Beach, designed to provide a variety of family entertainment, was launched in 1894. Perhaps the most ambitious construction project in Blackpool was the Tower, which opened to paying guests in 1894. Rising to 158 metres, the Tower was modelled on the Eiffel Tower but also served to differentiate Blackpool from its competitors. As well as a striking visual monument, the complex also contained an aquarium and menagerie. The Tower Ballroom remains a popular destination for ballroom dancing fans. These innovative developments ensured that Blackpool's success as a holiday resort continued. It is striking that many of these attractions continue to operate in the present day. The development of seaside resorts ensured that the economic impact of the Industrial Revolution spread beyond the areas surrounding the mills, factories and mines. Resorts also attracted wealthy businessmen and merchants. The Grand Hotel in Brighton, for example, served as a sophisticated holiday residence for wealthy families. Just as the railways radically changed the working lives of Britons during this period, they also reshaped how they spent their leisure time.

Chapter 9

The Modern Period

(1901 – Present)

My favourite walk takes me from my house to a local village. Following a lane past an old country churchyard, I cross farmland and join a footpath which passes a large hill before turning for home. Whilst the fields are empty save for horses and the occasional partridge, the landscape carries traces of a deeply embedded archaeological history. Undulations at ground level in the fields are ridge and furrow marks created by medieval ploughing. The large hill which I pass is in fact a large slag heap left by a now abandoned coal mine. Indeed, one of the fields hides a mass grave from a local mining disaster, commemorated by a still tended memorial in the local churchyard. Beside the slag heap there stood a bomb shelter constructed during the Second World War. Until recently, you could still step within it and imagine the sheer terror of its occupants as Luftwaffe bombers passed overhead. Yet two years ago the shelter was bulldozed as part of the rural regeneration of the former mining landscape. Only small lumps of concrete mark the site of the shelter now. The paradox of the archaeological history of the modern period is that, despite being the most recent remains, they are probably the most threatened.

DEFENCE

The twentieth century was the most violent period in human history. The Second World War alone can be quantified as our greatest non-natural catastrophe.[1] The violence of this period is reflected in the archaeological history of Britain in the form of defensive structures created in response to the threat of invasion or outright destruction. It can be argued that Britain was more highly militarized during the twentieth century than at any other point in the past. Since many of the defences were constructed in urban locations, the military archaeology of the modern period is diminishing rapidly in the face of redevelopments. Yet these monuments to a period of existential crisis allow archaeologists to reconstruct what would have happened had Britain been invaded or experienced a nuclear attack. From 1995 – 2001, the Council for British Archaeology organized a major investigation to record the military archaeology of Britain. Over 600 amateur and professional archaeologists were involved in the project, which surveyed almost 20,000 individual sites. The project database remains a fundamental resource for understanding how Britain was poised to respond to attack.[2]

The first major threat to British security during the twentieth century came with the outbreak of the First World War in 1914. Although we often associate the conflict with trench warfare on the Western Front, there were real concerns that Britain itself would be attacked by enemy forces. These fears were not unfounded as communities on the east coast were bombarded by sea and air during the war. Anti-aircraft batteries were constructed at key points to deter bombing raids. Their operation was supported by the use of large sound mirrors, particularly along the north eastern coast. These structures were used to amplify the sound created by incoming bombers and allowed trained listeners to predict their intended targets thus facilitating a defensive response.[3] The strategy for protecting against coastal incursions was to establish formidable defences around major ports and naval bases. Fifteen of the twenty-three artillery batteries constructed during the First World War were clustered on the east coast.[4] The defensive strategy implemented between 1914 and 1918 was primarily concerned with deterring attacks rather than repelling an invasion force. Its focus was predominantly strategic with little official protection for civilians in the form of bomb shelters.

The outbreak of the Second World War in 1939 saw Britain facing the very real possibility of invasion by German forces. The Wehrmacht had proved adept at seizing enemy territory through their swift Blitzkrieg campaigns. The fall of France and the evacuation of the British Expeditionary Force from Dunkirk left Britain under imminent threat of a military onslaught. As a result, a massive programme of anti-invasion defences was begun under the leadership of General Ironside, commander-in-chief of Home Forces. Their presence is still visible across Britain in the form of pillboxes, tank traps and ditches (Fig 19). After the withdrawal from Dunkirk, the British army was short of armaments and equipment. The Wehrmacht favoured the coordinated use of seaborne invasions, glider incursions, paratroopers and terror in commencing their invasions. For these reasons, the anti-invasion programme was designed to provide defence in depth through a series of stop lines which would hold up the enemy advance and provide a series of fall back positions for defending forces. The so-called 'Coastal Crust' was designed to prevent the enemy from landing troops and establishing a beachhead through which further reinforcements and supplies could be brought. Inland stop lines were intend to slow the enemy advance and allow military forces to muster for a concerted attack. At a local level, defences focussed on nodal points in the form of settlements or transport junctions which would serve as centres for resistance. Key areas such as airfields, reservoirs and utility stations received additional protection. Open areas in strategic locations which could have been used as temporary airfields by an invasion force were put beyond use through the deployment of obstacles or trenches.[5] The strategy of defence in depth essentially acknowledged that invading forces could not necessarily be prevented from landing. Instead, it focussed on limiting their advance to gain time for the defenders to mass their forces. Thus many of the initiatives undertaken during this period were in the form of anti-tank ditches or obstacles. Whilst the army would bear the brunt of the fighting, at a local level defence fell to the Local Defence Volunteers or Home Guard. A secretive resistance organisation, known as the Auxiliary Units, was recruited to wage guerrilla warfare in the event of a Nazi conquest. These small teams were to operate from hidden rural Operational Bases. The secrecy attached to the Auxiliary Units was such that many families were unaware that their relatives had joined.[6] In July 1940, General Alan Brooke relieved General Ironside as commander-in-chief of Home Forces. Brooke feared that the stop lines and emphasis on limiting enemy movement would hinder defending forces and lead to the static warfare experienced during the First World War. Instead, Brooke implemented a system of focal defensive positions supported by mobile military units.

SHOOTERS HILL

The stop lines worked at a number of levels, from the main GHQ line to those with a local focus. Shooters Hill, close to the city of London, has been the subject of a recent investigation to uncover how Second World War defences worked on the ground. Given its location, Shooters Hill formed part of a larger system which was intended to hinder invading forces in reaching London. The construction of the Shooters Hill defences was undertaken with a keen appreciation of the local terrain and topography. In particular, a dense wood nearby ensured that tanks and armoured vehicles would be funnelled down the road rather than dispersing across the countryside. The defences were composed of a number of related features which would work in concert to attack the invaders as they moved along what is now the A207 main road. Destroying individual vehicles would block the road and prevent the movement of armoured vehicles. Shooters Hill was crowned by a pill box and roadblock. This defensive position created a valuable field of fire over vehicles and troops attempting to pass through to London. Attempts to remove the roadblock would be prevented by suppressing fire from the pillbox. Supporting roadblocks were positioned on nearby roads to funnel the invaders along the required route. Elsewhere a large mine was disguised in the form of a garage next to the road. Such explosive devices would sow terror and panic among the Wehrmacht. A nearby machine-gun post was intended to capitalize on any explosion through cutting down reinforcements. Trenches dug near the road provided improvised defences as well as limiting the movement of vehicles off the road. A spigot-mortar pit also enhanced the capabilities of the defenders. Camouflage was an essential weapon in the armoury of the Home Guard. Aside from the mine disguised as a garage, the pillbox on the summit of Shooters Hill took the form of an off licence attached to the public house, which could also have served as a defensive position. The archaeology of the area also betrays civilian measures deployed in the event of attack in the form of air raid shelters, some of which remain as substantial structures. Whilst the defences of Shooters Hill were formidable and could easily have slowed the German advance, they are unlikely to have halted the invasion. Instead, they were designed to concentrate invading forces and harass their movement towards London. In doing so, the defenders of Shooters Hill would have granted the British Army time to regroup and prepare a robust counter attack.[7]

PEVENSEY CASTLE

Although Britain was last successfully invaded in 1066, as an island nation it has a long history of defence against attack both internally and from mainland Europe. It is therefore unsurprising that sites of historical importance were reactivated to serve within the defensive system of this period. Thus, the summit of an Iron Age hillfort at Old Bewick in Northumberland was crowned with two pillboxes which formed part of the local stop line attached to the central GHQ line.[8] Recent excavations at Shooters Hill have unexpectedly revealed a Bronze Age enclosure close to the later site of a barrage balloon.[9] Pevensey Castle in Sussex has a sustained history of involvement in defence against invasions owing to its proximity to the coast line. Established as a Saxon Shore Fort during the late Roman period, Pevensey was the site of the Norman landings in 1066. It became a Norman castle and remains a formidable structure. In 1940, Pevensey was identified as a location vulnerable to attack. Indeed, German military maps from the same period reveal a particular interest by the invasion planners in the defences around the castle. Pevensey Castle was designated as a nodal point by the British Army and therefore was subject to a robust defensive system. Aside from its proximity to the coast, the importance Pevensey lay in its position within the landscape. Pevensey occupies a spur of high ground surrounded by lower lying former marshland. British military officers feared that the castle would become a hub for the invasion force, allowing them to dominate the local landscape whilst protected by the structure of the castle.

In response to the perceived vulnerability of Pevensey, the castle was remilitarized and refortified. Pevensey functioned as the keep of the local area (a term used without irony by British military planners) which meant that it functioned as the central defensive position within the landscape. A large number of pillboxes and roadblocks were constructed with particular emphasis on the castle and local road junctions. Their creation expresses the desire of the British Army to prevent the castle from being utilized during an invasion, particular by mobile armoured forces. Machine gun positions were placed on the walls, one of which sat at the top of a medieval tower, and an anti-tank emplacement by the Roman gate. A battle headquarters was established within the castle. Attention was also paid to the fabric of the castle itself. Brick and concrete walls closed off some of the gates. More than fifty anti-tank cubes surrounded the castle. Any approach to the site by the Wehrmacht was therefore limited by the numerous anti-tank obstacles and a sustained barrage of machine-gun fire from the emplacements in the castle. The refortification of Pevensey demonstrates the adaptability of the British Army during this period of crisis. Many of the Second World War defences attached to the castle are still visible and demonstrate continuity in the defensive role of the site for almost two millennia.[10]

NUCLEAR DEFENCE

With the end of the Second World War, fears of invasion in Britain gradually subsided. Yet they were replaced by a new and potentially more horrific threat in the form of nuclear attack by Soviet Russia. The archaeology of the Cold War is strikingly different to that of earlier twentieth century conflicts. It is characterized by a pervading sense of secrecy, which to a certain extent continues to the present day. Indeed, some of the defences remain in active use. The focus of Cold War defences was both on protecting the population, or at least select elements of it, during a nuclear attack and sustaining some form of central and localized government in the aftermath. Despite the covert nature of many Cold War structures, a number remain ostentatiously visible in the landscape. A series of microwave communication towers were constructed to provide an alternative communication network in the event of nuclear attack. The nature of their purpose demanded that they were visible to each other, rather like earlier beacon chains. One such tower remains as the famous BT Tower in London.[11]

In the event of nuclear attack, maintaining continuity in government and effectiveness in military command structures was essential for the future of Britain. During the 1960s, eleven bunkers which would serve as regional seats of government in the aftermath of a nuclear explosion were established, including Brecon, Dover and Nottingham. One such seat of regional government was established in tunnels beneath Dover Castle which in parts dated back to the Napoleonic period. The avowed purpose of these bunkers was not to preserve an elite group, but rather to maintain a core local government who would provide leadership, support and sustenance for the surviving population. Those in the bunker were primarily shielded from the fallout of a nuclear explosion, allowing them to continue their roles. The survival of door signs at the seat of regional government in Cambridge has allowed the theoretical composition of the bunker community to be identified. Aside from rooms assigned as dormitories, conference rooms and power generators, offices were allotted to representatives from a number of arms of government. Representatives of the Ministries of Health, Transport, Public Buildings and Works were all to be housed within the bunker. The Home Office, Civil Defence and the Post Office would also have been present. The BBC were allocated a small studio from which they would have broadcast announcements and updates. The RAF, army and navy retained space within the bunker. In essence, the seat of regional government acted as a microcosm of central government. Indeed, in an apocalyptic scenario it may have been required to act as such.[12]

During a nuclear war, the Government would rely upon the provision of accurate information concerning the location, number and nature of explosions, with particular emphasis on the spread of radioactive fallout across Britain. A network of over 1500 underground monitoring posts was established to track the impact of a nuclear attack.[13] These posts were manned by volunteer members of the Royal Observer Corps, which moved from its primary role in observing aircraft to the scientific monitoring of nuclear war. In a quiet suburb of York can be found the bunker which served as the headquarters of the Royal Observer Corps (ROC) No. 20 Group (Fig 20). The purpose of this structure was to co-ordinate the information received from a number of small monitoring posts from across the region. The York bunker was opened in 1961 and formed part of a network of twenty-nine headquarters bunkers across Britain. It was manned by up to sixty male and female ROC volunteers drawn from the local population, scientists and engineers who maintained the power generator and air filtration equipment. In the event of an impending nuclear strike, the volunteers would have raced to the bunker where they would have remained for up to thirty days. Local engineers would have been selected by the police to enter the bunker alongside the ROC. The bunker was not equipped to operate after this thirty day period and therefore the inhabitants would have had to risk re-emerging into the post-apocalyptic landscape. The bunker itself was dug into an orchard and consists of three storeys covered over with earth. Although the structure was designed to protect the inhabitants from fallout, it could not have resisted a direct nuclear strike. Volunteers would have been required to emerge from the bunker on a regular basis to check recording equipment on the roof. The most important room in the bunker was the operations room, which coordinated reports flowing in from monitoring posts across the region and communicated with other centres in the network. Information received from monitoring posts would have been plotted on maps and used to anticipate the direction and nature of radioactive fallout. A large amount of space in the bunker was used for the machinery necessary to support life, including air filtration and conditioning equipment. It is impossible to predict what life in the bunker would have been like during nuclear war. The inhabitants of the bunker slept in dormitories according to a shift system. Conditions within the bunker were inevitably cramped and uncomfortable. There was limited space for personal effects. The colour scheme of the bunker was deliberately designed to inculcate a calming atmosphere. It is likely that ROC workers would have plotted and recorded the obliteration of their own loved ones during a nuclear strike. The Government was clearly worried about the possibility of suicides within the bunker community. Like many of the structures and plans for use in the event of a nuclear attack, it is impossible to know whether they would have worked effectively. The York bunker ceased operations in 1991. It is now owned by English Heritage and serves as a poignant reminder of a past which never happened.[14]

URBAN REGENERATION: NEWCASTLE & GATESHEAD

In the later twentieth century, a number of major British cities pursued a strategy of urban regeneration as a means of revitalising their economies in light of the decline of British heavy industry. Examples of such regeneration projects include Cardiff, Manchester and Liverpool. These shifts in the urban landscape represent a desire to diversify from reliance on a few industries to engage with dynamic sectors such as science, culture and education. The transformation of Newcastle and Gateshead during the twentieth century is in many ways an exemplar of the ability of cities to reinvent themselves and their communities.

The origins of Newcastle can be traced to the Roman period, when a fort was constructed to oversee a strategically important crossing of the Tyne. The river has been of continuing importance to the wellbeing of the city. For several centuries, the economy of Newcastle rested on two major industries, namely shipbuilding and coal. Shipyards on both sides of the Tyne produced some of the largest sea-going vessels in Europe and supported communities of skill workers. The Tyne also acted as a major conduit for the exportation of coal from collieries in Northumberland and County Durham. A large volume of coal was transported by sea to London. The sand used as ballast for returning vessels was used by the glassmaking industry on Wearside. The twentieth century witnessed a gradual decline in these vital industries for Tyneside and therefore a negative impact on the economic health of the region. Foreign competition began to drive the shipyards out of business. Although the fall in productivity was arrested by the Second World War and the emergence of the armaments industry close to the city, the reversal was only temporary in nature. Coal exports to France and Germany declined due to the opening of new mines in mainland Europe. From the 1960s, the coal trade with London also fell into decline. The demise of traditional industries coincided with a desire by some elements of the City Council to rejuvenate Newcastle through a programme of regeneration which would enable Newcastle to appear as the 'Brasilia of the North'. This led to a series of development projects which are widely regarded to have been unsuccessful if not harmful to the fabric of the urban environment.[15] The passionate pursuit of a modernist style led to the destruction of a number of historic buildings including the Royal Arcade. The erection of multi-storey buildings, including high rise flats, was seen by many as detrimental to the landscape of Tyneside. Not all of the buildings constructed during this period were perceived in a negative light. Just outside the city stands the Byker Wall. Designed by the architect Ralph Erskine, the Byker Wall varies from three to twelve stories in height and displays a colourful textured façade. It possesses listed status and was included on the UNESCO list of outstanding twentieth century buildings.

From the 1990s renewed attempts to regenerate the city focussed on improving its image as a place of culture and leisure. The Grainger Town Project sought to redevelop a central section of the inner city which, although possessing a large number of buildings of historical or architectural importance, had suffered as a result of the economic decline. Sustained investment resulted in an area known for the quality of its shops and leisure facilities. The Quayside of Newcastle and Gateshead suffered through neglect after the importance of the river for industry faded away. Recent developments have revitalized the banks of the Tyne. The Baltic flour mill in Gateshead is a prominent local landmark and a reminder of the industrial heritage of the area. Its redevelopment into a major gallery for contemporary visual arts displayed sensitivity towards its past. The Baltic has hosted exhibitions from leading artists from around the world and has contributed significantly to the local economy. Another former industrial building, the Co-operative flour warehouse has been revamped as a prestigious boutique hotel.[16] These developments mark not the removal of the past but its remodelling to serve a new cultural context. The distinctive Sage regional music centre on the Gateshead Quayside is the result of a design by the renowned architect Norman Foster. Although its appearance is startlingly modern, the curves of its exterior recall the nearby Tyne Bridge (Fig 21). The creation of the Baltic and Sage have cemented Tyneside's reputation for culture and the arts.

Higher education has proven to be increasingly important for Newcastle over the last century, not least due to the economic benefits of having a large student population within the city. Whilst universities have traditionally been campus based and therefore distinct from the rest of the urban environment, recent developments challenge the use of space for higher education. The Centre for Life occupies an area close to the Central Railway Station. The complex was created as a partnership between a number of bodies including Newcastle University, the National Health Service and private companies. It also hosts a popular science visitor attraction. Construction work is currently ongoing for a new complex entitled Science Central through a collaborative partnership between Newcastle University and the City Council. As well as educational, administrative and research facilities, the complex will include sustainable housing, green spaces and allotments. The Centre for Life and Science Central challenge preconceived notions of the binary opposition between 'town and gown'. They present a unified vision for the future of urban spaces where applied research and technical expertise underpin new developments for the greater wellbeing and economic prosperity of the wider community.

LANDSCAPE & MEMORY

In the contemporary world, our appreciation for the landscapes in which we live and work is arguably as strong as that of our ancestors. Although such appreciation tends to aesthetic rather than practical, it is clear that perceived threats to the beauty of particular landscapes invoke strong emotions. The medieval market town of Ludlow, for example, has striven to maintain the character and quaintness of its urban terrain. The development of a new superstore close to the railway station was achieved through a remarkable level of sensitivity concerning the place of the structure within the local landscape. The roof of the structure was deliberately shaped to echo the contours of surrounding hills. For this reason, the superstore appears not as an alien imposition on a historic area but rather a sensitive development which shares a sense of place with the local community.

Features within the landscape, either natural or manmade, contribute to our sense of identity at a local and national level. The white cliffs of Dover are synonymous with memories of twentieth century conflicts and the threat of invasion. More recent additions to the landscape can also act as powerful symbols of community identity. The Angel of the North sculpture near Gateshead has become intrinsically linked with the people of Newcastle and Gateshead. The industrial angel whose form evokes the industrial heritage of the local area is highly visible by motorway and rail. The site selected for the sculpture contains remains from a former colliery. The sculptor Anthony Gormley has stated that the Angel represents a focal point for a community challenged by the end of the industrial era.[17] Gormley's project Another Place is now exhibited on Crosby beach near Liverpool. Formed from a hundred cast iron human sculptures standing on the seashore, the work engages directly with the tides and the daily movement of people, animals and maritime traffic along the seashore. Gormley's works demonstrate an unusual depth of understanding of the power of monuments within the landscape.[18] It is difficult to look at the Angel of the North and not be reminded of some of the great archaeological sites of early prehistory, which similarly attempted to mark the human presence within the landscape.

The contemporary British landscape is imbued with a deep symbolism which connects precise localities with the distant past. Such symbolism affects not only our place within the landscape, but also how we choose to move through it. The threads of a journey can reconnect us with a real or imagined past at an almost visceral level. Topographic symbolism is rarely as important as it is during times of social or political crisis. The deposition site of Lindow Man was probably carefully selected for its ritual and religious connotations. One of the most traumatic national events in Britain in recent years was the death of Diana, Princess of Wales, in 1997. The geography of Diana's funeral and burial reflected her importance to the British people by passing through a series of locations which resonated with royal and ancestral symbolism. The funeral cortege left from Diana's home at Kensington Palace. In the days since her death, members of the public had left floral tributes at the palace gates. These served to focus public grief on a specific location associated with the princess and the royal family. The funeral itself was held at Westminster Abbey, a site associated with the royal family as a venue for coronations, weddings and funerals. As such the Abbey represents the monumentalisation of royal rituals since the medieval period and connected a specific event with a broad historical narrative of monarchy. The route of the funeral cortege was publicised and followed by the media allowing the public to participate in the event. Yet in contrast to the visibility and public focus of her funeral, the burial of Diana took place in private at Althorp, the seat of the Spencer family since the sixteenth century. The princess was interred on a lake island, a choice which resonates with Arthurian connotations. The context of her burial marked the return of Diana from the public role of a member of the royal family to the privacy of the Spencer family home. In death, Diana's funeral procession retraced the steps she had taken in life from being a private citizen to a very public personality. In doing so it consciously linked sites which demonstrate the status of both of her families.[19]

FUTURES

This book ends where it began, on the coast at Happisburgh in Norfolk. Eight-hundred thousand years ago Happisburgh was where some of our earliest ancestors struggled to maintain a foothold on the edge of their natural range in the face of adverse climatic conditions. Today, Happisburgh faces new challenges in the form of severe coastal erosion which imperils the future of the settlement. Coastal erosion has probably been ongoing in this area for over 5,000 years and consists of losses of up to 10 m per year.[20] Although defensive measures may slow down the rate of erosion, on average one house has disappeared annually in recent years as the coastline recedes.[21] Climate change threatens to rapidly increase the rate of erosion in this area. The measures required to combat or adjust to changing climatic conditions have already begun to leave their traces on the British landscape. The search for renewable energy sources, in particular, will determine much of the archaeological record of the contemporary world.[22] Wind farms are a frequent source of contention for local communities on account of their perceived visible impact on the countryside. In some quarters, they are perceived as spoiling or mutilating the landscape. Yet, as this book has shown, the archaeological history of Britain has never been static. Humans have consistently imposed and monumentalized their presence within the landscape in varied and diverse forms. Archaeologists often refer to the archaeological record as a palimpsest. The term refers to a page of a manuscript which has been reused. In the same way, the British landscape contains visible traces of all the generations to have gone before. There is no such thing as pristine British countryside untouched by humans. Each generation has left their mark in an ever-changing vista of human life in Britain. Since the earliest presence of our ancestors, we have attempted to shape and control the terrain to our advantage. Considering the challenges faced by the inhabitants of Happisburgh and their prehistoric forebears, it is impossible not to be moved by the vast continuum of archaeological history in Britain and our own small place within it.

Notes

CHAPTER 1

1. Cunliffe 2012: 39
2. Our understanding of the activities of archaic humans in Britain has been greatly enhanced in recent years by the findings of the Ancient Human Occupation of Britain project. Stringer 2006 outlines how this research has changed our understanding of prehistoric Britain.
3. See Parfitt *et al* 2010; Stringer 2006: 63-66.
4. On *Homo Heidelbergensis*, see Stringer & Andrews 2005: 148-151.
5. See Stringer 2006: 95-100.
6. Pryor 2004: 20-30.
7. On Boxgrove, see Pitts & Roberts 1997.
8. For an overview of our understanding of Neanderthals, see Stringer & Andrews 2005: 154-157.
9. Schreve 2006
10. For a useful summary of current theories, see Stringer & Andrews 2005:164-165.
11. Stringer 2011: 192-193.
12. Pryor 2004: 45-51.
13. See Bello *et al* 2011.
14. On the discovery of prehistoric rock art at Creswell Crags, see Bahn *et al* 2005.
15. Cunliffe 2013: 54-56.
16. Pryor 2004: 85.
17. Evidence of religious belief during the Mesolithic is unsurprisingly scarce. However, a recent investigation at Warren Field in Scotland has interpreted the site as a ritual calendar used during this period. This discovery has the potential to revolutionise our understanding of Mesolithic rituals. See Gaffney 2013.
18. A site of Star Carr's significance inevitably attracts a substantial bibliography. See Pryor 2004 82-90; Conneller *et al* 2012.
19. Oppenheimer 2007: 470.
20. Cunliffe 2013: 128-131.

CHAPTER 2

1. For a broad view of the Neolithic and its impact see Foster McCarter 2008.
2. The pioneering research which led to a revised chronology for the emergence of the British Neolithic can be found in Whittle *et al* 2010.

3. Morris 2012: 172.
4. Cunliffe 2013: 162-168.
5. Pryor 2011a: 61-62; Thomas 1999: 54.
6. Ritchie 1994: 12-14; Pryor 2004: 246-248.
7. Organized violence occurs in hunter gatherer communities - see Diamond 2012: 129-170. Yet it only becomes clearly visible in the British archaeological record during the Neolithic.
8. Schulting & Wysocki 2005.
9. Mercer 2009.
10. Mercer 2009: 149.
11. Cunliffe 2013: 165.
12. This case study draws on the findings of the Stonehenge Riverside Project, as summarised in Parker Pearson 2012.
13. Parker Pearson & Ramilisonina 1998.
14. Darvill 2006.
15. For a particularly innovative approach to understanding Neolithic belief systems, see Lewis-Williams & Pearce 2003.

CHAPTER 3
1. Bradley 2007: 184-185.
2. Parker Pearson 1996: 83-84.
3. See Bradley 2005 on the connections between domestic life and religious belief in prehistory.
4. Jay *et al* 2011.
5. For a description of these burials see Catling 2012.
6. Cunliffe 2013: 286-288.
7. Pope 2008.
8. Bradley 2007: 208-209.
9. Parker Pearson 1994: 99.
10. The classic study is Fleming 1988.
11. Cunliffe 2013: 253.
12. Parker Pearson 1994: 99-100.
13. Pryor 2011a: 99-102.
14. Pryor 1991 presents a comprehensive overview of the site.
15. Bradley 1998.
16. Pryor 2002.
17. Parker Pearson & Ramilisonina 1998.

CHAPTER 4
1. Pytheas' journey deserves to be more widely known. His itinerary is reconstructed in Cunliffe 2001.

2. Cunliffe 2005: 70-86. The concept of the 'Celts' as a distinct people is a matter of great controversy, which is not explored here due to textual constraints. The best treatment is James 1999.
3. Pryor 2004: 332-334.
4. Strabo, *Geography* 2.5.8; 4.5.1-4.
5. Caesar, *Gallic Wars* 5.12-14.
6. Cunliffe 2013: 325-326.
7. On the Arras Culture see Cunliffe 2004: 84-86, 546-549.
8. Pope 2008.
9. Payne *et al* 2006: 44 – 47.
10. Waddington 2011.
11. Perhaps the most famous examples comes from accounts of the fall of Troy, see Virgil, *Aeneid* 2.760.
12. For a discussion on understanding the function of hillforts, see Payne *et al* 2006: 151-162.
13. The major text is Cunliffe 1983.
14. For an overview of Danebury see Payne *et al* 2006: 58-62.
15. On Bury Hill see Payne *et al* 2006: 54-58.
16. Cunliffe 2013: 323-324.
17. Ritchie 1994: 67-71.
18. Foster 1989.
19. On crannogs, see Pryor 2011a: 152-153.
20. Russell 2006: 66.
21. For a unique perspective on an unusual element of Iron Age religion, see Armit 2012.
22. Caesar, *Gallic Wars* 5.13-16.
23. Pliny the Elder, *Natural History* 16.249-51.
24. The best treatment of Lindow Man is Joy 2009.
25. Caesar, *Gallic Wars* 4.20-36.
26. Caesar, *Gallic Wars* 5.1-23.
27. Cicero, *Letters to Atticus* 4.15.10; 4.16.7; 4.18.5.
28. Creighton 2000: 76.
29. Augustus, *Res Gestae* 32.
30. Creighton 2000: 108
31. Creighton 2000: 192.
32. Cunliffe 2005: 156-158.
33. For a regional perspective, see Sharples 2010.

CHAPTER 5

1. *Roman Inscriptions of Britain* (*RIB*) 1065 add.
2. *RIB* 1171 add.

3. For a critical survey of the historical sources for the period between Caesar's raids and the pacification of northern Britain, see Braund 1996.
4. Suetonius, *Gaius* 44.
5. Dio 60.19.1-60.22.2.
6. Suetonius, *Claudius* 17.
7. Erim 1982.
8. Suetonius, *Vespasian* 4.
9. Tacitus, *Agricola* 14.
10. *RIB* 91 add.
11. Dio 60.21.1.
12. Tacitus, *Annals* 12.36, 12.40; Tacitus, *Histories* 3.45.
13. Tacitus, *Annals* 14.31-37.
14. Mattingly 2007: 110-112.
15. Tacitus, *Annals* 14.38.
16. Tacitus, *Agricola* 21.
17. Grant 2007: 79.
18. Tacitus, *Agricola* 29-37.
19. Tacitus, *Annals* 14.38.
20. *RIB* 12.
21. Mattingly 2007: 166.
22. Reported in *Britannia* 2006 37: 468 no. 3.
23. For a series of useful papers on the concept of the army as a community, see Goldsworthy *et al* 1999.
24. *RIB* 816, 823.
25. Virgil, *Aeneid* 1.279.
26. See Campbell 2012 on the importance of rivers for the Roman worldview.
27. For an overview of the army in the north, see Breeze & Dobson 1991; Bidwell & Hodgson 2009.
28. Breeze 1994 summarises our understanding of forts in Britain.
29.Birley 1977.
30. Bowman 2003 offers a comprehensive introduction to the tablets.
31. *Tab. Vindol.* III 628.
32. *Tab. Vindol.* II 154.
33. *Tab. Vindol.* II 164.
34. *Tab. Vindol.* II 344.
35. *Tab. Vindol.* III 650.
36. *Tab. Vindol.* II 291.
37. Mattingly 2007: 166.
38. *Britannia* 1977 8: 430 no. 8.
39. *ILS* 4751.
40. *AE* 1973 370.

41. Cunliffe 2013: 383.
42. Armit 2012.
43. *RIB* 200.
44. *RIB* 2201 add.
45. *RIB* 959.
46. See Henig 1984. Rüpke 2011 provides an overview of religious practices across the empire.
47. E.g. *Britannia* 1982 13: 404-5 no. 7.
48. On military religions, see Irby-Massie 1999.
49. Gordon 2011 summarises our present understanding of Mithraism.
50. *RIB* 2.4.2447.20.
51. For differing approaches to the evidence for Christianity see Thomas 1981 and Mawer 1995.
52. Mattingly 2007: 255-291.
53. The extent of Romanisation is explored in Russell 2010 and Russell & Laycock 2010.
54. On the rural landscape of Roman Britain see Mattingly 2007: 352-378.
55. Hodgson 2013.
56. *RIB* 191.
57. On the impact of Rome in Scotland, see Hunter 2012.

CHAPTER 6

1. Zosimus 6.5.3.
2. Mattingly 2007: 530.
3. Mattingly 2007: 225-254.
4. See Collins 2012: 154-169.
5. Fleming 2011: 32-35.
6. On the links between Britain and Byzantium, see Harris 2003.
7. Halsall 2013.
8. A heavy reliance on the fragmentary historical records can mislead. See, for example, the ill-received account in Morris 1993.
9. Halsall 2013: 60.
10. Pryor 2005: 135-143.
11. Oppenheimer 2007: 443.
12. Gelling 2011.
13. See the synthesis in Frodsham & O'Brien 2005.
14. Williamson 2008 outlines the topographic context of the site.
15. Care Evans 1986 catalogues the finds in detail.
16. See the discussion on Wood 2005b: 61-79.
17. Klemperer 2013 summarises our current understanding of the hoard.
18. Mercia has had a notable impact on twentieth century literature. J.R.R.

Tolkien, author of The Lord of the Rings, has the people of Rohan refer to their country as the Mark. The term almost certainly is derived from the contemporary name for Mercia, well known to Tolkien in his role as Professor of Anglo-Saxon. See Shippey 2005: 139-140.
19. For a collection of papers on the history of Mercia, see Brown & Farr 2011.
20.Wood 2005b: 81-110.
21. Semple 2011.
22. Fleming 2011: 165.
23. Bede, *Ecclesiastical History of Britain* 1.13.
24. Fleming 2011: 143.
25. Bede, *Ecclesiastical History of Britain* 1.30.
26. Bede, *Ecclesiastical History of Britain* 2.15.
27. Cramp 2005 describes the site in full.
28. Forster 2004 is an excellent introduction to the period.
29. Cunliffe 2013: 434-437.
30. For a synthesis of recent thinking on this topic, see Catling 2010.
31. Fleming 2011:227-232.
32. Richards 2007.
33. For what follows, see Ferguson 2010; Richards 2011.
34. The Viking archaeology of York is summarised in Hall 1994.

CHAPTER 7

1. Scully 2013 identifies the Classical allusions in the Mappa Mundi.
2. See Carpenter 2004: 1-25.
3. Different perspectives on Domesday are presented in Williams 1995 and Roffe 2000.
4. Wood 2005a reconstructs the English landscape based on Domesday.
5. Carpenter 2004: 31.
6. Morris 2013 is the best introduction to the Conquest and its immediate aftermath.
7. Goddall 2011.
8. Liddiard 2005: 20-22.
9. Morris 2012: 52-54.
10. See Morris 2012: 94-142.
11. Morris 2012: 127-132.
12. Goddall 2011.
13. Liddiard 2005: 131-134.
14. Liddiard 2005: 134-139.
15. See Fiorato *et al* 2007.
16. Monastic life is reconstructed in Brooke 2003.

17. Gilchrist 1999:230 summarises the history of the monastic orders in Britain.
18. Carpenter 2004: 39.
19. Cannon 2007: 305-315.
20. Yeoman 1995: 25-28.
21. Keene 2000.
22. This case study draws on the fundamental works of Lloyd 1996; 2008.
23. See Shoesmith & Johnson 2000 for the development of the castle.
24. Mann 2002.
25. Symonds 2012.
26. Rackham 1996: 168.
27. Pryor 2011a 298-301.
28. Rackham 1996: 123.
29. This case study utilises the comprehensive treatment in Beresford & Hurst 1990.
30. The first results from the excavation and initial analysis have been published in Buckley *et al* 2013.

CHAPTER 8
1. For the context of this episode, see Wood 2003: 7-13.
2. Aston 2000: 158-169.
3. Stirland 2000: 149.
4. Stirland 2000: 153.
5. See Bell 2009.
6. Thurley 1993: 50-56.
7. Pryor 2011a: 465.
8. Rackham 1996: 390.
9. See Colls 2010.
10. See Thomas 2012.
11. Wood 2003: 224.
12. Bowsher & Miller 2009.
13. Harrington 2004: 106.
14. Harrington 2004: 20-21.
15. Harrington 2004: 28.
16. Harrington 2004: 49-51.
17. Tabraham & Grove 1995: 11-12.
18. Tabraham & Grove is the best overview of the archaeology of the Jacobite rebellions. Duffy 2007 analyses the revolt of 1745.
19. This thesis is advanced by Osborne 2013.
20. Sutton & Trinder 1997: 37-38.
21. Osborne 2013: 77.

22. Trinder 2013: 47.
23. Stratton & Trinder 1997: 27.
24. Osborne 2013: 19.
25. Trinder 2013: 203.
26. Osborne 2013: 258.
27. Figures drawn from Osborne 2013: 281.
28. Trinder 2013: 107.
29. Hoskins 1955: 264.
30. Stratton & Trinder 1997: 98.
31. See Pryor 2011b: 106-115.
32. Osborne 2013: 163.
33. Figures taken from Osborne 2013: 164.
34. Trinder 2013: 387.
35. Trinder 2013: 398-400.
36. Newell 2011:14; Osborne 2013: 214.
37. Osborne 2013: 219.
38. Trinder 2013: 495-496.
39. Nevell 2010: 19.
40. Osborne 2013: 252.
41. This case study is drawn from a synthesis of unpublished excavation reports produced in Symonds & Casella 2006: 159-166.
42. Osborne 2013: 268.
43. See Hoskins 1955: 250-251.
44. See Trinder 2013: 570.

CHAPTER 9

1. See Ferguson 2006: xxxiv.
2. The database is accessible online: http://archaeologydataservice.ac.uk/archives/view/dob/
3. Osborne 2004: 168-169.
4. Osborne 2004: 13.
5. Foot 2006: 7-11.
6. Osborne 2004: 88.
7. See Brockman 2009.
8. Osborne 2004: 66.
9. Pryor 2011: 267.
10. Foot 2006 512-518.
11. Pryor 2011: 268.
12. See Cocroft & Thomas 2003: 205-207)
13. Cocroft & Thomas 2003: 174.
14. The best source for the York bunker is the guide produced by English

Heritage 2010.
15. Purdue 2011: 297-303.
16. Purdue 2011: 321.
17. See http://www.antonygormley.com/sculpture/item-view/id/211 (last accessed 25/09/13).
18. See http://www.antonygormley.com/sculpture/item-view/id/230#p0 (last accessed 25/09/13).
19. Pointon 1999.
20. Clayton 1989.
21. Poulton 2004.
22. See Gore 2006 on the potential impact of global climate change.

Bibliography

Aldhouse-Green, M. (2010) *Caesar's Druids: An Ancient Priesthood*. Yale: Yale University Press.

Armit, I. (2012) *Headhunting and the body in Iron Age Europe*. Cambridge: Cambridge University Press.

Aston, M. (2000) *Monasteries in the Landscape*. Stroud: Tempus.

Bahn, P.G., Ripoll, S., Pettitt, P., & Muñoz, F. (2005) Creswell Crags: Discovering cave art in Britain. *Current Archaeology* 197: 217-227.

Barron, C.M. (2000) London 1300-1540. In D.M. Pallister (ed), *The Cambridge Urban History of Britain*. Volume 1, pp. 395-440. Cambridge: Cambridge University Press.

Bell, L.S., Lee-Thorp, J.A. & Elkerton A. (2009) The sinking of the Mary Rose warship: a medieval mystery solved? *Journal of Archaeological Science* 36: 166-173.

Bello, S., Parfitt, S. & Stringer, C. (2011) Gough's Cave, Somerset. *British Archaeology* 118:14-21.

Beresford, M. & Hurst, J. (1990) *Wharram Percy Deserted Medieval Village*. London: Batsford.

Bidwell, P. & Hodgson, N. (2009) *The Roman Army in Northern England*. Newcastle upon Tyne: Arbeia Society.

Birley, A.R. (2000) *Hadrian: The Restless Emperor*. London: Routledge.

Birley, R. (1977) *Vindolanda: A Roman frontier post on Hadrian's Wall*. London: Thames & Hudson.

Bowman, A.K. (2003) *Life and Letters on the Roman Frontier*. London: British Museum.

Bowsher, J. & Miller, P. (2009) *The Rose & The Globe – Playhouses of Shakespeare's Bankside, Southwark: Excavations 1988 – 1990*. London: MOLA.

Bradley, R. (1998) *The Passage of Arms: An archaeological analysis of prehistoric hoards and votive deposits*. Oxford: Oxbow.

Bradley, R. (2005) *Ritual and Domestic Life in Prehistoric Europe*. London: Routledge.

Bradley, R. (2007) *The Prehistory of Britain and Ireland*. Cambridge: Cambridge University Press.

Braund, D. (1996) *Ruling Roman Britain: Kings, Queens, Governors and Emperors from Julius Caesar to Agricola*. London: Routledge.

Breeze, D.J. (1994) *Roman Forts in Britain*. Princes Risborough: Shire Archaeology.

Breeze, D.J. & Dobson, B. (1991) *Hadrian's Wall*. third Edition. London: Penguin.

Brockman, A. (2009) Digging up Dad's Army: The archaeology of World War II on Shooters Hill. *Current Archaeology* 228: 35-42.

Brooke, C. (2003) *The Age of the Cloister: The Story of Monastic Life in the Middle Ages.* Stroud: Sutton.

Brown, M.P. & Farr, C.A. (2011) *Mercia: An Anglo-Saxon Kingdom in Europe.* London: Continuum.

Buckley, R., Morris, M., Appleby, J., King, T., O'Sullivan, D. & Foxhall, L. (2013) 'The king in the car park': new light on the death and burial of Richard III in the Grey Friars church, Leicester, in 1485. *Antiquity* 87: 519-538.

Cannon, J. (2007) *Cathedral: The Great English Cathedrals and the World that Made Them*. London: Constable.

Campbell, B. (2012) *Rivers & The Power of Ancient Rome*. Chapel Hill: University of North Carolina Press.

Care Evans, A. (1986) *The Sutton Hoo Ship Burial*. London: British Museum Press.

Carpenter, D. (2004) *The Struggle for Mastery: The Penguin History of Britain 1066 – 1284*. London: Penguin.

Catling, C. (2010) Raiders and traders: New research on the Vikings. *Current Archaeology* 245:12-21.

Catling, C. (2012) Gold in their hair: Pioneering Travellers along the Copper Road. *Current Archaeology* 265: 26-33.

Clarke, D.V. & Sharples, N. (1985) Settlements & Subsistence in the Third Millenium BC in Renfrew, C. (1985) *The Prehistory of Orkney BC 4000 – 1000 AD*, pp. 54-82. Edinburgh: Edinburgh University Press

Clayton, K.M. (1989) Sediment input from the Norfolk cliffs, Eastern England - a century of coast protection and its effects. *Journal of Coastal Research* 5:433-442.

Cocroft, W.D. & Thomas, R.J.C. (2003) *Cold War: Building for Nuclear Confrontation 1946-1989*. Swindon: English Heritage.

Collins, R. (2012) *Hadrian's Wall and the End of Empire: The Roman Frontier in the fourth and fifth Centuries*. London: Routledge.

Colls. K. & Mitchell, W. (2010) Dig for Shakespeare. *British Archaeology* 113 pp. 24-29.

Conneller, C., Milner, N., Taylor, B., Taylor, M. (2012) Substantial settlement in the European Early Mesolithic: new research at Star Carr. *Antiquity* 86: 1004-1020.

Cramp, R. (2005) *Wearmouth and Jarrow Monastic Sites*. London: English Heritage.

Creighton, J. (2000) *Coins and Power in Late Iron Age Britain*. Cambridge: Cambridge University Press.

Cunliffe, B. (1983) *Danebury: Anatomy of an Iron Age Hillfort*. London: Batsford.

Cunliffe, B. (2001) *The Extraordinary Voyage of Pytheas the Greek*. London: Penguin.

Cunliffe, B. (2005) *Iron Age Communities in Britain*. fourth Edition. Abingdon: Routledge.

Cunliffe, B. (2012) *Britain Begins*. Oxford: Oxford University Press.

Darvill, T. (2006) *Stonehenge: The Biography of a Landscape*. Stroud: Tempus.

Diamond, J. (2012) *The World Until Yesterday*. London: Allen Lane.
Duffy, C. (2005) *The '45: Bonnie Prince Charlie and the untold story of the Jacobite rising*. London: Phoenix.
English Heritage (2010) *York Cold War Bunker*. London: English Heritage.
Erim, T.K. (1982) A new relief showing Claudius and Britannia from Aprodisias. *Britannia* 13: 277-81.
Ferguson, N. (2006) *The War of the World: History's Age of Hatred*. London: Allen Lane.
Ferguson, R. (2010) *The Hammer and the Cross: A New History of the Vikings*. London: Penguin.
Fiorato, V., Bolyston, A. & Knüsel (2007) *Blood Red Roses: The Archaeology of a Mass Grave from the Battle of Towton AD 1461*. Oxford: Oxbow Books.
Fleming, A. (1988) *The Dartmoor Reaves: Investigating Prehistoric Land Divisions*. London: Batsford.
Fleming, R. (2011) *Britain After Rome: The Fall and Rise 400 to 1070*. London: Penguin.
Foot, W. (2006) *Beaches, fields, streets and hills: The anti-invasion landscapes of England, 1940*. York: Council for British Archaeology.
Forster, S.M. (2004) *Picts, Gaels and Scots*. London: Batsford.
Foster, S. (1989) Analysis of spatial patterns in buildings (access analysis) as an insight into social structure: examples from the Scottish Atlantic Iron Age. *Antiquity* 63: 40-50.
Foster McCarter, S. (2008) *Neolithic*. London: Routledge.
Frodsham, P. & O'Brien, C. (eds) (2005) *Yeavering: People, Power & Place*. Stroud: Tempus.
Gaffney, V., Fitch, S., Ramsey, E., Yorston, R., Ch'ng, E., Baldwin, E., Bates, R., Gaffney, C., Ruggles, C., Sparrow, T., McMillan, A., Cowley, D., Fraser, S., Murray, C., Murray, H., Hopla, E., & Howard, A. (2013) Time and a Place: A luni-solar 'time-reckoner' from eighth millennium BC Scotland. *Internet Archaeology* 34
Gelling, M. (2011) Place-Names and Archaeology. In Hamerow, H., Hinton, D.A. & Crawford, S. (eds)*The Oxford Handbook of Anglo-Saxon Archaeology*, pp. 986-1002. Oxford: Oxford University Press.
Giles, K., Masinton, A. & Arnott, G. (2012) Visualising the Guild Chapel, Stratford-upon-Avon: digital models as research tools in buildings archaeology. *Internet Archaeology* **32**.
Gilchrist, R. (1999) Landscapes of the Middle Ages: Churches, castles and monasteries. In Hunter, J. & Ralston, I. (eds.) (1999) *The Archaeology of Britain: An Introduction from the Upper Palaeolithic to the Industrial Revolution*, pp. 228-246. Oxford: Routledge.
Goddall, J. (2011) *The English Castle 1066-1650*. Yale: Yale University Press.
Goldsworthy, A., Haynes, I. & Adams, C. (eds) (1999) *The Roman Army as a Community*. Journal of Roman Archaeology Supplementary Series 34. Portsmouth: JRA.
Gordon, R. (2011) Institutionalised Religious Options: Mithraism. In Rüpke, J.

(ed.) (2011) *A Companion to Roman Religion*, pp. 392-405. Oxford: Wiley Blackwell.
Gore, A. (2006) *An Inconvenient Truth: The planetary emergence of global warming and what we can do about it*. London: Bloomsbury.
Grant, A.E. (2007) *Roman Military Objectives in Britain under the Flavian Empire* BAR British Series 440. Oxford: Archaeopress.
Greene, K. & Moore, T. (2010) *Archaeology: An Introduction*. fifth Edition. Abingdon: Routledge.
Haigh, B. & Gillooley, S. (2000) *A Century of Huddersfield*. Stroud: Sutton Publishing.
Hall, R. (1994) *Viking Age York*. London: English Heritage.
Halsall, G. (2013) *Worlds of Arthur: Facts & Fictions of the Dark Ages*. Oxford: Oxford University Press.
Hamerow, H., Hinton, D.A. & Crawford, S. (eds) (2011) *The Oxford Handbook of Anglo-Saxon Archaeology*. Oxford: Oxford University Press.
Harrington, P. (2004) *English Civil War Archaeology*. London: Batsford.
Harris, A. (2003) *Byzantium, Britain and the West: The Archaeology of Cultural Identity AD 400-650*. Stroud: Tempus.
Henig, M. (1984) *Religion in Roman Britain*. London: Routledge.
Henig, M. (1995) *The Art of Roman Britain*. London: Routledge.
Hodgson, N. (2013) Divide and Conquer: Hadrian's Wall and the native population. *Current Archaeology* 277: 20-27.
Hoskins, W.G. (1955) *The Making of the English Landscape*. London: Penguin.
Hunter, F. (2012) Beyond Hadrian's Wall: War and Diplomacy on the Edge of the Roman World. *Current Archaeology* 265: 18-25.
Hunter, J. & Ralston, I. (eds.) (1999) *The Archaeology of Britain: An Introduction from the Upper Palaeolithic to the Industrial Revolution*. Oxford: Routledge.
Hutton, R. (2009) *Blood and Mistletoe: The History of the Druids in Britain*. Yale: Yale University Press.
Irby-Massie, G. L. (1999) *Military Religion in Roman Britain*. Leiden: Brill.
James, S. (1999) *The Ancient Celts: Ancient People or Modern Invention*. London: British Museum.
Jay, M., Parker Pearson, M., Richards, M.P., Nehlich, O., Montgomery, J., Chamberlain, A. & Sheridan, A. (2011) The Beaker People Project: an interim report on the progress of the isotopic analysis of the organic skeletal material. In M.J. Allen, J. Gardiner, A. Sheridan & D. McOmish (eds) *The British Chalcolithic: people, place and polity in the later third millennium*. Prehistoric Society Research Paper 4. Oxford: Oxbow.
Joy, J. (2009) *Lindow Man*. London: British Museum.
Keene, D. (2000) London from the post-Roman period to 1350. In D.M. Pallister (ed), *The Cambridge Urban History of Britain*. Volume 1. Cambridge: Cambridge University Press. pp. 187-216.
Klemperer, D. (2013) A treasure of astonishing richness: Researching the Staffordshire hoard. *British Archaeology* 131: 14-19
Lewis-Williams, D. & Pearce, D. (2003) *Inside the Neolithic Mind:*

Consciousness, Cosmos and the Realm of the Gods. London: Thames & Hudson.
Liddiard, R. (2005) *Castles in Context: Power, Symbolism and Landscape 1066-1500*. Oxford: Windgather Press.
Lloyd, D. (1996) *The Concise History of Ludlow*. Ludlow: Merlin Unwin Books.
Lloyd, D. (2008) *The Origins of Ludlow*. Ludlow: Logaston Press.
Mann, M.E. (2002) .Medieval Climatic Optimum. In MacCracken, M.C. & Perry, J.S. (eds) (2002) *Encyclopedia of Global Environmental Change Vol. 1 The Earth System: Physical and chemical dimensions of global environmental change*, pp. 514 – 516. Chichester, John Wiley & Sons.
Mattingly, D. (2007) *An Imperial Possession: Britain in the Roman Empire*. London: Penguin.
Mawer, C.F. (1995) *Evidence for Christianity in Roman Britain: The Small Finds*. BAR 243. Oxford: Tempus Reparatum.
Mercer, R.J. (2009) The Origins in Warfare in the British Isles. In J. Carman & A. Harding, *Ancient Warfare*, pp. 143-156. Stroud: History Press.
Morris, J. (1993) *The Age of Arthur: A History of the British Isles from 350 to 650*. London: Weidenfeld & Nicolson.
Morris, M. (2012) *Castle: A History of the Buildings that Shaped Medieval Britain*. London: Windmill Books.
Morris, M. (2013) *The Norman Conquest*. London: Windmill Books.
Morris, R. (2012) *Time's Anvil: England, Archaeology and the Imagination*. London: Weidenfeld & Nicolson.
Nevell, M. (2010) Dark Satantic Mills? The archaeology of the world's first industrial city. *Current Archaeology* 242: 12-19.
Oppenheimer, S. (2007) *The Origins of the British*. London: Constable.
Osborne, M. (2004) *Defending Britain: Twentieth-Century Military Structures in the Landscape*. Stroud: Tempus.
Osborne, R. (2013) *Iron, Steam & Money: The Making of the Industrial Revolution*. London: The Bodley Head.
Parfitt, S., Ashton, N. & Lewis, S. (2010) Happisburgh. *British Archaeology* 114:14-23.
Parker Pearson, M. (1994) *Bronze Age Britain*. London: Batsford.
Parker Pearson, M. (2012) *Stonehenge: Exploring the Greatest Stone Age Mystery*. London: Simon & Schuster.
Parker Pearson, M. & Ramilisonina. (1998) Stonehenge for the ancestors: the stones pass on the message. *Antiquity* 72: 308-26.
Payne, A., Corney, M. & Cunliffe, B. (2006) *The Wessex Hillfort Project: Extensive survey of hillforts in central southern England*. London: English Heritage.
Pitts, M. & Roberts, M. (1997) *Fairweather Eden: Life in Britain half a million years ago as revealed by the excavations at Boxgrove*. London: Century.
Pointon, M. (1999) Funerary and Sexual Topographies: the Death and Commemoration of Diana Princess of Wales. *New Formations* 37: 114-129.
Pope, R. (2008) Roundhouses: 3,000 years of prehistoric design. *Current Archaeology* 222: 14-21.

Poulton, C.V.L. (2004) Disappearing Coasts. *Planet Earth* Summer 2004: 26-27
Pryor, F. (1991) *The English Heritage Book of Flag Fen*. London: Batsford.
Pryor, F. (2002) *Sea Henge: A Quest for Life and Death in Bronze Age Britain*. London: Harper Collins.
Pryor, F. (2004) *Britain BC: Life in Britain and Ireland before the Romans*. London : Harper Perennial.
Pryor, F. (2005) *Britain AD: A Quest for Arthur, England and the Anglo-Saxons*. London: Harper Perennial.
Pryor, F. (2011a) *The Making of the British Landscape*. London: Penguin.
Pryor, F (2011b) *The Birth of Modern Britain: A Journey through Britain's Remarkable Recent Archaeology, 1550 to the Present*. London: HarperPress.
Purdue, A.W. (2011) *Newcastle: The Biography*. Stroud: Amberley.
Rackham, O. (1996*) The History of the Countryside*. London: J.M. Dent & Sons.
Renfrew, C. (1973) 'Monuments, mobilization and social organisation in Neolithic Wessex' in Renfrew, C. (ed.) *The Explanation of Culture Change: Models in Prehistory*, pp. 539-58. London: Duckworth.
Richards, J.C. (2001) *Blood of the Vikings*. London: Hodder & Stoughton.
Richards, J.D. (2011) Anglo-Scandinavian Identity. In Hamerow, H., Hinton, D.A. & Crawford, S. (eds)*The Oxford Handbook of Anglo-Saxon Archaeology*, pp. 46-61. Oxford: Oxford University Press.
Ritchie, A. (1994) *Scotland BC*. Edinburgh: HMSO.
Roffe, D. (2000) *Domesday: The Inquest and the Book*. Oxford: Oxford University Press.
Ross, A. (1974) *Pagan Celtic Britain*. London: Sphere Books.
Rüpke, J. (ed.) (2011) *A Companion to Roman Religion*. Oxford: Wiley Blackwell.
Russell, M. (2006) *Roman Sussex*. Stroud: Tempus.
Russell, M. (2010) *Bloodline: The Celtic Kings of Roman Britain*. Stroud:Amberley Publishing.
Russell, M. & Laycock, S. (2010) *UnRoman Britain: Exposing the Great Myth of Britannia*. London: History Press.
Schreve, D.C. (2006) The taphonomy of a Middle Devensian (MIS 3) vertebrate assemblage from Lynford, Norfolk, UK, and its implications for Middle Palaeolithic subsistence strategies. *Journal of Quaternary Science*, 21.5: 543-556.
Schulting, R. J. & Wysocki, M. (2005) In the Chambered Tumulus were found cleft skulls: An Assessment of the Evidence for Cranial Trauma in the British Neolithic. *Proceedings of the Prehistoric Society* 71:107-38.
Scully, D. (2013) Augustus, Rome, Britain and Ireland on the Hereford mappa mundi: Imperium and salvation. *Peregrinations: Journal of Medieval Art and Architecture* 4 (1): 107-133.
Semple, S. (2011) Sacred Spaces and Places in Pre-Christian and Conversion Period Anglo-Saxon England. In Hamerow, H., Hinton, D.A. & Crawford, S. (eds)*The Oxford Handbook of Anglo-Saxon Archaeology*, pp. 742-763. Oxford: Oxford University Press.
Sharples, N. (2010) *Social Relations in Later Prehistory: Wessex in the First Millennium BC*. Oxford: Oxford University Press.

Shippey, T. (2005) *The Road to Middle Earth*. Second Edition. London: HarperCollins.
Shoesmith, R. & Johnson, A. (eds) (2000) *Ludlow Castle: Its History & Buildings*. Logaston: Logaston Press.
Stamper, P. (1999) Landscapes of the Middle Ages: Rural settlements and manors. In Hunter, J. & Ralston, I. (eds) (1999) *The Archaeology of Britain: An Introduction from the Upper Palaeolithic to the Industrial Revolution*. Oxford: Routledge. pp. 247-263.
Stirland, A.J. (2000) *Raising the Dead: The Skeleton Crew of Henry VIII's Great Ship, the Mary Rose*. Chichester: John Wiley & Sons.
Stratton, M. & Trinder, B. (1997) *Industrial England*. London: Batsford.
Stringer, C. (2006) *Homo Britannicus: The Incredible Story of Human Life in Britain*. London: Allen Lane.
Stringer, C. (2011) *The Origin of Our Species*. London: Allen Lane.
Stringer, C. & Andrews, P. (2005) *The Complete World of Human Evolution*. London: Thames & Hudson.
Symonds, J. & Casella, E.C. (2006) Historical archaeology and industrialisation. In Hicks, D. & Beaudry, M.C. (eds) (2006) *The Cambridge Companion to Historical Archaeology*, pp. 143-167. Cambridge: Cambridge University Press.
Symonds, M. (2012) London's Volcanic Winter: Spitalfields Cemetery and the Famine of 1258. *Current Archaeology* 270: 12 – 19.
Tabraham, C. & Grove, D. (1995) *Fortress Scotland and the Jacobites*. London: Batsford.
Thomas, C. (1981) *Christianity in Roman Britain to AD 500*. London: Batsford.
Thomas, C. (2012) Raising the Curtain: Excavating Shakespeare's Lost Playhouse. *Current Archaeology* 269: 10-13.
Thomas, J. (1999) *Understanding the Neolithic*. London: Routledge.
Thurley, S. (1993) *The Royal Palaces of Tudor England*. New Haven: Yale University Press.
Trinder, B. (2013) *Britain's Industrial Revolution: The making of a manufacturing people, 1700-1870*. Lancaster: Carnegie Publishing.
Waddington, C. (2011) Massacre at Fin Cop: New Evidence of an Iron Age Hillfort at War. *Current Archaeology* 255: 18-27.
Whittle, A., Healy, F. & Bayliss, A. (2010) *Gathering Time: Dating the Early Neolithic Enclosures of Southern Britain and Ireland*. Oxford: Oxbow Books.
Williams, A. (1995) *The English and the Norman Conquest*. Woodbridge: Boydell.
Williamson, T. (2008) *Sutton Hoo and its landscape: The Context of Monuments*. Oxford: Windgather Press.
Wood, M. (2003) *In Search of Shakespeare*. London: BBC Books.
Wood, M. (2005a) *The Domesday Quest: In Search of the Roots of England*. London: BBC Books.
Wood, M. (2005b) *In Search of the Dark Ages*. London: BBC Books.
Yeoman, P. (1995) *Medieval Scotland*. London: Batsford.

Index